Practitioner Research in the Primary School

Edited by
Rosemary Webb

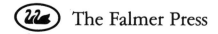 The Falmer Press

(A member of the Taylor & Francis Group)
London • New York • Philadelphia

UK   The Falmer Press, Rankine Road, Basingstoke, Hampshire, RG24 0PR

USA   The Falmer Press, Taylor & Francis Inc., 1900 Frost Road, Suite 101, Bristol, PA 19007

LA
633
P73
1990

First published 1990

British Library Cataloguing in Publication Data

Practitioner research in the primary school.
1. Primary school education. Research
I. Webb, Rosemary
372.072
ISBN 1-85000-807-8
ISBN 1-85000-808-6 pbk

Library of Congress Cataloging-in-Publication Data

Practitioner research in the primary school/edited by Rosemary Webb.
     p. cm.
   Includes bibliographical references and indexes.
   ISBN 1-85000-807-8 — ISBN 1-85000-808-6 (pbk.)
   1. Education. Elementary—Research—Great Britain.
  2. Teaching—Research—Great Britain. I. Webb, Rosemary.
LA633.P73 1990
372'.072041—dc20   90-39820
                                          CIP

Jacket design by Caroline Archer

Typeset in 11/13 Garamond by
Chapterhouse, The Cloisters, Formby L37 3PX

Printed in Great Britain by Burgess Science Press, Basingstoke on paper which has a specified pH value on final paper manufacture of not less than 7.5 and is therefore 'acid free'.

Contents

Acknowledgments   vii

Introduction   1
Rosemary Webb

1 The Origins and Aspirations of Practitioner Research   12
  Rosemary Webb

2 Why do Pirates Have Peg Legs? A Study of Reading for
  Information   34
  Doreen Gregson

3 Towards Reading?   55
  Beatrice Reed

4 Writing in the Infant Classroom   77
  Linda Russell

5 Information Gathering in Topic Work: The Pupil Experience   96
  Rosemary Webb

6 Language Counts in the Teaching of Mathematics   126
  Susan Wright

7 A Process Approach to Science   153
  Virginia Winter

8 Culture and Behaviour: A Study of Mirpuri Pakistani
  Infant Pupils   183
  Avrille McCann

9 Towards a Policy of Equal Opportunities through Research   202
  Jenny Vickers

10 Procedural Rules in the Management of Pupils in the Primary
   School   222
   Alastair Horbury

11 The Processes and Purposes of Practitioner Research   244
   Rosemary Webb

Notes on Contributors   271
Author Index   273
Subject Index   277

Acknowledgments

My thanks go to the contributors to this book who, despite their respective heavy workloads, put much time and effort into their chapters and managed to meet agreed deadlines.

I owe a debt of gratitude to the Department of Education at York for funding research into the Outstation Programme and to Professor Ian Lister for his continuing support.

I am especially grateful to Graham Vulliamy for the encouragement that he gave me, for his helpful comments on the innumerable draft chapters that we generated and for his editorial assistance with the final version.

Introduction

Rosemary Webb

Stenhouse (1975) suggested that teachers should possess a 'capacity for autonomous professional self-development through systematic self-study, through the study of the work of other teachers and through the testing of ideas by classroom research procedures' (p. 144). Central to this vision of teachers researching their own practice was the belief that the improvement of teaching and learning in schools could best be achieved through the development of the critical and creative powers of individual teachers. The research studies in this book, which reflect and extend that vision, serve as accounts of the learning experiences of a group of practitioner researchers. Here the term practitioner research is used to refer to case-study research and evaluation and action research undertaken by teachers, advisers, lecturers and others who work within the education system.

The book has two closely interrelated purposes. The first is to provide information and ideas on the areas of the formal and hidden curriculum into which the practitioners enquired. Although the studies were carried out prior to the implementation in England and Wales of the National Curriculum as set out by the 1988 Education Reform Act, the issues which they address remain central to teaching and learning in primary schools. Also, where appropriate, contributors have discussed the likely implications of their findings for the implementation of the National Curriculum. Readers are invited to reflect critically on these research accounts and the findings presented by the authors and where appropriate, to generalize from the events portrayed and analyzed to their own situations. It is hoped that through providing opportunities for vicarious experience and alternative descriptions of the familiar, both those in initial teacher training and experienced teachers may gain deeper insights into some of the issues that concern them. In this way the findings reported in this book may contribute to the increased understanding and improvement of practice. The second purpose is to provide methodological ideas and assistance for those already engaged in practitioner research and to motivate others to seek an opportunity to undertake some form of research-based enquiry. The two purposes are closely interrelated because of the value the contributors ascribe to taking a research stance to teaching.

Before describing further the book's content and rationale, it might be helpful to provide a few biographical details to explain the impetus for its publication. Its origins are in my introduction to the notion of teacher research in 1981 when I enrolled for a full-time MA at the Centre for Applied Research in Education (CARE), University of East Anglia. This provided the opportunity for direct access to the work and ideas of members of the Centre particularly Barry MacDonald and Rob Walker. It was a challenging, sometimes bewildering and threatening, but always tremendously exciting place to be. When I returned to teaching 'hooked on research' I registered at the Centre for a part-time MPhil. I count myself as extremely fortunate in that for the last year of his life Lawrence Stenhouse was my supervisor. Despite his illness he was the model supervisor who set aside as much time as I needed to talk through my work. Subsequently, the award of a DES studentship enabled me to return to the Centre to carry out doctoral research on a full-time basis. Profoundly influenced by the work of CARE and the potential of research-based courses to challenge one's thinking and push back horizons I sought the opportunity to share in the provision of such a course. The Outstation Programme run by the Department of Education, University of York, presented this opportunity.

All the chapters in this book result from school-based research carried out in the context of participation in a higher degree programme at the Department. Six of the eight other contributors were members of one of the Outstation Programme's part-time MA courses for practising teachers (for a description of the course, see Lewis, 1988). Reed carried out her research while participating in the Department's full-time MA Programme. Horbury, who is a tutor on the Outstation Programme, like Reed began his research as a full-time MA student. However, the potential scope of the study led him to pursue it at doctoral level. The fieldwork for my PhD, part of which is the subject of Chapter 5, was carried out while I was at CARE. However, it was actually written up while I was organizing and teaching on the Outstation Programme.

The Outstation Programme made this book a possibility — not just for the obvious reason that the majority of the contributors were course members — but because of the learning I and other staff have undergone through working with teachers on their projects, together with the insights provided by course evaluations (Munn, 1986; Webb, R., 1984; Webb, K., 1986) and by past and current research into the Outstation Programme and its effects. The programme which opened in Cleveland Local Education

Authority (LEA) in 1983 evolved from the Department's extensive experience in in-service work. Its aim is to enable teachers to address their own concerns and the practical problems of their schools within the context of a higher degree. It is sponsored by LEAs, taught in local teachers' centres and supervisions are conducted in participants' schools — features which made it innovatory when it was first initiated. A special characteristic of the programme is that it recruits teams of teachers in acknowledgment of Fullan's (1982) point that 'It is very hard to be a lone innovator' (p. 273). Although team members have tended not to collaborate on their research projects in the ways initially envisaged, the team approach has been found to be of vital importance in encouraging applications, supporting progress through the programme and helping to create an environment in schools which facilitated the research process (Webb, 1988).

The educational theory grounded in practice, which is a characteristic of practitioner research, contrasted sharply with my initial experience of the educational theory generated by the more traditional styles of quantitative research. During my first years of teaching, in vertically-streamed infant classes, I encountered a number of difficulties arising from the fact that I had been junior trained. I looked to the research literature for guidance and ideas. The language and tone of the studies, together with their remoteness from the pressures of classroom life as I knew it, soon led me to share Anning's (1986) view that: 'We seemed to live in separate worlds. A prestigious research industry seemed to be thriving at the expense of school practitioners rather than in support of them' (p. 57).

Bassey (1983) draws a distinction between 'disciplinary research' and 'pedagogic research'. He sees the former as being carried out by psychologists, sociologists, philosophers and historians primarily for the development of their discipline, although they may also be concerned with the advance of education. Their conceptual structures, research paradigms, methods of data collection, styles of reporting and publication outlets are characterized by the parent discipline. He argues that such traditional research, pursued from the vantage point of specialists and couched in their terms, has been rejected by practising teachers as of little use in assisting them to analyze classroom situations and in devising solutions to practical problems.

In contrast, 'pedagogic research', which is how the research reported in this book can be characterized, is research into the processes of teaching and learning and/or the factors which directly affect these processes. It employs methods of enquiry, ways of presenting findings and publication outlets that are eclectic, pragmatic and readily accessible to teachers. Bassey (1983) states that:

> its prime purpose is to find ways of improving pedagogic practice, and this is not deflected by other purposes. Theory is created in the pursuit of improvement and for the achievement of that improvement, not as the ultimate purpose of the research. (p. 111)

The research within the following chapters is primarily concerned with the advance of pedagogy. However, as all the contributors submitted accounts of their research in order to obtain higher degrees it was an important aim that their research should give rise to theory. The shared intention was that it should be theory that was grounded in the data. Such theory has the potential to be of direct relevance to teachers and to heighten their awareness of the beliefs, assumptions and conditions that determine their practice. This may lead to a critical appraisal of their own situation and subsequent changes to existing practice.

Besides distinguishing between disciplinary research and pedagogic research, Bassey (1981 and 1983) draws attention to the dichotomy between research aiming to provide generalities from which the outcomes of similar sets of events can be predicted and research involving the detailed 'study of singularities'. He argues that the former provides few empirical generalizations of direct use to teachers. He combines these two dichotomies to form a fourfold typology of empirical research into education which draws attention to pedagogic research into singularities. It is this latter form of research which Bassey views as potentially the most valuable for teachers. Thus, he suggests that:

> the educational research community . . . should distinguish between pedagogic research and other forms of educational research, and in relation to pedagogic research should eschew the pursuit of generalisations, unless their potential usefulness is apparent, and instead should actively encourage the descriptive and evaluative study of single pedagogic events. In this way pedagogic research will contribute effectively to the improvement of pedagogic practice. (1981, p. 86)

The following chapters provide 'descriptive' and 'evaluative' studies of single pedagogic instances, events and issues. As stated in the opening paragraphs of this chapter readers are invited to generalize from these studies to their own situations in order to better understand the latter. However, the authors also make generalizations based on their findings in order that readers may test these out in their own situations and refine, extend or refute them. Developing generalizations and grounded theories to inform the thinking of other practitioners appears an important element in practitioner research which seeks to improve practice beyond the individual classroom or situation in which it was carried out.

Practitioner research which adopts an action-research approach is currently regarded as a powerful vehicle for the improvement of 'pedagogic practice'. Oberg and McCutcheon (1989) define action research as:

> any systematic inquiry, large or small, conducted by professionals and focusing on some aspect of their practice in order to find out more about it, and eventually to act in ways they see as better or more effective. (p. 117)

According to this definition most of the research reported in this book could be classed as action research. However, as discussed in Chapter 1, in the last five years more specific understandings of what is meant by action research have been agreed upon. Most definitions now incorporate the notion of an action-research cycle which involves establishing the nature of the problem, designing and implementing a solution and monitoring the effects of that solution. The research of Gregson and Winter align most closely to that definition. The other contributions were conceived as school-focused case studies.

The concept of case study itself is ambiguous. Smith (1978) treats 'educational ethnography, participant observation, qualitative observation, case study, or field study...as synonyms' (p. 316). As pointed out by Adelman, Jenkins and Kemmis (1980) the techniques for collecting information for a case study:

> are held in common with a wider tradition of sociological and anthropological fieldwork. Case study methodology is eclectic, although techniques and procedures in common include observation (participant and non-participant) interview (conducted with varying degrees of structure), audio-visual recording, field-note-taking, document collection, and the negotiation of products (for example discussing the accuracy of an account with those observed). (pp. 48–9)

However, Stenhouse regarded case study as generally different in essence from both ethnography and participant observation:

> Case study, he said, may draw upon the techniques of ethnography as evolved through social anthropology, yet it is not the same as ethnography since it is not primarily a participant-observation study but rests on documents including those created through interviews and observation. These documents are to

become a public record and they contribute to the education of the subjects (not the objects) of the study, that is, they are not merely an outsider's register of behaviour; nor are the concepts of case study 'imposed' on communities where they are not part of the discourse of those communities. (Skilbeck, 1983, p. 15)

This description characterizes the majority of the practitioner-research projects carried out within the context of the department's MA courses — particularly the Outstation Programme. Stenhouse's model of case study both involves practitioners in the research process and seeks to educate them through that process. His vision of case study makes it appear an appropriate one for pedagogic research, which begins with the issues in the consciousness of practitioners, involves collaboration with practitioners to gain understanding of those issues and seeks to inform their professional judgment.

In his influential book *An Introduction to Curriculum Research and Development* Stenhouse (1975) presented a powerful argument to support his belief that 'It is not enough that teachers' work should be studied: they need to study it themselves' (p. 143). In the last decade and a half, teacher research has generated increasing interest and support because of its potential to bring about the personal and professional development of individuals and contribute to change in schools. Many British institutions of higher education now offer research-based higher degree and diploma in-service courses. As Nias (1988) points out, the participation of teacher educators from countries such as Canada, the United States, the Netherlands, Austria, West Germany and Norway in the third international conference on 'Teaching Enquiry-Based Courses' suggests that the field is expanding world-wide. Also, LEAs have come to view the teacher-researcher model of in-service work as a means of developing and disseminating good practice (see, for example, Treacher, 1989). The growth of the movement has led Bell (1985) to claim that 'what was once thought a radical movement seems now to be developing into the new orthodoxy' (p. 175).

The notion that teachers should study their own practice is now accepted. The value of such work is generally acknowledged within the research community. For example, at the National Foundation for Educational Research (NFER) Northern Conference held in 1989 five of the contributors to this book were invited to present their research findings. However, to date, the growing literature in this area has been almost exclusively written by academics who extol the virtues of practitioner research, discuss the methodology underpinning it and provide guidance on data-gathering techniques. Only very rarely do such academics apply the approaches that they advocate to their own practice (a significant exception is Winter, 1989). Also, there are as yet very few published accounts of the findings and outcomes of such research by teachers in either the educational journals or in books. Those that exist tend to be isolated examples in edited collections (see, for example, Prisk, 1987) or included in the publications of specific groups which have limited circulation (see, for example, the bulletins of the Cambridge Action Research Network and the outcomes of the Arts in Schools Project; Treacher, 1989). Even where books have been co-written by academics and teachers (for example, Hustler, Cassidy and Cuff 1986; Nixon, 1981), they have chosen to concentrate mainly on practitioners' experiences of using research methods, exploring the possibilities of practitioner research in differing contexts and ways of facilitating such research rather than on presenting research findings and the uses to which they have been put. This is the reason that this book has the twin purposes of providing substantive accounts and methodological discussion and why, although a balance between the two is achieved across the book as a whole, the emphasis in the chapters providing research accounts is on findings.

Oberg and McCutcheon (1989) also call for more accounts of teacher research to be written by practitioners in order that teachers contemplating carrying out research may gain insights into the likely benefits to be gained and the problems encountered. They recognize that there is little incentive for busy teachers to devote the time and energy required to produce published accounts. Therefore they suggest that 'perhaps it is important for outsiders to collaborate with teachers, not to "take over" the teacher's research, but to report the process, findings and changes in practice that result' (p. 126). Those involved in facilitating teacher research may usefully publicize its processes and outcomes in order to generate greater awareness of its potential. However, if teachers are to retain ownership of their research, become further accepted into the wider educational research community and contribute to theoretical and political debate at local and national level, it is essential that they disseminate their own work. My experience on the Outstation Programme suggests that despite time constraints practitioners, who have invested a great deal of time, energy and commitment into their research, are keen to disseminate their findings. However, initially they may need practical assistance and moral support to identify appropriate opportunities and mediums for dissemination particularly in relation to publications. This book demonstrates the commitment of the nine of us, who collaborated to produce it, to develop a vehicle for the publication of our work.

Over half of the participants on the Outstation Programme are teachers from infant and primary schools. The majority of these are women. This is why — with one exception — the contributors to the book are female. However, as according to the Equal Opportunities Commission (EOC, 1988) in 1985 78 per cent of primary teachers were female this could provide a justification for such a gender bias. Weiner (1989) who argues that action research has been developed and directed by men points out that:

> Significantly the 'important' authors and theorists, and those mentioned in the teacher-researcher networks — for instance, in the Classroom Action Research Network (CARN) (see Bulletins 6 and 7; Holly and Whitehead, 1984, 1986) — were predominantly male . . . (p. 47)

Certainly men such as Stenhouse, Elliott, Adelman, Nixon, Kemmis and Walker were the most influential figures in initiating the teacher-researcher movement. However, increasingly important contributions to the movement are being made by women (see, for example, Bell, 1987; Grundy, 1987; Lomax, 1986; Nias and Groundwater-Smith, 1988; Rudduck, *et al.*, 1986). Unfortunately, Weiner's claim that the pronoun 'he' is frequently used to denote teacher-researchers continues to be borne out, as is revealed in many of the quotes from the literature in the following pages. Rather surprisingly, even Jean McNiff (1988) tells us that action research 'encourages a teacher to be reflective of his own practice in order to enhance the quality of education for himself and his pupils' (p. 1). A sub-text of this book could be to emphasize that there are many committed female practitioner researchers and to demonstrate the relevance of the practitioner research movement to their interests and concerns.

The first chapter sets the scene by documenting the origins, aims and fortunes of different movements which have contributed to, and promoted, the development of practitioner research in education during this century. In Chapter 2 Gregson portrays a collaborative action-research project on literacy within topic work. Detailed observations of pupils provide insights into their strategies for finding information in the school library and their interactions with text. Her frank account of the trials and tribulations of the research process bring home to the reader both the potentially threatening nature of researching one's own practice and the benefits in terms of personal learning.

The focus remains on reading for Chapter 3 which examines the factors informing approaches to the teaching of reading, the implications of these approaches and teachers' explanations for pupils' failures to become effective readers. While some of the issues are closely related to those discussed by Gregson, the approach to data collection was totally different. Reed negotiated access into a school with which she was unfamiliar in order to carry out her research in the role of participant observer. She acknowledges that this created an element of tension which she had to try to overcome in order for teachers to share their views and experiences with her.

In Chapter 4 Russell in the role of teacher-as-researcher describes how she studied the writing experiences of groups of infants through tape recording writing sessions and classroom observation employing the use of 'an invisible cloak'. Through gaining a deeper understanding of the pupils' likes and dislikes in regard to writing and the practical and cognitive difficulties that they encountered, she was able to identify ways of improving her teaching in this area. Chapter 5, which discusses some of the issues for consideration when collecting pupil data, returns to examining aspects of topic work from the pupils' perspective. Implications for teaching and learning are suggested by an analysis of the different ways in which information for topic tasks was gained, the purposes to which it was put and the forms in which it was presented.

In Chapter 6 Wright describes the problems that she encountered in researching her teaching of mathematics in her corridor classroom. She studied her own use of mathematics language and that of a group of middle infants and identified the confusions and misunderstandings that occurred and the effects of these on concept development. Like Russell, she explains the changes in practice that have resulted from her findings. Winter's account of her action research into science teaching forms Chapter 7. She devised, implemented and monitored a range of investigations to provide pupils with the opportunities to develop the skills of questioning, problem-solving, hypothesis-testing, and planning and evaluating their work. Readers similarly concerned to develop a process approach will find her study a useful source of ideas and pointers for consideration.

The last three case studies focus on whole school issues. Chapters 8 and 9 describe research carried out in order to inform school policies. Vickers, as part of her job description as a deputy head, was required to produce an Equal Opportunities Policy. She tackled the task by gathering information on the values and attitudes in relation to gender roles held by pupils, staff and parents. She describes how her understanding of the issues was particularly aided by data obtained from the mothers and the ways in which this influenced the initiatives taken by the staff to raise awareness both within the school and the community. McCann, in her role as home-school liaison teacher carried out extensive participant observation and video-taped observations to collect data for her research into the effects of the culture of Mirpuri pupils on their behaviour in school. She documents her increasing understanding of the pupils' experiences at home, in the Mosque and at school and describes the numerous changes in school practices brought about by the research. In Chapter 10, Horbury looks at the taken-for-granted routine activities of school life and identifies a set of classroom-based rules which both infant and junior teachers use to socialize pupils into becoming 'effective' members of a class. Acknowledging the difficulties posed by data analysis, he illustrates how the categories which he uses emerged through the continual process of organizing, re-examining and interpreting the data in the quest to determine meaning.

Chapter 11 concludes the book by drawing together the issues relating to research design, data gathering and analysis which have been discussed in the other chapters. It describes the ways in which practitioner research can influence the personal and professional development of individuals, change classroom practice, shape policy and generate theory. Finally, in considering the range of purposes which practitioner research might serve it looks at the research agenda created by the implementation of the National Curriculum.

References

ADELMAN, C., JENKINS, D. and KEMMIS, S. (1980) 'Rethinking case study: Notes from the second Cambridge conference', in SIMONS, H. (Ed.) *Towards a Science of the Singular*, Norwich, CARE, University of East Anglia.

ANNING, A. (1986) 'Curriculum in Action', in HUSTLER, D., CASSIDY, T. and Cuff, T. (Eds.) *Action Research in Classrooms and Schools*, London, Allen and Unwin.

BASSEY, M. (1981) 'Pedagogic research: On the relative merits of search for generalization and study of single events', *Oxford Review of Education*, 7, pp. 73–94.

BASSEY, M. (1983) 'Pedagogic research: Case studies, probes and curriculum innovations', *Oxford Review of Education*, 9, pp. 109–21.

BELL, G. H. (1985) 'Can schools develop knowledge of their practice?', *School Organisation*, 5, pp. 175–84.

BELL, J. (1987) *Doing Your Research Project*, Milton Keynes, Open University Press.

EQUAL OPPORTUNITIES COMMISSION (1988) *Facts ... That Figure; Equal Opportunities and Education*, EOC: Manchester.

FULLAN, M. (1982) *The Meaning of Educational Change*, Toronto, OISE Press.

GRUNDY, S. (1987) *Curriculum: Product or Praxis*, Lewes, Falmer Press.

HUSTLER, D., CASSIDY, T. and CUFF, T. (Eds.) (1986) *Action Research in Classrooms and Schools*, London, Allen and Unwin.

LEWIS, I. (1988) 'Learning Together: Issues Arising from Outstation MA Course Experience', in NIAS, J. and GROUNDWATER-SMITH, S. (Eds.) *The Enquiring Teacher: Supporting and Sustaining Teacher Research*, Lewes, Falmer Press.

LOMAX, P. (1986) 'Action researchers' action research: A symposium', *British Journal of In-service Education*, 13, (1) pp. 42–9.

MCNIFF, J. (1988) *Action Research: Principles and Practice*, London, Macmillan Education.

MUNN, P. (1986) 'Teachers' Perceptions of Year One of the Outstation Programme: Bramley Grange Cohort 1984–1985', Department of Education, University of York

NIAS, J. (1988) 'Introduction' in NIAS, J. and GROUNDWATER-SMITH, S. (Eds.) *The Enquiring Teacher: Supporting and Sustaining Teacher Research*, Lewes, Falmer Press.

NIXON, J. C. (Ed.) (1981) *A Teachers' Guide to Action Research*, London, Grant McIntyre.

OBERG, A. and McCUTCHEON, G. (1989) 'Teachers' experience doing action research', *Peabody Journal of Education*, **64**, (2), pp. 116–27.

PRISK, T. (1987) 'Letting them get on with it: A study of unsupervised talk in an infant school', in POLLARD, A. (Ed.) *Children and Their Primary Schools*, Lewes, Falmer Press.

RUDDUCK, J., HOPKINS, D., SANGER, J. and LINCOLN, P. (1986) *Collaborative Enquiry and Information Skills*, British Library Research Paper 16, London, British Library.

SKILBECK, M. (1983) 'Lawrence Stenhouse: research methodology', *British Educational Research Journal*, **9**, pp. 11–20.

SMITH, L.M. (1978) 'An evolving logic of participant observation, educational ethnography and other case studies', in SHULMAN, L. S. (Ed.) *Review of Research in Education*, Chicago, Peacock.

STENHOUSE, L. (1975) *An Introduction to Curriculum Research and Development*, London, Heinemann.

TREACHER, V. (Ed.) (1989) *Assessment and Evaluation in the Arts*, Berkshire LEA SCDC Arts in Schools Project, Reading, Berkshire LEA.

WEBB, K. (1986) 'Teachers' Perceptions of Year One of the Outstation Programme: Banney Royd 1985–6', Department of Education, University of York.

WEBB, R. (1984) 'An Evaluation of the Cleveland Outstation Programme', Department of Education, University of York.

WEBB, R. (1988) 'Outstation Teams: a collaborative approach to research in schools', *British Educational Research Journal*, **14**, No.1, pp. 51–64.

WEINER, G. (1989) 'Professional self-knowledge versus social justice: A critical analysis of the teacher-researcher movement', *British Educational Research Journal*, **15**, pp. 41–51.

WINTER, R. (1989) *Learning from Experience: Principles and Practice in Action Research*, Lewes, Falmer Press.

Chapter one

The Origins and Aspirations of Practitioner Research

Rosemary Webb

In the introductory chapter I mentioned the initial perceptions of educational research as irrelevant and unhelpful to the development of classroom practice which I held as a beginning teacher. These sentiments are echoed throughout the literature of teacher research and are probably still held by some teachers. However, as will be shown in this chapter, the growth of practitioner research — especially during the last decade — has fostered collaboration between teachers and researchers in institutions of higher education and has done much to demonstrate and promote the inter-relationship between research and action, and theory and practice.

This chapter identifies the diverse strands of the teacher-researcher movement and examines their origins and changing fortunes. The different ways in which researchers within the pyschological, sociological and pedagogic traditions have sought to involve teachers in research are described. The pragmatic and ideological reasons underlying this involvement within these traditions are contrasted, revealing some strong similarities. Notions of teacher-as-research students, research critics, research workers, curriculum-problem-solvers and initiators of their own investigations emerge. These notions are analyzed to reveal their value positions, the demands in terms of skills and knowledge that they make of teachers and their underlying expectations of changing practice in classrooms and influencing educational policy. The chapter thus provides a map of the main influences which have shaped practitioner research, as it is currently practised, which can be pursued in greater depth through the references by the reader who so wishes.

A historical overview of the teacher-researcher movement provides important lessons for the conduct of such work today. Whereas teacher research is currently identified both with qualitative research strategies, such as case study and action research, and with a focus upon teachers' rather than educational researchers' concerns, neither of these have always been the case.

Thus, I will show how teacher-researcher developments have at different times been incorporated into the more traditional positivist research paradigms in both psychology and sociology (for the essential differences between positivist and qualitative research strategies, see Finch, 1986). The motivations for this have varied, from recognizing the important role that teachers could play in collecting data for educational researchers to a conviction that the practice of teaching might be improved by conveying to teachers the theories of educational researchers. In each case, this led to styles of teacher research in which the priorities of teachers were almost totally subordinated to those of researchers. The lessons of history indicate, however, that the problems arising from this are certainly not restricted only to traditional positivist research strategies. Thus, the chapter concludes by suggesting that some of the currently influential approaches to practitioner research are in danger of suffering a similar fate.

Practitioner Research and the Psycho-Statistical Paradigm

In 1981 in his AERA Conference address, May (1981) argued that if research and teaching aspired to achieve a more creative relationship it would be necessary for both the language and style of accounts of the research process and findings to be couched in language which would make them accessible to practitioners. He identified the early attempts to bridge the gap between the theory generated in academic institutions and the reality as experienced by the class teacher as based on the notion of 'teacher-as-research-student'. This is the notion that comes across in American writing on the subject at the turn of the century. For example, Boone (1904) argued that:

> for reliable results there are needed trained observers . . . there is needed a body of earnest teachers who are also students, and who are ready to make every day's undertakings an object of thoughtful, critical direction . . . open-minded, as if working in a laboratory. (p. 200)

Teachers were required to develop an understanding of the research concerns and methods of experimental psychology. As May (1981) pointed out, such involvement required the teacher community 'to give more credence to the "realities" of the research community, whilst the latter maintain their established position' (p. 2).

This is the stance elaborated in the work of Buckingham (1926) who emphasized that educational research needed the involvement of teachers because psychological problems should be pursued 'in their immediate and practical bearing' (p. 374). Participation in research by teachers ensured a ready supply of research subjects, as teachers had access to a large number of learners for a long period of time. Also, 'in the case of the teacher the application may be made to the very persons from whom the data were secured and in respect to whom, therefore, their validity is less doubtful' (p. 374). Teacher involvement was seen as a means to get teachers to value and act on research. The likely relevance of that research to the wider teaching community was not questioned.

However, Buckingham believed that there were benefits for the teacher to be derived from participating in the research process:

> If teaching these children is to include studying them, the job of teaching takes on new dignity. Its scope is broadened. Its meaning is enriched. No other calling may then be compared with it. It is the great adventure. (p. 380)

Thus in his book entitled *Research for Teachers* he exhorts his audience to become 'research workers':

> Some of the experiments performed by the psychologist can be conducted by you, and there are others, available to you, which he cannot easily manage. You will need some direction and at first you will make mistakes. But you will be at the heart of teaching and learning; and if you use good sense you will profit much and so will your pupils. (p. 371)

He describes two laboratory experiments on learning that could have been located within schools and conducted by teachers concluding that 'If you substitute the teacher for the psychologist, the schoolroom for the laboratory, and a class of pupils for the half dozen learners, you have the conditions for a very much more fundamental and satisfactory experiment' (p. 372).

Although Buckingham is predominantly concerned with testing and experimental research, he acknowledges that 'among the many types of research work available to teachers, the making of case studies is by no means unimportant' (p. 378). However, by case studies he means the kinds of investigation carried out by clinical psychologists whereby the characteristics, antecedents, needs and achievements of individuals are recorded in detail. For him 'A collection of such cases would be a priceless legacy from an experienced teacher' (p. 378). More recently the argument for the cumulation of educational case studies in order to build up a bank of professional knowledge has been forwarded by Stenhouse (1978) as the basis for developing a history of contemporary education. Also, as argued by

Ebbutt and Elliott (1985), such a bank of expertise and collective insights into common problems could provide a resource for teachers to build upon when reflecting on problems in their own situations, rather than simply 'reinventing the wheel'. It also facilitates the generation of theory by encouraging generalizations to be made across cases and by providing a wider research community with access to hypotheses which they may wish to test and refine in the context of their own particular situations and the possibilities open to them.

Buckingham goes on to assure teachers that 'if you do your work carefully . . . reports of what you have done will be gladly received by periodicals for publication' (p. 371). He backs up this claim by referring to some 'reports of a research character' by teachers which 'recently appeared in a single volume of one of our foremost educational journals'. The subject matter of these ranged across extra-curricular activities, accounting systems for athletic organizations, student publications, the high school assembly, the proper use of the teacher's time and 'the pupil of low intelligence quotient'. He does not foresee a tension between the teachers' interests in, and perspectives on, the issues that they chose to write about and the agenda likely to be set for them by the psychologists. It is interesting to read his view on teachers writing reports for academic journals in the light of the comments made by Oberg and McCutcheon (1989), which are discussed in the introduction (see p. 7), and the problems teachers have experienced in getting their work accepted by the 'traditional' research community located within research institutes and institutions of higher education. Either he attributed that community with considerable flexibility and openness to alternative accounts, or he was confident that the teachers would be both willing and able to work within the experimental paradigm and write up their experience according to its established criteria. However, if a coherent body of pedagogic knowledge is to be contributed to and utilized by practitioners, ways of co-ordinating and disseminating findings need to be found which must include facilitating the publication of their work by teachers.

Referring to the *Lists of Researches in Education and Educational Psychology* compiled by Blackwell (1950, 1952, 1954, 1956 and 1958), May (1981) draws attention to the vast range and quantity of educational research within the 'psycho-statistical' paradigm that has been undertaken, primarily by teachers, for higher degree qualifications in education at British universities since 1918. This is also apparent in the *Register of Theses on Educational Topics in Universities in Ireland* which goes back to 1911 (McKernan, 1985). Teachers participating in such research had to learn the language and methods associated with the paradigm.

Dewey (1929), like Buckingham, was very concerned about the fact that educational theory appeared to have little impact on classroom processes. He argued that while educational theory derived from research was merely transmitted to teachers their understanding of the implications for classroom practice were likely to go unrecognized or become distorted. He viewed the contributions that might be given by classteachers as 'a comparatively neglected field' (p. 46) and argued for the involvement of 'the teacher as investigator'. This was necessary because:

> As far as schools are concerned, it is certain that the problems which require scientific treatment arise in actual relationships with students. Consequently, it is impossible to see how there can be an adequate flow of subject-matter to set and control the problems investigators deal with, unless there is active participation on the part of those directly engaged in teaching. (p. 48)

He attributed the problem largely to the limitations of quantitative methods of data collection which, if their importance is exaggerated:

> tend to cramp judgement, to substitute uniform rules for the free play of thought, and to emphasise the mechanical factors that also exist in schools . . . they do not give any help in the larger questions of reconstruction of curriculum and methods. (pp. 65–6)

He recognized the inadequacy of an approach to practitioner research which merely engaged teachers in experimental work and surveys. He suggested that both the research agenda and the research methods needed to change if research was to become meaningful to teachers and to suggest practical solutions to problems.

The Origins of Action Research

Lewin, a social psychologist in the field of human relations, shared Dewey's view that research findings ought to provide insights for practitioners or policy-makers to suggest to them ways in which to act in order to bring about change. Believing that 'research that produces nothing but books will not suffice' (1946, p. 35), Lewin devised a model of action research designed to enable the effective management of social situations in order to achieve certain prespecified objectives. This model took the form of 'a spiral of steps each of which was composed of a cycle of planning, action and fact-finding about the result of the action' (p. 38). Fact-finding or 'reconnaisance to show us whether we move in the right direction and with what speed we move' (p. 38) was vital for the necessary modification and ultimate successful implementation of the overall plan. Unlike current educational action research, which at least in rhetoric and generally in practice, aspires to be open-ended and democratic, Lewin's model was functionalist and prescriptive. Also, given that his research was aimed at the improvement of intergroup relations, the choice of a reconnaisance plane assessing the situation after a bomber raid on Germany seems an extraordinary example of the fact-finding process.

For a decade Lewin's approach was very influential in the United States within the work on human relations and he is widely referred to as the founder of action research. However, McKernan (1989) argues that this is undeserved because a few other writers had already used the notion of action research and indeed the actual term. For example, Collier (1945), Commissioner for Indian Affairs from 1933–45, used the expression action research and urged the administration to adopt such an approach to social planning. He was convinced that 'since the findings of research must be carried into effect by the administrator and the layman, and must be criticised by them through their experience, the administrator and the layman must themselves participate creatively in the research, impelled as it is from their own area of need' (p. 276).

McKernan (1989) describes how in the USA during the period 1930–45 state and local authorities increasingly involved teachers in research and curriculum development activities. The view that this could be best achieved through quantitative studies continued to predominate. This is illustrated in a short book aiming to promote teacher involvement in educational research as part of the process of rebuilding post-war education in Britain. Written by Oliver (1946), the then Professor of Education at Manchester University, it states the requirements for teachers' investigations to count as research:

> To define objectives . . . to define results clearly, and if possible express them exactly in the quantitative terms of measurement. This procedure may seem rigorous, and even far removed from the work of teaching. it is necessary, however, if we wish to lift teaching from the plane of opinion towards that of proof. (pp. 32–3)

However, during the post-war period several writers drawing on the work of the progressives and the social psychologists championed the use of action research to achieve curriculum reform. Their models of action research, although influenced by Lewin, seem closer in espoused philosophy to the aspirations of current practitioner research. For example, one can note the open-minded, open-ended ways in which Passow *et al.* (1955) suggest that an action researcher should behave:

> The action researcher is a person who does not feel that he has all the facts and knows all the answers. He tries to gather facts and carefully assess and delineate the problem. Rather than resorting to propaganda techniques, he tries to ask and search for evidence when he himself or other members present opinions. Rather than having a pre-designed solution, and predefined judgments, he states solutions tentatively as hypotheses to be tested. He withholds judgments and conclusions until evidence is collected and analysed. (p. 143)

Corey (1949), concerned that 'very little has been written in the field of education which will be particularly helpful to persons who are interested in action research' (p. 511) put together a collection of journal articles to form a handbook on *Action Research to Improve School Practices* (1953). In the handbook he identifies the two main tenets of his particular approach to action research. Firstly, the approach is based on the formulation and testing of an 'action hypothesis'. An action hypothesis is a hunch or prediction that a particular procedure will lead to a desired goal. Such hypotheses are derived both from teachers' beliefs and convictions and from 'traditional research investigations' which 'frequently are fruitful sources of hypotheses to test in actual school situations' (p. 30). One of the examples he gives is:

> Curriculum committees made up of volunteers [action] will be more productive [goal] than curriculum committees constituted by appointment [alternative action].

Hypotheses such as the above can be put to the test by putting the procedures into practice and collecting evidence to determine the degree to which the goal has been realized. As a result of the findings, further action hypotheses can be formulated and tested as part of a cyclical process until the problem is satisfactorily resolved. It is interesting that the process of systematically gathering and analyzing data does not begin until after the solution has been formulated. Current models of action research (see, for example, Carr and Kemmis, 1986) have an enquiring stance from the outset in order to ensure that before any action is taken the nature of the problem is adequately understood.

Secondly, Corey emphasizes the importance of 'co-operative action research' which involves all those who are known to be concerned about the problem being tackled or those who will be affected by whatever is done to solve it. The main advantages he argues for this approach are that if a number of interested parties are involved in tackling a problem they are more likely to devise feasible solutions. Also, if the data indicate that changes are required, there will be greater staff commitment to bring this about and a supportive framework within which to take the risks that are necessarily involved in trying out new practices. However, he warns of the need to maintain good relationships with other staff and to keep them informed about the research because 'unless precautions are taken, the research group may become something of a pedagogical island in a generally hostile faculty environment' (1953, p. 39). This aptly describes the situation in which Holly (1984) and a group of teachers undertaking action research found themselves because their school's hidden curriculum, the organizational structures, the management styles and the relationships between teachers and pupils were in direct conflict with the values and processes of the research.

For Corey, the merits of an action-research project should be determined by the extent to which the methods and findings have brought about improvement in practice. He acknowledges that the action researcher's concern with improvement 'make it unlikely, though not impossible, that his findings will contribute to the systematic body of information known as the science of education' (1949, p. 512). In this statement he pre-empts the growing dilemma experienced by practitioner researchers, especially those who are submitting accounts of research primarily designed to bring about change in the classroom as theses for the award of higher degrees. In the current climate, understandably, there is an increasing requirement by schools and LEAs for practical research outcomes, at least in the first instance, in return for various forms of support such as the payment of course fees. This pressure is occurring at a time when an expanding body of knowledge on practitioner research makes possible more sophisticated research designs drawing on a wider range of data-gathering techniques, such as videos of classrooms, group interviews, teachers' diaries and the use of simulations with pupils. Increasingly, there is an expectation that a more thorough approach should be capable of generating more in-depth theorizing and generalizable hypotheses. However, within the timescale available, if the major orientation of the research is a situation-specific practical classroom concern, the potential for theory generation may be left unexploited as it usually requires an additional level of data analysis aided by further reading. But, as Pollard (1984) has argued, systematic rigorous research is the kind that both makes the most effective contribution to shaping policy, whether at school, regional or national level, and to theory generation. Unfortunately, Corey has no suggestions on how to address this issue. Recognizing that theory generation is a difficult process for all researchers he counters with the accusation that 'although professional researchers are inclined to emphasise theory when their attention is called specifically to it, this emphasis is not at all evident in most of their research reports' (1953, p. 30).

After a period of growth in the 1940s and 1950s the practitioner-research movement fell into decline as once again theory and practice, research processes and action became separated out. Carr and Kemmis (1986) offer an explanation for this rooted in the social and economic climate during a period when the technological model of research and development was highly successful:

> As academic researchers in the social sciences began to enjoy unprecedented support from public funding bodies, they began to distinguish the work of the theorist-researcher from that of the 'engineer' responsible for putting theoretical principles into practice. The rising tide of post-Sputnik curriculum development, based on a research-development-diffusion (RD and D) model of the relationship between research and practice, legitimated and sustained this separation . . . By the mid-1960s, [this] model had established itself as the pre-eminent model for change. (p. 166)

The RD and D model can be illustrated by a brief description of two inter-related projects sponsored by the British Library Research and Development Department (BLRDD). A report (Irving and Snape, 1979) based on an interview survey of 200 teachers and school librarians in Nottingham and Cheshire identified the gap between the skills teachers felt that pupils needed, and those that they were actually taught. As a follow-up to this Hounsell and Martin (1983) mounted a two-year development project in 1978 which resulted in the national distribution of a resource folder in order to provide teachers with further information about these skills and some practical assistance in teaching them. While Hounsell and Martin felt that their project had raised the awareness of the teachers who were able to participate in project workshops the receipt of materials alone appeared a weak strategy to initiate change.

An acknowledgment of the problem of trying to achieve widespread or in-depth change in schools by projects following the RD and D model has caused recent BLRDD funding to favour action-research projects such as Information Skills in the Curriculum Research Unit (Norris, 1983) and Teaching, Information-Handling and Learning (Sanger, 1987). The advantages and disadvantages of an action-research approach to the development and dissemination of work in the area of information skills are explored in a collection of papers by Rudduck, Hopkins, Sangar and Lincoln, (1987).

Practitioner Research within the Sociology of Education

Sociologists, like their psychologist counterparts, have also sought to induct teachers into their methods and for similar reasons. This was particularly the case for researchers working within the ethnographic 'interpretive' paradigm such as the proponents of the 'new sociology of education' (Gorbutt, 1972). They challenged approaches to teaching predicated on the assumption that education or 'academic' knowledge was necessarily superior to everyday commonsense knowledge. This challenge created a need for detailed investigations of the nature of curricular knowledge and the implications of this for teaching and learning which both demonstrated the need for, and encouraged the development of, an interpretive research paradigm in education. This paradigm contained the possibility of a central role for the teacher as researcher and agent of change:

> If teachers could operate in various forms as researchers, it may be possible for them to gain new insights and understanding of their world, on which new practices may be based. Teachers' knowledge need no longer be treated as something which researchers study, but as a resource and having a value, which can contribute to new understandings. (Bartholomew, 1973, p. 21)

The underlying tenet of the 'new sociology' was that school knowledge is socially constructed and ideological and should be rendered as problematic and open to sociological examination. This was expressed through the contributions to *Knowledge and Control* (Young, 1971) which opened up 'some alternative . . . and fruitful directions for sociological enquiry into education' (p. 2). The literature which emerged during the brief period following the book's publication suggests that it was a time of considerable excitement and exploration. A number of ex-teachers, working within this analytical framework, conducted participant observation studies. These questioned taken-for-granted aspects of the curriculum and of teachers' perspectives and offered alternative explanations of pupil failure which were located within school provision rather than the supposed deficiencies of pupils and their backgrounds (see, e.g., Vulliamy, 1976, on music teaching and Whitty, 1976, on social studies teaching).

Early on in this movement Gorbutt (1972) recognized the potential of the new sociology of education, which 'challenges prevailing practices and assumptions in colleges and schools' (p. 7) for developing 'professional awareness'. At the North East London Polytechnic he developed the notion of 'the self-critical researching teacher who would constantly monitor the effectiveness of his own and colleagues' activities and modify his behaviour accordingly' (p. 10). The subsequent creation of new knowledge structures and alternative pedagogical approaches arising from this new understanding were poised to 'revitalise schools and colleges and possibly fulfil the promise of education for all' (p. 10).

However, such hopes were shortlived. As Whitty (1981) has argued, early criticisms of the 'new sociology of education', which considered it to have an over-optimistic view of the possibilities of change at school level based on an inadequate analysis of institutional and societal constraints, caused the movement to split in two directions. One group followed the lead of Althusser (1971) and Bowles and Gintis (1976) and engaged in Marxist critiques and considerations of social and cultural reproduction in capitalist societies. The well-known study of progressive primary education by Sharp and Green (1976) is an example of such an ethnography conducted within a Marxist framework. Teachers are portrayed as unaware of the discrepancies between the reality of their classroom practices and their aspirations. The study denies 'the possibility that the teachers theorise as much as they, as researchers, do, although within different realms of discourse with different sources of significance' (Adelman and Young, 1985, p. 50). Teachers are once again relegated to the role of subjects to be researched.

The second group focused on conducting ethnographies on the minutiae of school life (Hammersley and Woods, 1976; Woods, 1980a and 1980b) and within this approach the perceptions of teachers continued to be valued and various ways of actually involving them in research were explored. For example, Burgess (1980a) describes a series of in-service courses that had been provided for teachers since 1977 which introduced them to the current concerns of sociological research in education, taught them how to evaluate such research and how to conduct small-scale studies. His experience with course participants led him to believe that if teachers were trained to evaluate and conduct research it would be possible to promote research groups within schools to inform school policy and decision-making. This would be achieved by summarizing relevant research reports and circulating them to staff and by conducting small-scale studies within schools. The Teachers' Centre was envisaged as coordinating the work between particular groups and disseminating it over a wider area.

The study of particular cases is obviously a much more viable proposition for the practising teacher than the study of representative samples which characterizes the 'psycho-statistical' paradigm of educational research. However, alternative paradigms continued to exist which involved teachers as researchers within the positivist tradition. At the Centre for Educational Sociology, University of Edinburgh, a Collaborative Research Programme enabled practitioners to pursue enquiries on topics of interest to them through accessing a specially designed computerized data-bank of information on the school and post-school experiences of Scottish school leavers — the Scottish Education Data Archive (SEDA) (Cope and Gray, 1979). A fundamental aim of the programme was to enable teachers 'to understand the implications of survey data and critically to examine practice in the light of these implications' (pp. 238–9). Also, it was hoped that through experiencing the same kinds of knowledge bases open to government and administrators, teachers would be better equipped to participate in public debate.

In claiming the programme represented 'something markedly different' from naturalistic classroom-based research, Cope and Gray point out that they 'do not need teachers in order to acquire the core data' and 'we are therefore inducting teachers not from the direct practical necessities of data collection but from theoretical conviction' (p. 239). While this chapter shows how the notion of teacher-as-research worker was an essentially pragmatic move by the research community, progressives such as Dewey were also motivated by theoretical conviction that teachers who understood, participated in and utilized research for their own purposes would be in a stronger position to initiate change. Also, as will be demonstrated in the remaining sections of this chapter, those currently concerned to develop the teacher-as-researcher movement share Cope and Gray's concern to empower teachers 'to operate in the world of policy, resources and curriculum innovation' and 'to infiltrate into that world alternative modes of comprehending' (p. 250).

The Teacher-as-Researcher Movement

In Britain the national curriculum research and development projects of the 1970s provided the main impetus and support for teachers concerned to research their own practice through a 'naturalistic' or case-study approach. As discussed in the Introduction (see p. 3-5) this approach, which focused on pedagogic concerns, adapted and extended the techniques of data collecting employed by ethnographers. The Schools Council's Humanities Curriculum Project (HCP) (1967–1972) based at CARE ascribed fundamental importance to the role of the teacher researcher. Research and teaching were viewed as interdependent processes and it was suggested that the characteristics of a professional teacher might include:

> The commitment to a systematic questioning of one's own teaching as a
> basis for development;
> The commitment and skills to study one's own teaching;
> The concern to question and to test theory in practice by the use of those
> skills. (Stenhouse, 1975, pp. 143–144)

Both HCP and the Race Relations Project (1972–5) which followed it
were concerned to develop a radical new pedagogy for the study of
controversial issues in classrooms. Elliott (1983) identified what Stenhouse
offered teachers through these projects as 'a curriculum conceived as a set of
hypotheses they could experiment with as the basis for a reflective translation
of educational ideas' (pp. 108–9). The notion was that practitioners should
not merely accept and implement the ideas of academic researchers but
rather that they should test them out in their own classrooms in order to
evaluate, reject and/or develop them. A parallel can be drawn between this
and Corey's (1953) idea of developing and testing out 'action hypotheses' in
school situations described earlier in the chapter. Also, through the process
of enquiring into their own practice, Stenhouse (1983) considered that
practitioners would become more aware of the reasons underpinning their
assumptions and actions and recognize the constraints and pressures exerted
on them by societal norms and expectations. This developing understanding
was regarded as potentially emancipatory:

> The essence of emancipation, as I conceive it, is the intellectual,
> moral and spiritual autonomy which we recognise when we eschew
> paternalism and the rule of authority and hold ourselves obliged to
> appeal to judgement. (p. 162)

The Ford Teaching Project (1975), which focused on the problems of
implementing enquiry-discovery methods across the curriculum, took
further the potential of teacher research apparent from the experience of
HCP and developed some influential strategies for the collection and
analysis of data, such as triangulation (Elliott and Adelman, 1976) and the
negotiation of accounts with research participants in order to diminish bias
and increase the reliability of interpretations. The Classroom Action
Research Network (CARN), which now has an international membership,
was set up in 1976 with a grant from the Ford Foundation to provide a forum
for the discussion and dissemination of the project's work. The project on
Teacher-Pupil Interaction and the Quality of Learning (TIQL) (1981–83)
based at the Cambridge Institute of Education (CIE) further refined and

documented these strategies through the production of working papers such as 'Action-research: A framework for self-evaluation in schools' (Elliott, 1981). Through the involvement of 'outer network' groups TIQL contributed to the dissemination of the ideas and practices of teacher research — for example, several of the contributors to *Action Research in Classrooms and Schools* (Hustler, Cassidy and Cuff, 1986) were influenced by their participation in the project.

Since the exploratory work in action research undertaken at CARE and the CIE in the early 1970s the number of action-research projects and networks set up to support practitioner researchers has steadily expanded, often centred on institutions of higher education. As such groups evolve, they sometimes develop their own philosophy, underlying principles and procedures which inform and guide the ways in which research is carried out within the group. An example of one such distinctive British group is that centred on the University of Bath (McNiff, 1988) which is led by Jack Whitehead. The central concern of this group is to develop the idea of a 'living educational theory' embodied in the action researchers' claims to know how and why they are attempting to overcome practical educational problems and the form of their own professional development. Whitehead (1989) argues that educational theorizing is the reflexive process that arises from a teacher's awareness of his/her 'self' as 'a living contradiction' whose practice negates the realization of desired aims and values and the experience of overcoming that negation. The validity of individuals' 'claims to knowledge' contained within their research accounts are judged according to methodological soundness and the degree of reflexivity demonstrated in relation to the effects of the personal and social contexts in which the theories were located.

Groups like the one at Bath, which have a distinctive corporate identity, can provide teachers with a supportive but critical forum for generating ideas and discussing and refining their work. Such groups have the potential to provide practitioner research with direction, a strong sense of purpose and the possibility of individuals contributing to the development of a house style. However, there seems to be a danger that groups which have a particular intellectual tradition or strong theoretical perspective could create a straitjacket for intending practitioner researchers, who feel they must conform to the methods advocated by their mentors. Although teachers are encouraged to reflect critically upon their practices and upon the ways in which the educational system shapes those practices, they may not be similarly encouraged to reflect on and question the values, beliefs and processes that they are participating in as a group member.

Ironically, there seems a particular danger of teachers being channelled into certain ways of interpreting their world in forms of research which specifically set out to 'emancipate' them. This raises questions about how far facilitators of learning can take responsibility for the emancipation of those with whom they work and the criteria that they use to determine when and to what degree such emancipation has been achieved. For example, Lawn (1989) advocates forms of what he has called 'schoolwork research' which 'builds from life history to institutional change' and 'aims to emancipate from isolation and from institution' (p. 157). He describes how primary in-service teachers engaged in school-based research would begin with ideas for 'rather neat research projects on curriculum content' which then changed after several weeks because of 'their growing confidence about what educational research could be and with a recognition that it could be relevant to their concerns' (p. 157). On the one hand, he claims that 'I have never determined the nature of the research, only the method of achieving it (participant observation/interview)' (p. 157). On the other hand, when giving examples of the teachers' choice of topics they can be seen to relate closely to his own theoretical interests in the labour process (see, for example, Lawn, 1987; Lawn and Ozga, 1981). Thus the topics which he cites are: relations with the headteacher, relations with each other, finding a role, school labour disputes, and mid-term career analyses. Even the apparently unrelated and familiar topic of display was subsequently viewed as 'an innocuous subject [which] turned out to be a significant feature of the labour process' (p. 158). Thus those of us who lead such groups should examine and acknowledge our potential influence over the selection of research topics and the frameworks within which data are analyzed. It is necessary to question the depth of understanding and the level of emancipation that can be achieved in situations where teachers may only control the surface features of their research, such as the choice of data-collection techniques. This problem is compounded, of course, within the context of an award-bearing course.

A concern for emancipation and a blueprint for achieving it is central to the work of the currently most influential group promoting action research, which is based at Deakin University, Victoria. The group's publications, which are designed to facilitate teacher research, particularly within the University's own award-bearing courses offered to off-campus students, give detailed guidance on how to follow their formal schema. This comprises a self-reflective action-research spiral which represents a much reworked version of Lewin's original concept (see, for example, McTaggart and Kemmis, 1981). While the schema demonstrates the need for action research to be rigorous and systematic and provides ways in which this might be achieved, Groundwater-Smith (1988) suggests that for the practitioners on Deakin's courses it has become 'a set of technical rules for the conduct of the action research game complete with a snakes and ladders spiral which would allow movement around the board, leading ultimately to the granting of a credential' (p. 261).

This group's approach to action research has a strong theoretical framework derived from the Frankfurt School of Critical Theorists, especially the contemporary philosopher Jurgens Habermas. Habermas (1978) identifies three knowledge-constitutive interests: technical-cognitive, practical and emancipatory-cognitive. These three, which determine how knowledge is generated and organized, can be recognized as characterizing all human activity. Grundy (1987), who acknowledges her intellectual debt to Kemmis, argues that the knowledge-constituitive interests are manifest in three distinct models of action research: technical, practical and emancipatory. The technical interest gives rise to instrumental action research which becomes a vehicle for assessing and refining teaching skills and disseminating sets of ideas which remain unquestioned by the research process. The practical interest is characterized by a general concept of 'the good' and gives rise to deliberative and collaborative action research designed to gain in-depth understanding of curricular specifications and classroom situations in order to effect improvements in practice. However, the assumptions underpinning what constitutes an improvement, the structure of the education system and social norms remain unchallenged. Only emancipatory action research, she suggests, transforms the ways in which practitioners think and act. It does this through requiring them to recognize and understand the historical and social origins of their actions and the consequences that these have for others involved in the schooling process. In the project descriptions which Grundy provides to exemplify these models she makes no attempt to examine how in reality they overlap and interrelate. Reflection and action stimulated by practical concerns can serve to feed reflection and action arising from emancipatory interests and vice versa.

Critical theorists attack practitioner research, which like most of the studies reported in this book, have their origins within the CARE tradition for its emphasis on the 'practical' as opposed to the emancipatory. Carr (1984) makes the claim that:

> where the 'critical' approach differs from the 'practical' view is in its explicit recognition of how the practitioner's own understanding of his educational values may become distorted by various non-educational forces and pressures and of how the practical realisation of those values may be impeded by institutional structures and political constraints. (p. 4)

However, as Cicourel (1981) points out, micro- and macro-data and theory are integrated in everyday settings as a routine feature of all cultural or social organization 'because all daily life settings reflect several levels of cultural complexity' (p. 52). He argues that:

> Neither micro- nor macro-structures are self contained levels of analysis, they interact with each other at all times despite the convenience and sometimes the dubious luxury of only examining one or other level of analysis. (p. 54)

When reflecting on everyday classroom practice, practitioners immediately come up against the context of power and authority in which that practice is located. Thus Elliott (1983) claims that teacher-researchers investigating issues of importance to them 'tend to develop critiques of the macro-context of their practices during the process of reflectively developing and testing their practical theories' (p. 14). For example, the teachers that Elliott (1976) worked with on the Ford Teaching Project were concerned to deepen their understanding of the factors facilitating or constraining the promotion of enquiry/discovery learning in order to improve this aspect of their practice.

Carr (1984) views it as part of the role of the critical theorists:

> to indicate to practitioners what needs to be done for these misunderstandings to be removed and the adverse effects of these organisational arrangements eliminated. (p. 5)

They see their role as the achievement of the professional emancipation of teachers, by replacing uncritical attitudes with reflective ones derived from outside the study of education. However, there appears to be a danger that research facilitators may preside in judgment over teachers, thereby imposing on them the researchers' decisions as to what constitutes reasoned arguments and which statements are based on false consciousness. Proponents of the 'practical' approach attach importance to the perspectives, values and predilections of both teachers and researchers. They acknowledge that the biography or the 'false consciousness' of both groups always affects what is regarded as important data in a piece of research and the ways in which these data are likely to be interpreted.

Within emancipatory action research, it is intended that the understanding of the effects of structural practices and the empowerment that this understanding brings, should be achieved through self-reflective discourse within an Ideal Speech Situation (ISS). ISS requires a climate of justice and equality where all speakers can freely communicate their views and question the assertions of others. Groundwater-Smith (1988) acknowledges the likely impossibility of creating a collaborative critical community of the kind envisaged by Habermas within the context of award-bearing courses which reward individual competitive effort and vest authority in the facilitators of the research. Using the Action Research Planner (McTaggart and Kemmis, 1981) as an example she speculates as to whether through:

> the reification of certain practices . . . some enquiry-based teacher research has become a strategy for reproducing technical behaviour more expertly. (p. 261)

Even without the additional constraint of working towards an award conditions in schools do not readily lend themselves to establishing an ISS. Although increasingly the individualist culture of schools is breaking down and staff are working collaboratively on school policies and schemes of work, a climate has yet to be established in most schools where views are openly exchanged and reciprocal critique encouraged. There are a number of important factors which prevent the achievement of such a climate, such as the hierarchical nature of staffing, school micro-politics and the expertise traditionally considered to be vested in the academics, advisers or members of the school's senior management who might facilitate such research.

Conclusion

The historical overview of the rise and fall of teacher-research movements during this century reveals the extent to which these movements imposed on teachers particular ways of thinking and acting in relation to their practice. For example, in the very different traditions of both the psycho-statistical paradigm and the interpretive paradigm of the 'new sociology of education' it was necessary for teachers to accept and to learn to work with the specific methods, conceptual frameworks and purposes laid down by their facilitators in academic institutions.

The rhetoric of the more recent teacher-research movements acknowledges that permanent changes in practice arise from fundamental shifts in attitudes which can only be achieved through teachers grappling with, and therefore achieving an understanding of, school and classroom issues. This suggests that the research concerns and ways of gathering evidence and interpreting that evidence are the prerogative of the teachers. However, closer examination shows how current traditions of teacher research are also moulding and categorizing teachers' investigations. Given that any movement which introduces teachers to new ideas and ways of working will necessarily 'indoctrinate' to some extent, some traditions attempt to exert greater influence over teachers than others. For example, the model of action research located at Bath and the 'emancipatory' model of action research developed at Deakin University contain notions of appropriate topics for research, a specific language over and above that generally associated with the research process, theoretical frameworks to guide data analysis, expectations in terms of both product outcomes and ways of thinking and specific criteria by which successful progress through the research process can be judged.

Two traditions have retained the greatest autonomy for the teachers: 'practical' action research as developed at CARE and the CIE and the work of the post-war action-researchers as represented by Corey (1953) who shared similar concerns and approaches. In so doing the proponents of 'practical' action research have incurred criticisms that they have failed to encourage teachers to critique the macro-context of their practice and recognize the social, economic and political constraints on change in schools. However, I have argued that self-critical reflection, which is an essential element of 'practical' action reseach, leads practitioners to critique the macro-context of their practice. Practitioner research is recognized as a vehicle for both exposing and working to alleviate the constraints under which teachers work. However, teachers have to work within the system and many of them are concerned to find ways of doing so more effectively for the benefit of their pupils. Therefore a major aim of practical action research is to enable practitioners to inhabit the system creatively in order to work towards change through action at the micro-level.

Strong theoretical positions like those underpinning both 'emancipatory' and 'schoolwork' research may serve to replace uncritical attitudes by 'critical' ones, but these may be applied in a similarly uncritical fashion. When adopting these new positions, how far are teachers encouraged to recognize and question the sociohistorical antecedents and institutional norms which give rise to them? If teacher research is to be genuinely deserving of this label, then teachers should be able to play a major role in determining its orientation and to make choices from a range of possible analytical frameworks.

Thus, the reader will find considerable individual differences between the research accounts in this book in terms both of approaches to data gathering and of analysis. For example, the chapters by Gregson and Reed both focus on aspects of reading. However, on the one hand, Gregson's action-research study poses uncomfortable personal questions for her which challenge previously held assumptions and cause her to totally revise her views and her practice in relation to the pupils' use of reference books. On the other hand, Reed, as a participant observer, analyzes the factors affecting the teaching and learning of reading in terms of social determinants, presenting a more sociological analysis of constraints upon the process of change. As described in the introduction, all the research accounts in this book can be characterized as 'pedagogic research' into the processes of teaching and learning and/or factors which directly affect these processes. However, within that tradition, the contributors have been encouraged to develop their own approaches to carrying out the research, interpreting the data and reporting the findings — exemplifying something of the wide variety of teacher-research work carried out at York.

References

ADELMAN, C. and YOUNG, M. F. D. (1985) 'The assumptions of educational research: the last twenty years', in SHIPMAN, M. (Ed.) *Educational Research: Principles, Policies and Practices*, Lewes, Falmer Press.

ALTHUSSER, L. (1971) 'Ideology and ideological state apparatuses', in *Lenin and Philosophy and Other Essays*, London, New Left Books.

BARTHOLOMEW, J. (1973) 'The teacher as researcher — a key to innovation and change', *Hard Cheese, A Journal of Education!*, 1, 1, pp. 12–22.

BOONE, N. (1904) *Science of Education*, New York, Scribner.

BOWLES, S. and GINTIS, H. (1976) *Schooling in Capitalist America*, London, Routledge and Kegan Paul.

BUCKINGHAM, B. R. (1926) *Research for Teachers*, New York, Silver, Burdett and Co.

BURGESS, R. G. (1980a) 'Some reflections on teacher-based research', *Insight*, 3, 2, pp. 20–3.

BURGESS, R. G. (1980b) 'Symposium on teacher-based research', *Insight*, 3, 3, pp. 1–51.

CARR, W. (1984) 'Theories of Theory and Practice', paper prepared for an Invitational Conference on Educational Theory held at the Philosophy of Education Department, London Institute of Education, 4 June.

CARR, W. and KEMMIS, S. (1986) *Becoming Critical: Education, Knowledge and Action Research*, Lewes, Falmer Press.

CICOUREL, A. V. (1981) 'Notes on the integration of micro- and macro-levels of analysis', in KNORR-CETINA, K. and CICOUREL, A. V. (Eds.) *Advances in Social Theory and Methodology: Toward an Integration of Micro- and Macro-Sociologies*, London, Routledge and Kegan Paul.

COLLIER, J. (1945) 'United States Indian Administration as a laboratory of ethnic relations', *Social Research*, 12, pp. 265–303.

COPE, E. and GRAY, J. (1979) 'Teachers as Researchers: Some experience of an alternative paradigm', *British Educational Research Journal*, 5, (2), pp. 237–51.

COREY, S. M. (1949) 'Action research, fundamental research, and educational practices, *Teachers College Record*, 50, pp. 509–14.

COREY, S. (1953) *Action Research to Improve School Practices*, New York, Teachers College, Columbia University.

DEWEY, J. (1929) *The Sources of a Science of Education*, New York, Liveright Publishing Company.

EBBUTT, D. and ELLIOTT, J. (1985) 'Why should teachers do research', in EBBUTT, D. and ELLIOTT, J. (Eds.) *Issues in Teaching for Understanding*, York, Longman.

ELLIOTT, J. (1981) 'Action-research: A framework for self-evaluation in schools', TIQL Project, Cambridge, Cambridge Institute of Education.

ELLIOTT, J. (1976) *Developing Hypotheses about Classrooms from Teachers' Practical Constructs*, Ford Teaching Project, Cambridge, Cambridge Institute of Education.

ELLIOTT, J. (1983) 'A curriculum for the study of human affairs: the contribution of Lawrence Stenhouse', *Journal of Curriculum Studies*, 15, 2, pp. 105–23.

ELLIOTT, J. and ADELMAN, C. (1976) 'Innovation at the classroom level; a case study of the Ford Teaching Project for OU course E203', *Curriculum Design and Development*, Milton Keynes, Open University Press.

FINCH, J. (1986) *Research and Policy: The Uses of Qualitative Methods in Social and Educational Research*, Lewes, Falmer Press.

GORBUTT, D. (1972) 'The new sociology of education', *Education for Teaching*, 89, pp. 3–11.

GROUNDWATER-SMITH, S. (1988) 'Credential bearing enquiry-based courses: Paradox or new challenge', in NIAS, J. and GROUNDWATER-SMITH, S. (Eds.), *The Enquiring Teacher: Supporting and Sustaining Teacher Research*, Lewes, Falmer Press.

GRUNDY, S. (1987) *Curriculum: Product or Praxis*, Lewes, Falmer Press.

HABERMAS, J. (1978) Appendix 'Knowledge and human interests: A general perspective', in *Knowledge and Human Interests*, translated by Shapiro, J.J., London, Heinemann Educational Books.

HAMMERSLEY, M. and WOODS, P. (1976) *The Process of Schooling*, London, Open University/Routledge and Kegan Paul.

HOUNSELL, D. and MARTIN, E. (1983) *Developing Information Skills in Secondary Schools*, Library and Information Research report 9, London, British Library.

HOLLY, P. (1984) 'The institutionalisation of action research in schools', *Cambridge Journal of Education*, 14, 2, pp. 5–8.

HUSTLER, D., CASSIDY, T. and CUFF, T. (Eds.) (1986) *Action Research in Classrooms and Schools*, London, Allen and Unwin.

IRVING, A. and SNAPE, W. (1979) *Educating Library Users in Secondary Schools*, British Library R and D report 5467, London, British Library.

LAWN, M. A. (1989) 'Being caught in schoolwork: The possibilities of research in teachers' work', in CARR, W. (Ed.), *Quality in Teaching: Arguments for a Reflective Profession*, Lewes, Falmer Press.

LAWN, M. A. (1987) *Servants of the State: The Contested Management of Teaching 1900–1930*, Lewes, Falmer Press.

LAWN, M. A. and OZGA, J. T. (1981) *Teachers, Professionalism and Class*, Lewes, Falmer Press.

LEWIN, K. (1946) 'Action research and minority problems', *Journal of Social Issues*, 2, pp. 34–46.

McKERNAN, J. (1985) (Ed.) *Register of Theses on Educational Topics in Universities in Ireland 1980–84 (Second Supplement)*, Dublin, Educational Studies Association.

McKERNAN, J. (1989) 'Action research and curriculum development', *Peabody Journal of Education*, 64, 2, pp. 6–20.

McTAGGART, R. and KEMMIS, S. (1981) *The Action Research Planner*, Geelong, Deakin University.

McNIFF, J. (1988) *Action Research: Principles and Practice*, London, Macmillan Education.

MAY, N. (1981) 'The Teacher-As-Researcher Movement in Britain', paper presented to the A.E.R.A. annual conference, Los Angeles, 1981.

NORRIS, N. (1983) *Information Skills an Educational Analysis*, The Evaluation of InSCRU Vol.4, Norwich, CARE, University of East Anglia.

OBERG, A. and McCUTCHEON, G. (1989) 'Teachers' experience doing action research', *Peabody Journal of Education*, **64**, 2, pp. 116–27.

OLIVER, R. P. C. (1946) *Research in Education*, Allen and Unwin, London.

PASSOW, A. *et al.* (1955) *Training Curriculum Leaders for Cooperative Research*, New York, Teachers College, Columbia University.

POLLARD, A. (1984) 'Ethnography and social policy for classroom practice', in BARTON, L. and WALKER, S. (Eds.) *Social Crisis and Educational Research*, London, Croom Helm.

POLLARD, A. (1985) *The Social World of the Primary School*, London, Holt, Rhinehart and Winston.

RUDDUCK, J., HOPKINS, D., SANGAR, J. and LINCOLN, P. (1987) *Collaborative Inquiry and Information Skills*, British Library Research Paper 16, London, British Library.

SANGAR, J. (1987) 'Action research and teacher empowerment', in RUDDUCK, J., HOPKINS, D., SANGAR, J. and LINCOLN, P. *Collaborative Inquiry and Information Skills*, British Library Research Paper 16, London, British Library.

SHARP, R. and GREEN, A. G. (1976) *Education and Social Control*, London, Routledge and Kegan Paul.

STENHOUSE, L. (1975) *An Introduction to Curriculum Research and Development*, London, Heinemann.

STENHOUSE, L. (1978) 'Case study and case records: Towards a contemporary history of education', *British Educational Research Journal*, **4**, 2, pp. 29–39.

STENHOUSE, L. (1983) *Authority, Education and Emancipation*, London, Heinemann Educational.

VULLIAMY, G. (1976) 'What counts as school music?', in WHITTY, G. and YOUNG, M. (Eds.) *Explorations in the Politics of School Knowledge*, Nafferton, Nafferton Books.

WHITEHEAD, J. (1989) 'Creating a living educational theory from questions of the kind, "How do I improve my practice?"', *Cambridge Journal of Education*, **19**, 1, pp. 41–52.

WHITTY, G. (1976) 'Studying society: For social change or social control?', in WHITTY, G. and YOUNG, M. (Eds.) *Explorations in the Politics of School Knowledge*, Nafferton, Nafferton Books.

WHITTY, G. (1981) 'Left policy and practice and the sociology of education', in BARTON, L. and WALKER, S. (Eds.) *Schools, Teachers and Teaching*, Lewes, Falmer Press.

WOODS, P. (Ed.) (1980a) *Teacher Strategies*, London, Croom Helm.

WOODS, P. (Ed.) (1980b) *Pupil Strategies*, London, Croom Helm.

YOUNG, M. F. D. (1971) *Knowledge and Control: New Directions for the Sociology of Education*, London, Collier Macmillan.

Chapter two

Why do Pirates have Peg Legs?
A Study of Reading for Information

Doreen Gregson

Background to the Research

School Visit, 1986: Monday 9.30 am: Reception class in an infant school:
'Huh!' voices the teacher to a small group of children sitting on the mat dutifully gazing at a flash-card with the letter 'h' on it. '*Huh is for hat. What is huh for?*'
Replies straggle in; the teacher presses for a more concerted effort. Gazes begin to wander . . . to the pictures on the wall . . . out of the window . . . to the jumper in front which has such an interesting pattern that one traces over it, making the occupant wriggle . . .
'HUHMARKWHATISHUHFOR?'

In the course of many years as an advisory teacher for reading and language I have witnessed this scene countless times. The role of observer enables one to stand back and question materials and methods that one has previously taken for granted; the role of team colleague working alongside others who are equally interested in the development of language and literacy enables debate and the formulation of grounded theories; the building of trust in the schools where one works enables the testing and modification of such theories by working in collaboration with class teachers.

What follows is an abridged account of one such collaboration. Maria Martin, a teacher of a class of 10–11 year olds, shared my enthusiasm for developing reading within the general curriculum. In particular, we were interested in the use of study skills, and widening the teaching of these to encompass children who had basic literacy problems.

Together we formulated an action-research project. Maria maintained overall responsibility for everything which happened in the classroom. She decided on the theme of the topic and we planned the literacy programme within this framework. The responsibility for teaching varied: sometimes we worked alongside one another; at times one took the teaching role and the other observed; when the children seemed totally perplexed and we could not see a reason for this one of us would work as a pupil alongside the class in order to share their experiences more fully. I produced any reading material which was thought necessary. I also kept detailed research diaries, which included transcripts of taped interviews and discussions with the children, recorded both during the teaching programme and in the following term (see Gregson, 1987).

It is important in any kind of team teaching that there is a common philosophy and shared aims, and that members are relaxed when working together. Maria and I were referred to in school as Little and Large, in reference not only to our relative physiques and our joint performances, but also because fortunately we could both see the funny side of situations which were fraught.

City Road, the school in which we worked, has a high proportion of bilingual children. By the age of 8 or 9, the only easily discernible language difference between them and the monolingual English speakers is one of accent. I was uncertain whether the problems which we encountered were due to the second language factor as they seemed equally represented in all ethnic groups. I felt it important to test this by repeating some of our work, but in a totally dissimilar school, before starting the main study. Interestingly, a similar picture did emerge from this pilot project.

The research question for the main research was as follows:

> What picture of the teaching and learning of reading emerges during a term's topic work with a class of 10-11-year-old children in a junior school?

The specific foci within 'reading' were:

(a) Study/reference/research skills
(b) Comprehension: children's ability to interact with a text.

Subsidiary to the main question was:

> Do any previously unconsidered issues affecting reading for learning emerge?

This chapter reports on aspects of the findings under (a) and (b) above.

Methodology

As a student teacher I was taught to analyze what went wrong and why in my lessons. My first headteacher taught me that it was equally important to recognize what went right and why. Thus I was introduced early to the habit of self-questioning. The people most closely concerned with the second stage of my career introduced me to many articles on research into the teaching of reading. The emphasis in these articles was to prove 'x' to be more effective than 'y'. From this I gained the impression that real research concerned the gathering of 'proof' of the measurable kind. I never questioned the need for variables to be controlled, subjects carefully matched, or the results to have statistical significance. For me, these were the elements of true research. Psychologists offered their help in setting up research projects in which I could measure the effectiveness of my methods against others. I was told that everything could be reduced to numbers and measured — even happiness. All I had to do was tell them what I wanted to measure and they would devise the test. I was very uneasy about this; often in the reports I read I saw no people or situations with which I could identify, but these seemed insufficient grounds for dismissing the content. Anning (1986) seems to have had similar feelings: '. . . I felt frustrated that teachers lacked the language to argue coherently with the researchers' (p. 54).

Learning about naturalistic research methodology released me from this tension. In particular, action research seemed to be the logical follow through to the earliest training I was given; the training which I now recognize has been most beneficial in my attempts to better the arts and crafts of my teaching. Research which helps teachers to question themselves and their practice is most likely to be of use to them in the long run. Investigations centred solely on children, where teachers appear as shadowy figures in an ill-defined background may have undesirable side effects. By focusing only on learning rather than teaching and learning, the commonsense knowledge of teachers may not be challenged:

> The point about taken-for-granted professional knowledge is precisely that it *is* taken for granted, and as such closes off certain aspects of how a teacher operates or could operate. (Cummings and Hustler, 1986, p. 47, their emphasis.)

Whitehead (1985) provided the framework to the research project which Maria and I formulated:

> I experience a problem . . .
> I imagine a solution to my problem.

I act in the direction of the solution.

I evaluate the outcomes of my actions.

I modify my problems, ideas and actions in the light of my evaluations. (p. 98)

In the event it was not quite so clear cut as this. The outcomes of our actions dredged up more problems of which we were previously less aware; problems which seemed in need of more urgent solution than the first ones, and were, I believe, composed mainly of our taken-for-granted knowledge. Our reactions to the realization of this led to major changes in our approach to the children, but unfortunately we were unaware of the effects of innovation on pupils (Rudduck, 1984). I, in particular, felt that I had lost my teaching skills:

> . . . educational innovations which involve the likelihood of increased amounts of noise . . . pose particular problems in practice because their implementation potentially jeopardizes the appearance of control in the classroom. (Denscombe, 1980, p. 79)

It was not just that there was an increase of noise; that in itself would have been no problem to us. But neither Maria nor I had ever experienced such widespread minor misbehaviour and disengaged attitudes in a class before, and the cumulative effect was to undermine my confidence to the extent of almost abandoning the work at half term. Its continuance was due entirely to the very great support we were offered from my MA tutor and our colleagues in the school and the language centre from which I work.

During the major part of the action-research programme I believed that Maria and I fully understood each other professionally, and were equal partners in the venture. It was not until Maria was commenting on my data analysis that I began to realize that this was not so:

> *Maria* I didn't know what you were going for . . . I was doing a holding job . . . I wasn't involved . . . I thought you knew definitely what you were after. I didn't realize how much you were ready to change; willing to modify. Which literally meant at the end of every lesson. I didn't realize you were open to suggestion. I was the follower.

This conversation illuminated a number of worries which I had had. The principal one was that there was no carry over from what we and the children engaged in and learned during topic sessions to other areas of the curriculum; Maria did not seem to capitalize on experiences or extend them. I was puzzled by this, for I did not realize Maria's position:

> I expected you would have lesson plans and know exactly what was
> going to happen. I did think that if I did anything I might be
> interfering with your data. I thought you had to be there to
> monitor it all.

My own lack of clarity at the outset, coupled with what amounts to blindness
in not recognizing the issue at the time, appeared to have caused the
problem. When I had been practising specific research techniques I had
asked Maria not to take any action in some circumstances. Further, although
I knew that I was aiming to develop children's ability to read to learn I was
unsure what modifications to our teaching techniques would need to be
made in the light of what we were learning, and Maria did not believe me
when I told her I could not predict outcomes, or felt at a loss.

I wondered if perhaps status played a part in this. I am an advisory
teacher, Maria a classteacher. The promotional structure in education does
not reward good teachers except by removing them more and more from the
classroom. I, and many teachers I have talked with, have often felt that
primary school teachers are at the very bottom of the education heap. I
would suggest that a major consequence of this might be that they devalue
themselves and their work. Although we discussed everything together,
Maria still saw me as the leader of the partnership, even though the
responsibility for the class was hers. I find it very sad that at the time she did
not recognize the parts her comments played in the progress of the work:

> . . . you came back with a re-think, a new strategy if something
> hadn't worked out, and I just waited for you to do that . . . I didn't
> realize that I was contributing to the modifications.

Perhaps at the time I did not recognize this, because I did not need to, being
the person in the 'superior' position. It might not matter how open the
person with higher status is; if the person with less rank perceives herself to
be the follower, then she most likely will be, regardless of what she has to
offer. Unless this danger is recognized and brought out into the open, there
might be less chance of true collaboration under these circumstances.

I feel another important factor was the growth of my overwhelming
insecurity and sensitivity to criticism during the work. Was I too preoccupied
with myself to consider how Maria felt? Was it that I was afraid to be seen to
be failing; not in full command of the situation? At the time I was too busy
trying to survive to be able to analyze my feelings; it was a salutary
experience. I felt that I was under her continual, critical scrutiny, and yet the
data revealed no evidence of this. I wondered whether subconscious self-
preservation caused me not to record the unflattering, but no:

...I should have criticized you...but I've never been asked to criticize before. I didn't really know where you were going or what you were after. I didn't know what I was criticizing on.

If a team is to work effectively its members must be able to give and take constructive criticism. The advisory teachers with whom I work have all learned this skill; I took it for granted when working with Maria. I feel that consideration should be given to this issue before expecting teachers to work closely together in a team. Maria and I had a fund of goodwill and personal regard to help us through; some newly-formed teams, or a part-time teacher newly entering a shared teaching role, may have neither.

Writing an account of the work carried its difficulties too. I wanted other teachers to be able to relate to our experiences. Groundwater-Smith (1983) argues a case for the 'photographic story' as a mode of presenting educational research:

> The photographic story by virtue of its immediacy, its attention to detail, its succinct expression is a powerful touch stone...as the readers take possession, their own revelations and insights continue to shape the meaning. (p. 14)

I could not claim that my writing is an example of the genre, but I hope that I manage to convey at least something of the atmosphere of the term, rather than present a bland record of incidents within it.

Research/Reference Skill Findings

My first impressions, gained during initial observations of children working on a specific information finding task in the library, were not only that children had few reference skills, but that also they were insufficiently motivated to persist with a task through to its conclusion. The evidence on which I based my impressions was of the following kind:

> Harpal restless, bouncing on library steps, talking...
> Girls giggling by card catalogue. Muhashra poking another girl repeatedly with her pencil...
> Arshad starts jumping down steps. Prepares to jump over bookshelves again...

Apparently many children could not make up their minds what subject to research. They had each been given a letter of the alphabet and told to choose a subject beginning with that letter (Torbe and Medway, 1981,

p. 79), and some children changed subjects several times. I thought that it was as a consequence of this that several children gained no information at all during their starter session, as measured by notes made by them in their jotters.

I had been told that the children had been allowed free access to the library during their previous year, and yet despite this they seemed unable to locate information quickly, going about the task in a seemingly haphazard way:

> Arshad walks slowly across to a bookshelf. Picks out a book seemingly at random . . .
>
> Shabida returns a book to the shelf and walks slowly around the library apparently aimlessly. She looks fed up. Takes a book from a shelf apparently at random . . .
>
> Roxana sits with a pile of books, looking at the covers, transferring them from one pile to another. Draws out more books from the shelves and repeats the process . . .

As a result of this type of observation, lessons were planned to teach children how to locate specific information in books quickly. Such lessons were to some degree needed, if judged by the difficulties raised by some of the children:

> The question 'What do you do if your book hasn't got an author?' came to me three times in slightly different ways. In one case there was an editor and the child did not know the term; in the second the child had not understood the phrase 'text by'; in the third the child had not realized that the name under the title was by convention that of the author.

Wray (1986) writes:

> . . . it ought to be possible for the teacher . . . (whilst children are using reference books) . . . to spot skill weaknesses and introduce activities to remedy them — activities of which children can see the point. (p. 141)

Oh, Mr. Wray! It ought to be possible, but it certainly is not easy. On the one hand, at the outset children present a multitude of problems all at the same time. On the other hand, there are the books . . . As will become apparent, I feel that the findings of Paice (1984), with regard to the perversity of books about bees, could be applied across a full range of reference books for children.

Individual difficulties were brought to the attention of the whole class as examples of what they might find themselves as they worked. It was stressed that as Maria and I did not always anticipate correctly what they were going to have difficulty with, they should always bring to our attention anything they did not fully understand. By doing this, I feel that our teaching became more relevant to more children. As the term progressed and children could trust us to make positive teaching points from their errors we spent far less time teaching 'skills'; we knew that any lack of them would be brought to our attention by the child concerned. By half term children were demonstrating their reference skills by using them appropriately whenever they could.

'Whenever they could' is a key phrase. At first I had interpreted my observations in the light of the work of Lunzer and Gardner (1979) which draws attention to children who, although they can describe what to do to find information quickly, do not use these skills in practice. I began to wonder if I was beginning to uncover reasons why this might happen. There had been evidence from the start, but I had not recognized its significance. For instance, at the beginning of the initial library sessions all children in the group, regardless of their apparent abilities or subsequent behaviour, had begun work by immediately going to the card catalogue to find the Dewey number of their chosen subject. These were the 'unmotivated' who could not use reference skills. They couldn't, but it was not for want of trying.

It was only when I myself tried to use the library that I began to realize what the children were having to cope with. I could not find many of the references I wanted in the card catalogue. When I followed up a reference I had difficulty in locating the actual books, as they were frequently out of order. Having found a book which I thought might be useful I felt compelled to skim through it in addition to referring to the index, because the index was often unsatisfactory:

> Found the limitations of the library even more frustrating...Children couldn't find specified books...Children couldn't find specific information: nothing on potholes or woodworm...
>
> How can you teach a child to survey the literature when it consists of one book, and that without a contents page? How can you teach a child to locate information quickly when the book has no index, or the entries are wrong? How do you use an index organized in numerical order of pages rather than alphabetical order of subject? And how, oh how in the world can you find an indexed page reference in a book with no numbered pages?

It was not surprising that there was little evidence of children using the contents or index pages; there were few of the former and the latter were often inaccurate, as I found myself. Gordon (1983) says that in her opinion badly indexed books daunt children and make them feel that research skills are irrelevant. My evidence strongly supports this, and I would echo her plea for the indexing of children's books to be of the 'highest standard' and not just 'farmed out to anyone willing to have a try' (p. 182).

These frustrating elements were a widespread feature of the library work. I found that even when I located a book which promised to be useful, I still had to deal with the content. I found texts simplified to the point of banality, as for example the book about windows. The first picture caption read 'This is a window', which most children would surely know; the second caption under a different type of window read 'This is a big window'. As the pictures themselves were exactly the same size, and there were no details by which to make comparisons, this could be said to be factually inaccurate. More importantly, what information is the text carrying? At the other extreme I found a book on anatomy impossible to understand, despite its attractive appearance and my 'O' level qualification.

The school library is one of the best I have come across in my work. It is organized on the Dewey system, which gives more potential to the teaching of reference skills in school. The girls of the photography topic group showed pleasure and astonishment after their spontaneous evening visit to the City Library in search of relevant books: 'Eh, Miss, did you know they have the same numbers on their books as we do?' The school library was also relatively new at that time, but the original date of publication of many books made them of limited value.

After I studied my own behaviour in the library, I looked on that of the children with new insight. What had seemed like aimless movement was perhaps simply an intelligent reaction to the realities of the situation, and the gradual breakdown of behaviour and growth of boredom a natural reaction to frustration. Take for example Harpal bouncing on the library steps, when seen in a wider context:

> *9.15:* Harpal walks away from card catalogue muttering a number. Goes to shelves. Looks at numbers on book spines.
>
> *9.17:* Harpal goes back to card catalogue, pushes in front of queue: remonstrations. Removed by children to back of queue.
>
> *9.29:* Harpal sits watching others; seems uninvolved, turning pages of a book idly.
>
> *9.38:* Harpal talks to others. Has a pile of books, but does not refer to them. Goes back to catalogue.
>
> *9.46:* Harpal restless, bouncing on library steps. Catches my eye and returns to pile of books. Takes one and flicks through it.

9.48: Harpal making silly noises.

9.54: Overhear Harpal say, 'I don't know what to do . . .'. Pervaz seems to be giving him advice.

9.57: Overhear: 'Harpal, you've only done one line of writing . . .'.

This picture was typical of many children; perhaps I was typical of many teachers when I responded to the behaviour rather than the cause of the behaviour at first. Yet *I* went backwards and forwards from card catalogue to bookshelves, each time with less and less heart, and *I* sat on the library steps, gazing into space, wondering what to do next. Unlike Arshad, I was not agile enough to attempt a leap over the bookshelves, but I did frequently feel like kicking them.

The apparently random way in which children retrieved books from shelves seemed also to be a response to the situation as they found it. During interviews children said that when they had walked round the shelves they were looking for books with the required number which were out of place. They knew that if there was an entry in the catalogue there had to be a book somewhere. We solved this problem to some extent by starting and ending each session by checking the shelves for misfits, and relocating them. Some books simply were not there, though, or proved irrelevant. It was in response to this, the children explained, that they took piles of books and looked through them. This was not entirely at random; the children used the titles of books as a guide, which would explain why they glanced at books as they transferred them from one pile to another.

I had been surprised by the reactions of some of the children when they did find information they wanted:

Shima: I've found it! (She bounds up the library steps, waving a book).

Jameela: Phew! (She catches my eye and smiles; shows me a page with a picture of eggs on it.)

Ravinder: (jerks up suddenly from a crouched position over a book.) Gorit! Gorit! Gorit! (He looks round smiling.)

Thus there was evidence that if the material was there the children were far from unmotivated. There was also evidence of great initiative:

Kieron shouts to Gulam, who is standing by the catalogue, 'Give me everything that begins with "w" from first to last!' Gulam reading 'w' entries to Keiron. Keiron goes up to him, exchanges talk. Keiron turns suddenly, muttering '595' and rushes to jotter. Picks it up and continues swiftly to shelf.

My first reaction to this was that it was typical of Keiron to order other people around. But how sensible not to waste time choosing a subject before referring to the catalogue to see if there are any resources to pursue it.

The novelty of finding that research skills could work under certain circumstances was illustrated for us when I made worksheets based on available library material. The children were told that providing they followed the instructions on the sheet, I could guarantee that they would find the information. At each stage of the work the children turned to the teacher:

> I've found the book. Finished Miss!
> I've found the word in the index. Finished Miss!
> I've found the page. Finished Miss!

As the term progressed this need for step by step reassurance disappeared. At the same time specific research skills were used more often as appropriate. I find it impossible to assess how far the appearance of these skills was due to the fact that we created situations in which they could be used, or because they were being taught in the context of need.

Although the problems which children showed gradually became more likely to be child- or teacher-centred ones, and less likely to be due to inadequate situations, we were still able to misjudge what was happening:

> Children have each been given a pile of new books and asked which Dewey number they think best for each book. Maria comes up and whispers, 'That idiot there has two books on rabbits and has given them different Dewey numbers'. Investigation shows child is right; one is a book on pet, and one a book on wild rabbits.

Specific problems were never common to the whole group, but frequently seemed to be caused by difficulty in relating to written instructions:

> Salamat and Jameela come to me, a book open at the index.
>
> *Salamat:* It isn't in, Miss. Gully isn't in the index. (I look. It isn't, but it was when I wrote the worksheet. Realize that the entries don't conform to what I would have expected for the subject matter on the sheet. Turn to the front cover; title is 'Days of the Week'.)
> *Me:* What is this book called?
> *Salamat:* 'Days of the Week'.
> *Me:* What is the title of the book on your sheet?
> *Salamat:* Ellis.
> *Me:* No, that's the author. Do you remember, author first, then . . .

Jameela:	(interrupts) Date.
Me:	Good . . .
Jameela:	(continues from before as if I had not interrupted) Oh! 'Pipes and Wires'!
Me:	Yes, that's the title . . . Well? (Pause, children look expectantly at me.) The book you need is called 'Pipes and Wires'. The book you've got is called 'Days of the Week' . . .
Salamat:	(lively) Oh! I see! It's got to be *that* book! Oh! Now I know! She grabs Jameela and rushes off leaving me holding 'Days of the Week'.

During earlier work I had noticed a problem with children taking a book seemingly at random when the instruction called for a specific one. I wonder whether it relates to inexperience of having to follow written instructions without verbal ones being given in addition. Frequently teachers talk through written instructions, which makes it unnecessary for children to work out any interpretation for themselves. In this instance the oral instruction was 'follow the instruction on your sheet'. I was pleased to note that many children, who were all working in pairs in this lesson, did discuss together what the instructions implied before they attempted to follow them. We praised all signs of initiative. As might be expected, some children needed more support than others to gain enough confidence to trust their own judgments, but as a tactic it seemed to work well. As more children asked fewer questions, it meant that we had extra time to devote to those children who had problems concerned with the work itself.

Looking back over the issue of the teaching of research skills, I wonder whether instead of asking myself 'What study skills do the children have?' I should have asked 'What factors interfere with children's ability to put study skills into practice?'

Comprehension of and Interaction with Text

It has been impossible to write this section without free use of value-laden and ill-defined terminology such as 'less able'. This is because at the beginning of the research Maria and I used these terms in just such a way; they were the 'commonsense understandings' of 'truth' and 'reality' which had to be 'cut through' (Bogdan and Taylor, 1975, p. 11). I hope, as the chapter progresses, to illustrate how I began to question the use of such terminology, gradually finding it inappropriate or irrelevant.

A major concern at the outset was that children should not be faced with texts they could not read. I intended to produce special worksheets for the less able, but from the first attempt I began to question the value of this. The worksheet concerned had two parts, the first of which was for children thought to have basic literacy problems, and the second for the rest of the class. None of the children doing part (a) had any difficulty; by contrast, the children working on part (b) had many problems which seemed mainly to be caused by an inability to put themselves in the position of someone else. After watching the 'less able', who had quickly finished their own work, begin helping the 'more able' and 'average' children I felt less committed to the making of special worksheets. My experiences during the personal topic periods reinforced this feeling. To illustrate this, I have taken the example of two strongly contrasting children, Muhashra who had chosen to study clothes, and Amina who had chosen photography.

Muhashra, considered the least able child in the class because of her language and literacy difficulties, enjoyed looking at books on clothes, aimed at the adult market. She frequently initiated comments on these, which made me aware that she was not just getting information from pictures. It has become something of a cliché to say that 'motivated' children can read texts far in advance of their 'reading ability'. Logically this cannot be so; what the children are demonstrating is that their ability has been underassessed. In this case I felt that it was her hesitant and strongly accented English which misguided us. During observation of a personal topic lesson I noted that Muhashra attempted to initiate conversation with the remedial teacher who was working with her group. The teacher, new to the situation, responded by taking the book Muhashra was looking at, and reading aloud from it, asking her if she understood. The teacher explained that she had done this to try to simplify a task which she thought too difficult for the child. During the reading, however, Muhashra exchanged glances with another girl several times, seemingly totally disengaged, as she waited for the teacher to finish and give her the book back. She then continued looking through the book, but only addressed comments on it to other children after that.

During this period the photography group was also in the room, being tutored by Maria. These girls often initiated social conversation which I found very enjoyable; they also showed great insights into their own personal problems. Because of this, and the fact that they had no overt difficulties with reading and writing, I thought of them as being able. Amina was a member of this group, and the following is an observation of her during the session:

1.37 Lesson begins. There is a pile of books on the table which the children are reading for background information. Maria spends time cajoling each member of the group in turn, trying to get them to say which aspects of photography they would like to follow up.

2.13 *Amina:* 'There's nowt in these books'. She pushes two books away from her as she leans on her elbow on the desk. She looks bored.

Maria: 'There's one, two, three, four, five, six black lines there. Surely they have *something* on them!'

2.14: Unexpected visitors enter, unescorted. They explain to Maria that they have come 'to see multicultural education'. They look round the room without moving and begin asking her questions.

2.15: Amina talks to Kate about playtime. Begins rocking backwards and forwards, beating a rhythm on the table top.

2.16: Kate joins in. Rebecca stage whispers 'Sshh!' They all giggle and general chat develops. They begin sliding books across the table to one another.

2.26: Still chatting, resting heads on hands, lounging over table.

2.29: Visitors leave. Maria returns to group.

The issue of motivation emerges here, but at the time, we simply questioned why Amina and others like her, who had no obvious learning problems, did less well at a reading task than Muhashra, who had several. Which child was the less able in this situation, and what would either of them have gained or lost by using tailored work sheets rather than books? At this time too we had not recognized subtle complications surrounding the issue of free choice, and therefore expected that, having chosen their own topic, children would be motivated to read.

The term 'less able' became obsolete as we began to qualify it so often: less able to do what? Through this qualification informal but thorough diagnosis began to develop for each child. Attempts to group children according to 'ability' were abandoned as we realized that there was no way of telling what any child's ability at a given task was going to be until the task got under way.

The main plan for the personal topic lessons was as follows:

(a) The children were formed into groups of six, and told to decide on a topic within the theme 'holes'. There was considerable freedom, not only of choice of subject, but also of organization, as they could all work together or split into sub–groups as they wished.

(b) When the choice had been made, groups were asked to collect material from the library for background reading.

(c) They were asked to note down any questions or reflections which occurred to them as they read.

(d) Finally a plan of action was drawn up specifying what form their work would take; how they would get required information (other than books);what visits they would need to make, and so on.

Our most fundamental problem occurred immediately. Regardless of their apparent ability the children would not read. They did not seem to recognize reading as 'work' and we were frequently asked, 'What do we have to do?'. When the instruction 'Read about your subject' was repeated children countered with 'Yes, but what do we have to *do*?'. Some of the 'able' attempted to help us out with suggestions: 'Shall we make notes about it?' 'Have we to write about it?'. Again and again we explained the purpose of background reading, dropping all reference to the questions. As this seemed so totally alien we thought it might be the cause of the problem. All the children had difficulties at this point, but it was the 'able' who were the hardest to help over the hurdle:

> *Maria:* (during discussion of our work with a third person) The middle range . . . they got on and did things . . . They were the ones who worked their way through the whole lot and actually got on very well . . . (The top range) were resentful when we stopped them copying out . . .

A possible reason for the 'middle range' to have managed more successfully was that they had had less experience of using the library unsupervised to develop their own topics. Thus they had not developed a pattern of working which had to be dismantled before another could be introduced.

We have no direct evidence as to the previous educational history of the class, but it would seem that during their time in school reading in itself had not acquired any status as an activity. Until we could persuade children to read we could not tell what problems they had. When the problems did begin to appear they varied tremendously in nature. The most easily discernable was the 'reading' of words outside the child's spoken vocabulary, where either the verbal or other contexts gave little clue to the word's meaning:

> Children have been asked to guess the content of a book from the front cover only. Sameena has a book called 'Man the Healer'. Picture on front cover is of an eighteenth-century surgeon operating. Sameena thinks the book is 'about killing'. Does not understand the word 'Healer' though she can 'read' it. Picture on cover is sole clue, and certainly looks gruesome.

In this case an explanation of the word sufficed. In the following example the text the child was using had been so simplified as to be misleading, and therefore although the child could read and understand, his lack of background knowledge led to mistaken assumptions:

> Aslam comes up with a book open at a picture of a pirate with a 'peg leg' and says: 'Why does pirates have to cut their legs off and put these on?'. The caption to the picture does not make clear that wooden legs are incidental rather than desirable.

This example was dealt with by filling in the missing detail orally. The child was quite able to relate to the new knowledge.

Greater difficulties arose when children were not so easily able to assimilate the information:

> Hafiz has misunderstood 'self rescuer', reading 'a self rescuer belt' rather than 'a self rescuer on his belt'. He cannot understand what I am getting at and perseveres in thinking that a self rescuer is a belt, despite all my explanations and references to the picture and text.

I spent over half an hour with Hafiz, discussing his problems. My fieldnotes record that two days later I 'checked Hafiz to see if he has grasped the idea. He has'. I was wrong. His finished work reflected the error rather than the teaching.

The inability to grasp an idea might be due to the wide perceptual-language distance (Blank, Rose and Berlin, 1978) and the difficulty of the teacher in helping the child to bridge it. In this case the child did not seem to be able to relate to the picture, and I had neither a concrete example nor a useful analogy to which he could relate more easily. In retrospect I felt that the explanations were merely circling around the problem instead of closing in on it; they were all at the same perceptual-language distance. With later, similar problems, I asked the child 'to leave it with me' in order to give myself time to think out a way of reducing the task to a point with which the child could relate, and then re-building it to the point of original misunderstanding. Children's interest did not seem adversely affected by the delay.

During the term we found more evidence of passive reading (Browne, 1985; Lunzer, Gardner, Davies and Greene, 1984). Some children did not expect to have to do more than decode a text, after which all 'reading' was finished:

> ...(the children studying the eye) wanted to do how the eye works. What they didn't realize was that the book was using

optical illusions to demonstrate how the eye works . . . I (Maria) sat
down with them and discussed each paragraph as they read it.
Usually it told them to do something and I made them do it. They
got interested then and involved, and began understanding.

As the problem had been noted with previous classes we had introduced
a weekly reading activity similar to that envisaged by Southgate, Arnold and
Johnson (1981): . . . 'it seems advisable to concoct goals where the outcomes
involve either, *doing* something or giving an oral response, (not oral
reading)' . . . (p. 291). Usually we took a short extract from the book
currently being read to the class, photocopied it and asked them to:

(a) underline details which could be included in an illustration;
 and
(b) produce the illustration using the underlinings as quick references.

The aim was to see how accurate a mental picture the children were forming
as they listened, and the activity was developed into one of converting
information from one form to another (for example, drawing a map from
information in a text). This not only uncovered children's misconceptions, it
also acted as a check on the clarity of our didactics; for example in the lesson
in which I was involved no-one knew the word 'niche' and the subsequent
drawings gave us a measure of how effective our explanations had been.

In an attempt to extend the use of this technique further I gave the girls
of the photography group the instruction booklet which came with the
equipment for developing films, and asked them to extract in list form:

(a) the required chemicals and quantities, so that when we went
 shopping we knew exactly what we needed to buy, and
(b) the sequence of steps to be followed, written out clearly so that we
 could read them in semi–darkness. I also thought that this part of
 the exercise would give the group, and me, some idea of what to
 expect in the practical sessions as none of us had any experience of
 developing and printing photographs.

The instructions in the booklet were written in several languages; I
photocopied the page which had the English version, and incidentally, the
French version too. What I expected the children to produce was a simple
shopping list, followed by a simple list of step-by-step instructions which we
could follow more easily than the rather verbose and minisc, ely printed
original. I felt the exercise valuable in that it reflected a reading experience
that they would be likely to encounter many times in different contexts in
real life.

Despite many attempts at explanation and demonstration, the result was a complete fiasco, as the girls seemed merely to have underlined words at random all over the sheet. The following extracts are from a taped discussion held with the group nearly two months after the event:

Me:	Did the fact that you had to read real instructions . . . help you at all?
All:	(subdued) Yeh . . . yes.
Me:	Did you feel you actually understood what you were reading?
Amina:	Not all the time, no.
Me:	Where did you fall down?
Amina:	Big words. Long words.
Robeena:	. . . those sheets you photocopied for us (the instructions) were too small. We couldn't read 'em. Nearly all the words were complicated . . .
Amina:	When we were doing it we underlined the French words too.

The underlining of the French words caused a major row at the time, as I interpreted it as yet another example of the group's unwillingness to work sensibly, and illustrates how a teacher's preconceptions may totally blind her to the reality of the situation. In this case the blindness was perhaps a reaction to previous difficulties in motivating the group and their propensity to indulge in mild disruptiveness. At the same time I saw a group of girls who I thought were capable of far more than they gave, complaining of having to do 'boring reading' and reverting to silly behaviour. But was I in fact placing these 'able' girls in a situation where they were unable to demonstrate the abilities they had? I did not analyze closely what I meant by able, but I have since begun to do so.

I am a very able reader of detective fiction. I can decode every word and follow the story line effortlessly. I am able to read textbooks on reading; my background knowledge enables me to reflect on what I have read. When I began to learn about qualititive research methodology I was a less able reader of the relevant texts; it took several weeks to link what I thought were the 'paradimes' of my tutor with the paradigms of the books. I am a virtually illiterate reader of books on nuclear physics; not only do I fail to recognize words on sight but I also have insufficient background knowledge to help me to use context or to relate to what I read. Does all this make me a more or less able reader? One has to ask the question, 'More or less able to read what?'.

The photography group had shown themselves able to read books on photography. In my efforts to 'stretch' them, in effect give them a task at which they were less able readers, I rendered them 'virtually illiterate'.

When I asked, in the same interview as quoted above, long after the heat had died, why they had underlined the French words Robeena replied, 'Because the other words were so complicated . . . and we knew they were English . . . but when we came to the other (French) words we just thought, "Oh, this is even more harder", and we carried on'. Tabberer (1987) says '. . . education is about putting students in a position where they will encounter many problems — and work towards their solution' (p. 193). Perhaps the mark of a good teacher is that she recognizes the degree of difficulty each child requires in order to be stimulated but not overwhelmed.

Recognition is a crucial skill. I asked the children why they had not felt able to tell us at the time that they did not understand the work. Amina replied, 'Sometimes you got mad at us because you told us twenty times and we kept forgetting'. What they had been asking for was the decoding of a single word each time, and I did not recognize quickly enough that the giving of these was not helping to build an understanding of the whole. This was partly due to the fact that there were two teachers involved; as each of us was approached in turn we only saw half the magnitude of the problem. Furthermore, both Maria and I were embroiled in a situation of constant minor misbehaviour in the classroom; once again we appear to have reacted to the behaviour rather than to the causes of it. If we learned only one thing from this experience, it was that theoretical knowledge of comprehension problems is not enough; one needs to be able to recognize all the manifestations of the problems in practice.

Conclusions

With regard to the teaching of research skills, Maria and I realized how important it was for the teacher to put herself in the place of the child, and try the work, as this uncovers hidden situational problems (Hill, 1980). The most important skill of all, we felt, was one which at first we not only did not teach, but positively tried to eliminate: the skill of coping with frustration when trying to find information. We no longer 'doctor' work in order to ensure success; we teach children strategies for coping with sometimes inevitable failure to find relevant resource material.

The issues arising from studying the children's comprehension were complex, and have led to a continuation of the research. The immediate result was the introduction of a deliberate policy for raising the status of reading in the classroom. Of equal importance was the development of strategies by which the classteacher could buy time to talk at length with groups of children about their work and its problems.

For me, the most important insight has been in finding how often I responded to symptoms rather than to causes. Furthermore, even when I recognized my assumptions in one context, I was very slow to transfer that knowledge into others. Time and workload are very important factors in this. During the practical work the sheer stress of day-to-day teaching and evening-to-evening preparation made it difficult to relax sufficiently, to be able to stand back and reflect on events. Stenhouse (1975) seems to recognize the realities of classroom life: 'The conditions of teaching . . . often make survival a more urgent concern than scholarship' (p. 92). Yet the 'scholarship' or 'reflection' might possibly make survival easier, and eventually render the word obsolete. During the spring term, Maria and I experienced some very rewarding lessons fashioned from our insights, but we acknowledge that we were unlikely to have reached this point had we not been given a great deal of support from colleagues. This ranged from pointing us in the direction of reassuring research which indicated that perhaps the problems we were experiencing were not simply due to us losing our grip, through to pressing cups of coffee into our hands as we staggered, sometimes close to tears, from the classroom.

The most important factor in developing professional classroom skills would seem to be one of creating conditions in which it is possible for a teacher to break out of the 'survival' cycle. At the outset of this work, as a convert to action research, I felt that all teachers should experience it as part of their in-service training. Now, having more than theoretical knowledge, I am not so sure. Unless the conditions are right, with wise counselling and time made available for teachers to stand back from their problems, action research may break a teacher completely as she exposes in more and more depth her taken-for-granted knowledge. This is not to argue against classroom-based action research, but a plea for conditions to be developed in which it can thrive.

References

ANNING, A. (1986) 'Curriculum in action', in HUSTLER, D., CASSIDY, T., and CUFF, T. (Eds.) *Action Research in Classrooms and Schools*, London, Allen and Unwin.

BLANK, M., ROSE, S. A. and BERLIN L. J. (1978) *The Language of Learning*, Orlando, Grune and Stratton.

BOGDAN, R. and TAYLOR, S.J. (1975) *Introduction to Qualitative Research Methods*, London, John Wiley and Sons.

BROWNE, A. (1985) 'Young children's attention to textual context', *Reading*, **19** (1), pp. 46–50.

CUMMINGS, C. and HUSTLER, D. (1986) 'Teachers' professional knowledge', in HUSTLER, D., CASSIDY, T. and CUFF, T. (Eds.) *Action Research in Classrooms and Schools*, London, Allen and Unwin.

DENSCOMBE, M. (1980) '"Keeping 'em quiet": The significance of noise for the practical activity of teaching', in WOODS, P. (Ed.) *Teacher Strategies: Explorations in the Sociology of the School*, London, Croom Helm.

GORDON, C. (1983) 'Teaching the young to use indexes', *The Indexer*, 13 (3) pp. 181–2.

GREGSON, D. (1987) 'Why do Pirates Have Peg Legs? A Study of Reading for Information', Unpublished thesis submitted for the Master of Arts degree, York University.

GROUNDWATER-SMITH, S. (1983) 'The Portrayal of Experienced Education and the Literature of Fact'. Unpublished paper presented to CARE Study Group, University of East Anglia, March 1983.

HILL, M. (1980) 'The teacher's craft and "basic skills" ', in RICHARDS, C. (Ed.) *Primary Education: Issues for the Eighties,* London, A. and C. Black.

LUNZER, E. and GARDNER, K. (Eds.) (1979) *The Effective Use of Reading*, London, Heinemann Educational Books.

LUNZER, E., GARDNER, K., DAVIES, F. and GREENE, T. (1984) *Learning From the Written Word,* Edinburgh, Oliver and Boyd.

PAICE, S. (1984) 'Reading to Learn', *English in Education,* 18 (1) pp. 3–8.

RUDDUCK, J. (1984) 'Introducing innovation to pupils,' in HOPKINS, D. and WIDEEN, M. (Eds.) *Alternative Perspectives on School Improvement*, Lewes, Falmer Press.

SOUTHGATE, V., ARNOLD, H., and JOHNSON, S. (1981) *Extending Beginning Reading*, London, Heinemann Educational Books for the Schools Council.

STENHOUSE, L. (1975) *An Introduction to Curriculum Research and Development*, London, Heinemann Educational Books.

TABBERER, R. (1987) *Study and Information Skills in Schools*, British Library R and D Report 5870. Windsor, NFER-Nelson.

TORBE, M. and MEDWAY, P. (1981) *The Climate for Learning*, London, Ward Lock Educational.

WHITEHEAD, J. (1985) 'An analysis of an individual's educational development: The basis for personally oriented action research', in SHIPMAN, M. (Ed.) *Educational Research: Principles, Policies and Practices*, Lewes, Falmer Press.

WRAY, D. (1986) 'Information skills through project work', in CASHDAN, A. (Ed.) *Literacy: Teaching and Learning Language Skills*, Oxford, Blackwell.

Chapter three

Towards Reading?

Beatrice Reed

> They can read alright, but they just don't want to, they have no concentration for reading, they haven't learnt to enjoy books and reading is boring to them. They just want books that make no demands on them.

It was comments such as this, made by a teacher about his year 6 junior class, which led to the teaching and acquisition of reading becoming the focus of a three month case study I made in a primary school. What struck me from the outset was that teachers' comments indicated that there was a sharp division between what they said they hoped to achieve in teaching reading and what they felt they could or were able to achieve. All teachers strongly stated that they wanted children to become keen volitional readers. However, it was apparent from their comments, such as the above, and from children's comments, that whilst the majority of children acquired the mechanics of reading many did not appear to develop an understanding of its purpose.

Although I shall briefly address a matter of some concern to me during the research, that of gaining and maintaining access, the discussion which follows will largely concentrate on three closely related issues which emerged during the research:

1 Factors informing approaches to teaching reading — in particular, the constraints of time and numbers of children and experience-related beliefs;

2 Implications of these approaches to teaching reading; that is, in order to become effective readers, in the teacher's eyes, children had to develop an understanding of reading beyond that which was taught in the classroom;

3 The influence of home background and parents in reading acquisition, and classroom teachers' rationalization for what they saw as many children's failure to become effective readers in relation to this.

Although it might appear that a black picture is painted of the classroom teacher, this is not intended nor is it in keeping with the findings of the research. What is illustrated, however, are the very real constraints within which classroom teachers have to work, which appeared to dictate the kinds of approaches they felt able to adopt in the teaching of reading, and which in turn have direct implications for how children learn.

Gaining and Maintaining Access

Within case-study research the instrument of investigation is the researcher who assumes the role of participant observer, and whose ultimate aim is to study the situation from the participant's, in this case teachers' and pupils', points of view. In the light of this a major methodological concern throughout the research period was that of gaining and maintaining access, initially to the school and then more critically, through the teachers, to the classroom. The teachers were the 'gate keepers' (Burgess, 1984) with the power to allow the research process to continue or otherwise.

Initial access was made through the headteacher by letter, introducing myself as a teacher from Canada, studying in England, and interested in spending time in a primary school. This was followed by a telephone call and then a visit to the school. During this visit some three hours were spent with the headteacher prior to my broaching the subject of undertaking research in the school, thus giving her time to develop an impression of me. It was my intention that she should see me as a sympathetic, unassuming person with an interest in education, who would be unlikely to cause disruption in her school. In requesting access I outlined my area of interest and indicated a 'research bargain'; my willingness to help out in the school when not observing. Her response was positive, but with reservations, as shown in the following extract from my fieldnotes:

Interview with headteacher — 24 November, 1986

> *HT*: I would be interested in getting a different perspective of language teaching in the school, but I wouldn't want the staff disturbed. I think a meeting at the beginning of term would be important to show them exactly what you were doing and to discuss any problems or reservations.

The headteacher did not tell the staff of my intended research prior to the meeting she mentioned. I recognized that this meeting was crucial as not only did I need access to teachers' classrooms, but I also needed their trust. I did not want this potential trust jeopardized by their viewing my presence as an initiative of the headteacher by implication of my introduction by her. The following extract from my field-notes outlines the presentation I made to the staff:

Meeting with staff — Monday 9 January, 1987

1 Teacher from Canada. Unfamiliar with the English education system. Undertaking research, in part, to remedy that.
2 Particular interest in language teaching and learning but interests extend across curriculum.
3 Understand any feeling of apprehension over presence of another adult in classroom, as felt similarly when a researcher first spent time with me.
4 Research bargain, help for access.
5 Would always request access and would disrupt as little as possible.
6 No hidden agenda.
7 Complete confidentiality.

The questions raised by two teachers after the presentation were related to the nature of the research, that is, whether I intended to look 'only at teachers' or to be 'prescriptive', and as to what exactly my 'focus' was. Suspicion of my intention by some staff was to linger through the first six weeks until my 'focus' became more specific. This was possibly brought about by the beginnings of the current stress on teacher accountability, as suggested by Adelman (1985), and by a new headteacher carrying out changes in the school.

It was my intention in stressing my lack of knowledge of English education to make way for my asking what teachers could feel were obvious questions about what were everyday classroom occurrences. This was necessary in order to validate my interpretations and to make the familiar strange, in ethnographic terms. Although, to some degree, this strategy worked there were occasions when teachers not only found my apparent lack of understanding peculiar, but also had difficulty in verbalizing their perceptions of what they saw as routine or common place actions. As a participant observer I felt there was always an element of tension, a need for reflexivity with regard to my relationships with the participants. With each individual, it was necessary to adapt my role slightly to fit their 'needs' in order to assure the flow of information and maintain access. During the period of research, although not all teachers welcomed me into their rooms to the same degree, I was not at any time refused access.

The adaptation of role to secure access to the pupils' perceptions and thoughts required careful handling, for as Corrigan (1979) points out, certain kinds of information would not be forthcoming if the children, in particular the older ones, saw the researcher in the teacher role. Feeling this to be true, in the light of relationships I saw between teachers and children, I found it necessary to make it clear on several occasions that I was most unwilling to teach. The children's acceptance of me as 'the visitor' was shown in comments such as: ' . . . but you're not one of them, you talk to us'. Although this refusal to teach classes of children could have been problematic as far as maintaining the original research bargain was concerned, I think my constant willingness to work with small groups, to read with them and go to the library with them prevented the issue arising and, further, was an important channel for information from children.

Whilst in the classrooms the roles I adopted were strongly influenced by circumstances. During more formal lessons, particularly in junior classrooms I tended to have to observe, this gave importance to the time I spent with groups of children in the library where it was possible to talk. In the less 'formal' infant classes the selection of role could be made in terms of what was the most expedient for securing a given type of information. I found the most successful means of 'interviewing' very young children lay in joining in their games, in sitting in the reading corner with them, and in reading and talking about stories with them.

Factors Informing Approaches to Teaching Reading

During the course of the research I carried out semi-structured interviews with all the teachers in the school; that is, seven class teachers, five support staff and the headteacher. Through this a picture emerged of their shared and conflicting views on approaches to teaching reading and of the factors which appeared to have shaped these views. I will identify and discuss some of the major issues in this area.

Throughout, the classes will be identified in terms of the National Curriculum description; that is, reception or R, five-years or under; Y1 or 2 for five- to seven-year-olds; through to, Y6 for ten- to eleven-year-olds.

The Importance and Purpose of Reading

Similar views on the importance and purpose of reading were held by all teachers and yet there were extreme differences in the manner in which these views were reflected in individual teachers' practice.

Reading was unanimously 'acclaimed' as the most important skill to be acquired at school, without which the ability to progress through life would be seriously impaired. Teachers' somewhat effusive comments clearly demonstrated their feelings on this matter: '(Reading is a)... meal ticket for life'; '(an)... opening to new vistas!'; '(the)... most important subject, needed for all others', and; '(the)... gateway to future learning!'

This strength of feeling was carried into the teachers' purpose in teaching reading which was that the children would become enthusiastic volitional readers, and acquire both knowledge and language skills. The following comment illustrates this view:

> *Mr L*: I hope to give them (the children) a love of books, to help them enjoy reading, to see that it can be fun and impart useful knowledge. I can't expect them to see that it will have other spin offs, like increasing their vocabulary, making them better writers and more eloquent — but it will.

There was a strong indication that the major contributing factor to teachers' perceptions of the importance and purpose of reading was subjective; that it was an emotional response to their own experiences of reading. They felt they wanted to give their pupils access to what they and their own children had found in reading. As one teacher said:

> *Mrs T*: I hope they will be beginning to read as I read, finding in reading what I find.

There was little further evidence of consensus amongst the teachers, their aforementioned views being only one factor of the many which, drawn together, appeared to inform each one's practice. These factors were related to such things as the teachers' situation within the school, and the perceived pressures and constraints associated with that. A definite distinction existed between the teachers' homogeneous view of reading as a subject, and their contrasting views of how it should or could be taught.

The 'Situational' and 'Global' Perspectives

Within the school there was a polarization of perspectives on the teaching of reading. This allowed for two broad categories to be classified. The two per-spectives identified in this way relate to the teachers' direct experience of dealing with teaching and the constraints associated with their particular situations. Although there were individual variations it is the shared features of teachers' perspectives which are explored here. As Pollard (1985) suggests

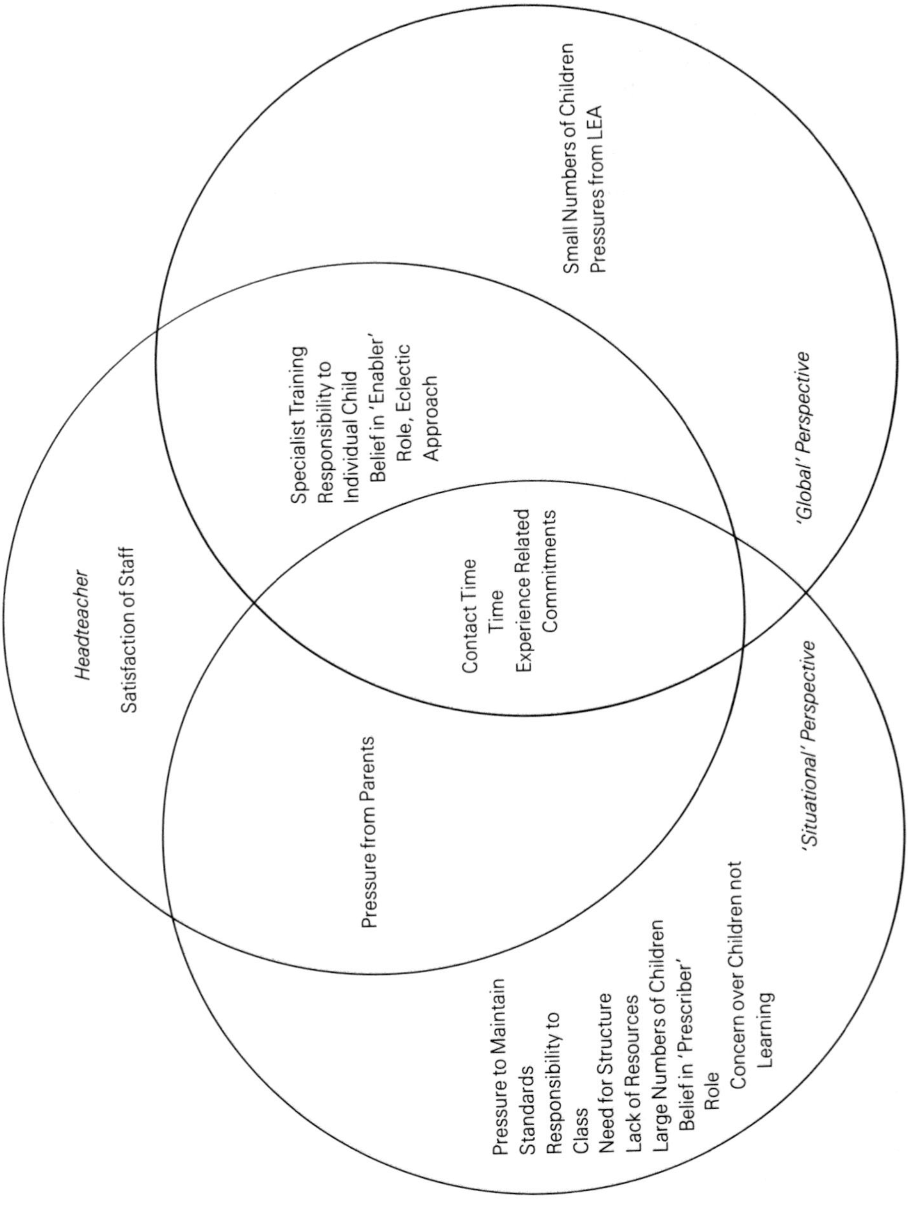

Figure 1   *Factors seen as informing teachers' practice*

' . . . in sociological terms, it is the nature of the similarities in perspective which is more significant' (p. 22). I have used the term 'situational' to refer to the shared perspectives of the class teachers, and 'global' to those of the support staff. Figure 1 is an overview of these categories and it also identifies the factors seen as influencing the headteacher's practice, her perspective being largely 'global'.

Discussion of these perspectives indicates, for the most part, that, as Hargreaves (1984) suggests ' . . . the pedagogical strategies which teachers employ are meaningful responses to experienced problems, constraints and dilemmas' (p. 66). The 'situational' perspective arose from factors associated with the responsibility for teaching reading within the classroom. These led the teachers, to different degrees, to see that the most effective means of teaching lay in the use of a commercial graded reading scheme, a mechanism which enabled the children, for the most part, to progress smoothly as a group.

The contrasting 'global' perspective was equally a response to the support staff's very different responsibility, that being to teach reading, in different locations, to small groups or individuals who had not succeeded within the classroom, as one said, 'We have to find something that works for them'. They did this by designing reading programmes which incorporated materials from a variety of sources in order to address the individual's needs. The headteacher's experience as an infant headteacher coupled with an interest and training in special needs education, have resulted in a view of how reading should be taught, closely aligned to that of the support staff. She felt that there was 'untapped' talent amongst the children which could only be developed through a more 'individualized', informal system. This led her to undertake initiatives to facilitate change in the teaching of reading.

The Move to Change

Through a discussion of the move to change reading in the school several factors seen as informing teachers' practices can be explored. These are: pressure from the local education authority; economic constraints; numbers of children; and experience-related beliefs. It was revealed that as a result of these pressures there appeared to be a divergence between what teachers felt they should do and what they felt they were able to do.

The underlying theme of the changes to reading was that the class-teachers should adopt an approach to teaching reading closer to that of the support staff. This was, in part, a result of the 1981 Education Act which specified that, where possible, children with special educational needs should be integrated into the classroom (Cox, 1985). This external factor placed pressure directly on the support staff and indirectly on the teachers, requiring the former to change their role from a teaching one to an advisory position, for as one support teacher said:

Mrs P: Teaching is impossible in most cases now. We are in charge of 250 children and offer advice. Classroom teachers have to take more responsibility.

The headteacher saw the implications for the teachers in this light:

HT: Traditionally those (children) who didn't learn were withdrawn. The others seem to learn despite the scheme. Now the teachers will have to start teaching them all.

This would necessitate a broadening of approach away from a reliance on a scheme and the inclusion of group and individual work. One member of the support staff clearly expressed what they saw as necessary:

Mrs N: They (the teachers) need to have a language programme for each child, viewing children individually (and thus) catering for and coping with problems.

It was generally agreed amongst the teachers that they would have liked more time to work with individual children, but that this was made impossible by the numbers they had to deal with, who made constant demands on them:

Mrs F: If only we could have a few minutes alone with every child it would make such a difference to their reading.

The following extract from my field-notes illustrates the difficulty Mrs F had in working with individuals during her reading lessons:

Field-notes — Monday 9 February, 1987, Y3

There are seven or eight children standing around the teacher's desk, obscuring her view of the other twelve children at their tables. While one child is reading to her the others are chatting as they wait to read or for a word from their reading book to be decoded. Mrs F spends about two minutes with each reader, but is frequently interrupted by those around her or by disruption in the classroom.

As Galton and Willcocks (1983) say:

It is a constant and exhausting battle to keep the queue of pupils as short as possible. In her efforts to achieve this the teacher had very little time for detailed discussion about the work itself. (p. 162)

Even those whose ideas on the teaching of reading were closest to those of the support staff and headteacher had reservations about the practicality of these ideas within the classroom, because of numbers of children:

Mrs K: There's two types of teaching, there's the support staffs', they have time to give their all to a small group without worry from the rest of the class. I can't do that, even if it is the best way.

This teacher had thirty-eight children in her reception class and one part-time assistant. She viewed the teaching position of the support staff as a form of 'Utopia', which could not be achieved in the classroom without extra resources and more assistance:

Mrs K: I need four quality assistants and more money for equipment, so that there are things to keep the children occupied effectively — things they can learn from.

The factors which she cited as shaping her practice were largely institutional and economic and beyond her control. Thus, although she had a 'global' perspective of how reading should be taught she felt bound by her circumstances to adopt, for the most part, an approach aligned to that of those with a 'situational' perspective. Wells (1986) says that '...under pressure teachers tend to fall back on the traditional transmission mode of teaching' (p. 119). This would appear to be indicated by the above comments from Mrs K.

The motivation to change was not only restricted in the classroom because of external factors. There was, for some teachers, a strong experience-related belief in the use of a reading scheme as the most effective medium through which reading could be taught. As one long-standing staff member said of the recently replaced *Ladybird Keyword Reading Scheme* (Murray, 1964/1972):

Mrs F: It did the most for the children in this school ... who found reading difficult, it encouraged them to read and their progress was rapid, and they enjoyed it.

This approach was in sharp contrast to that advocated by the headteacher and the support staff whose emphasis was on working with individuals. The following comment by a member of the support staff clearly reflects the dichotomy:

Mrs E: When I'm working with children I let them choose books from my selection box of books which I think will interest them, that they'll enjoy. They soon begin to predict sentences when they're involved in a story.

These comments by Mrs F and Mrs E also illustrate that despite the contrast between the two forms of practice, the stated principles for adopting them were very similar. Both approaches were seen as offering children the opportunity to learn to read quickly from materials relevant to their needs.

From these contrasting approaches emerged two very different views of the 'role' of the teacher: the support staff and headteacher perceived the role as one of an 'enabler', where the teacher works collaboratively with the children; alternatively, the teachers, to different degrees, viewed the teacher's role as a 'prescriber' who dictated what the children were to do and how they were to do it. These differing views underlay much of the tension which existed between the headteacher and several long-standing teachers.

The headteacher was the catalyst in the teaching of reading and her perception of the teacher as an 'enabler' strongly influenced the means she employed to facilitate change. Her belief in helping children individually towards understanding through experience was mirrored in the way that she was attempting to change the teachers' approaches to teaching reading. This was shown in the following comment:

HT: Reading is a sensitive area. I can't just say, 'Do this . . . ' I need to work with individual teachers, identifying certain problems, not necessarily doing it (the teaching) for them but offering a solution, showing them by example. Once people see the idea they are not so frightened to try it.

With this intention in mind her initiatives for change in reading were shown to staff through her teaching — the majority of her teaching time, both in and out of the classroom, being spent on reading related activities. In this way she was nurturing the staff, by not directing them, attempting to protect their professional integrity. She felt she had to: ' . . . let the teachers have their own way . . . and to try to dovetail the school's priorities into theirs'. To some extent, she appeared to be what Nias (1980) described as the 'positive head', whom her research found to be most popular amongst teachers, in that she had a high level of involvement, was available to her staff, gave leadership in setting aims and was interested in individual teacher development. Her manner in dealing with the staff bore close relation to her pedagogy.

Tension arose, however, in that those long-serving teachers who used more prescriptive approaches in their teaching would have preferred the headteacher to adopt a similar style in her direction of them. In addition, under the 'old head' they had become used to a paternalistic approach which, on reflection, they regarded as superior, in that he had had outlines for each year and subject:

> *Mrs M*: . . . you knew exactly where you stood, nothing left to chance, aims and objectives and plans for everything.

Although the new headteacher was the person with apparently the most power in the school, the influence of the 'old head' still lingered, contrasting strongly with, and thus undermining, her own. This resulted in a lack of unity amongst the staff, an insecurity, which affected their willingness to support her and thus her ability to effect change. To some extent, these staff were using their power to resist changes which they saw as threatening their control over their work, their professional stance and their ability to teach what they believed was best. The 'institutional bias' (Pollard 1985), the shared understandings of what a school is and what goes on there, was in a state of considerable flux as teachers attempted to re-define their positions and deal with what they saw as endangering the 'old' order of things. This was well illustrated through exploration of the teachers' responses to initiatives for change.

There was often, it appeared, a superficial willingness to incorporate new ideas or approaches but these were not always translated into classroom practice. An example of this was a series of events which took place in an infant classroom where a small group of children were identified by their teacher as having 'special needs' in relation to literacy. In line with the policy for integration a member of the support staff went into the classroom to set up a special programme. The intention was that the teacher, having seen the programme work and been advised of its purposes, would assume its responsibility. She acquiesced to this idea in principle. However, once the programme was established she was unwilling to continue. The result was that the headteacher undertook the extra teaching.

The Need for Structure

Several other factors were identified in relation to the teachers' reliance on commercial reading schemes, these reflecting a belief that they could not teach reading without a firm structure. There seemed to be a strong feeling amongst some teachers that children would not learn to read without a scheme:

Mrs T: Certain skills have to be known, but where do the basic skills come from? You have to have a scheme to teach the basic skills.

Teachers also felt that the reading scheme was necessary if they were to be able to measure progress effectively:

Mrs F: (with a scheme) . . . the teacher can quickly see what progress or otherwise the child is making. You know what they have learned.

A member of support staff commented on the teachers' need to have a concrete representation of the children's progress in this way:

Mrs E: They (the children) have to reach a standard, a norm, you (the teacher) have to have something to put down on paper that everyone at school will understand, will be able to see just where the children are. It's what some of them want, they feel safe and secure in their structure. They would be unnerved by the openness of being without a scheme.

To some extent, the teachers' need to have a structure related directly to the pressure they felt to ensure that children progressed as a group. There was also, for several teachers, an apprehension about their ability to teach children without a scheme stemming from a self-professed lack of knowledge about how children learn to read. They accounted for this in terms of the inadequacy of their initial training. As a recently qualified teacher said:

Mr T: We were never really taught (about reading) at college, we only had two or three sessions and they were on remedial reading.

The headteacher, however, expressed the view that, 'Teachers probably don't need the graded scheme as much as they think they do'.

There was a definite sense that the scheme 'did' the teaching (Reed and Horbury, 1988), as illustrated in the way teachers using the reading scheme frequently referred to what 'it' did — for example, 'They (the children) learn more quickly from it' or 'It just works'. This passive acceptance by teachers that someone knew better than they — in this instance the producers of the reading scheme — did not appear to occur to the same extent in relation to other subjects. It was something which enabled the teachers to spend their time on the job at hand without the responsibility of designing their own programmes.

The above discussion has illustrated that while the teachers had a shared view of the importance and purpose of reading, a variety of other factors related to the constraints under which they work and their experience-related beliefs also informed their approaches to teaching. Within the classroom this meant that teachers only saw a narrow range of pedagogical options as viable which resulted in the teaching of reading through the mechanism of the reading scheme. This allowed for the collective needs of the group, rather than those of the individual child, to be addressed. In the light of this it appeared that in order to read effectively in the teachers' eyes, to become keen volitional readers, the children had, to some extent, to fulfill their own needs. Many appeared unable to do this and it is to that matter that the discussion now turns.

Implications of Approaches to Teaching Reading

As I have mentioned, teachers felt the need to taper their reading pro- grammes in response to the constraints within which they worked. This meant that they felt unable to include more than what they described as 'the basics', that is, reading scheme related activities. What became apparent was that there were certain abilities teachers felt children needed to become effective readers but which they did not have time to teach. The implication of this was that children had to acquire part of their knowledge of reading outside its formalized teaching. This largely related to developing an under- standing of the purpose and possibilities of reading beyond a linear progression through the scheme. I have described the acquisition of these abilities as 'the jumps' children had to make between what was taught and what they needed to know in order to become readers. Discussion of these 'jumps' reveals the extent to which all participants saw children's home backgrounds and parents as a key influence in their learning to read. This will be addressed further in the final section of the chapter.

The Jumps

Within the infant department one of the major 'jumps' children appeared to have to make towards the acquisition of reading was connecting the meaning of words to their printed form, and to recognizing that the words held the story. Many children had difficulty in doing this and seemed to be 'barking at print'; that is, reading without understanding. This problem was identified by teachers as being of particular concern in the Y3 classroom. What became evident, through teacher's comments on this matter, was that some children were seen as coming to school with abilities which enabled them to understand what reading was about. This in turn enabled them to learn to read with comparative ease; they were considered by teachers to be 'natural readers':

> *Mrs K*: Some children, like Jane, are natural readers. From an early age she has realized that written words mean different things, that different shapes mean different words. She realizes that there is continuity in a book, that there are clues in pictures. She approaches reading in such a way as to use the clues. She wants to read. Now Nora, she sees each word individually, even if you ask her to tell the story she can't. She hasn't reached the stage of knowing she can help herself.
>
> *BR*: Why do you think that is?
>
> *Mrs K*: A lack of interest in books at home, probably nobody has bothered to sit with her so she hasn't reached the stage where she knows what books are about.

It is apparent from the above interview extract that there was an extreme difference between what the two children described knew of reading. Jane was seen as having come to school with a strong understanding of the nature of reading which she was able to apply to her reading with the teacher. In contrast Nora, without such an understanding, related reading to the recognition of individual words. If, as inferred, Nora has acquired her understanding of reading at school, it could be suggested that it must reflect those elements of reading which were stressed by the teacher as most important, as she was the key influence in the development of this understanding. Thus, as word recognition was given precedence, so Nora perceived that it was what reading was about.

At some point children, such as Nora, would appear to have to make the 'jump' in understanding from the perception they had developed of reading in response to its teaching, to 'recognizing what books were about' and being able to read effectively. It seems evident from Mrs K's comments that children's home background was considered to be a key element in the manner in which children learned to read and that a lack of involvement from home was seen as resulting in children facing difficulties.

Within the junior department the 'jumps' children had to make were largely related to their ability to make use of their knowledge of reading. That is, although many had acquired the ability to read a text they were without certain reading related skills which were regarded by teachers as necessary but which went untaught. These were such things as: the ability to select books; to use a library; to know what they liked to read and why; to enjoy reading; and to extract information from books. The key factors related to the 'jumps' in understanding which junior children had to make can be clearly illustrated through discussion of children's ability to select books.

Teachers believed that in order for children to attain the most benefit from their reading, and to enjoy it, they needed to read books which were of interest to them. In this, they had to be able to make appropriate selections of books. The development of this ability was, conversely, something which teachers felt unable to incorporate into their reading programmes. This applied to both children's selection of books in the classroom and to their use of the library.

Each junior class was given a 'library period' where the teacher could take the children to the library; they chose, however, not to use these. The teacher in charge of the library said:

> *Mrs F:* It concerns me very much that teachers do not use the library. I think that some members of staff have forgotten those books are there. I can't force them into the library, I have to find out why they don't use their library periods. If you have all the children in the library you can spend some time teaching them library skills, helping them choose, but it's changing into a purely mechanical thing, just change your library book and that's it.

What seems to be underlined in this comment is the lack of personal involvement of teachers in children's individual reading. Book selection had become, or was, the changing of books, a routine process carried on in isolation. The following comments from teachers indicate their rationale for neither using their 'library periods' nor becoming involved in book selection:

> *Mr T:* I took them a couple of times, but half of them didn't change their books, couldn't be bothered. It was a waste of time I didn't have, as children said they didn't know what they wanted.
>
> *Mr R:* I used to take them but I think it's more important to hear reading . . . They need help choosing books, to find the right ones but you never have enough time to do this. Ideally, you should have time to look at the book and discuss it and find out what the children want to read, then they would get more from their reading. You would have to have one teacher per child to help them all choose.
>
> *Mrs S:* There are some who don't know where to go, who have no idea of how to choose books they'll enjoy, this is the problem. And

> they are from homes where there are not many books. I try to
> give them as broad a selection as possible. I'd like to involve
> myself in selection, when I have time, when I get the scheme
> sorted out.

It seems to be apparent from these comments that while recognizing
that children were unable to select books which were of interest to them,
which meant that they were not enjoying reading, teachers felt unable to incorporate assistance in selection into their reading programmes. The
references to time and numbers of children underline the suggestion that in
response to these constraints teachers tapered their programmes to include
those elements of reading which they felt to be most important, that was the
use of the reading scheme and the hearing of reading. To some extent, there
were also those elements which required the least personal input from
teachers, in that they involved routine procedures which followed the same
pattern for each child. Galton, Simon and Croll's (1980) study found that
teachers' interaction with pupils tended to be of a routine nature and that
the kind of discussion which would be necessary, in this instance, to help
children select their books did not take place. They say:

> A teacher with a classroom populated by young children . . . can
> not easily afford either the time or the mental energy to engage in
> such discussion with individual children. On the contrary, she
> must always be conscious of the other twenty-nine pupils who, in
> this case are present . . . and also, if in varying degrees, demanding
> her attention. (p. 158)

In the light of the above, children who did not have the ability to select
books needed to acquire it independently. It could be suggested that this
required a considerable 'jump' in their understanding of the purpose of
reading in that they had to discover a reason to want to read for themselves.
In order to do this they had to move from reflecting in their reading those
elements which were given most stress by teachers. As one teacher said in
relation to why children read:

> *Mrs T:* The desire for adult approbation is strong, the system as a
> whole tends to incline children to read to adults and because
> they learn to read aloud that tends to be where the pleasure,
> the incentive, comes from.

Inferred in this comment is that children were reading largely for the sake of
getting what they did right in order to receive adult approval. As children
got older they were increasingly reading for the purpose of finishing the
reading scheme and becoming 'free readers'; that is, having finished the

reading scheme being free to choose what they read. The 'jump' that they had to make was to seeing the possibilities reading had outside the reading scheme and being heard read which had been the centre of their reading in school.

Meek (1984) says of the reading of 11-year-olds: 'When we look at children of this age whose reading can be accounted as expert, we find that much of what they know about reading has never been taught to them' (p. 294). The children she discusses could be considered to be those who made the 'jump' in understanding. Many children did not appear to make this jump in their interpretation of the purpose of reading. In this way, teachers' lack of involvement in children's selection of books could be seen as a contributing factor to the 'low' or 'negative' status children often seemed to give to reading. Once they finished the scheme and became 'free readers', being heard read only infrequently, much of the purpose the children had in reading was gone.

It could be suggested that the 'jumps' children had to make towards acquiring the ability to read effectively arose, at least in part, from teaching being carried out through routine procedures, such as hearing reading and teaching word recognition which worked for the 'natural reader'. Those who came to school with an understanding of, and thus purpose for, reading were those who succeeded. The others tended to be excused for not learning because of their home backgrounds. As Mrs K's earlier comment would indicate, children appeared to be differentiated against in terms of their position in relation to the 'natural reader'. Becker (1984) in his discussion of occupations, such as teaching, suggested that:

> Members of such occupations typically have some image of the 'ideal' client, and it is in terms of this fiction that they fashion their conceptions of how their work ought to be performed, and their actual work techniques. To the degree that actual clients approximate this ideal the worker will have no client problem. (p. 98)

The 'natural reader' would appear to closely resemble Becker's 'ideal client'. It would seem that in developing the concept of 'natural readers', and suggesting that children who did not share their qualities could not learn as effectively, offered teachers a means of dealing with the fact that the children were not learning within the approaches which they felt constrained, by classroom circumstances, to adopt. Throughout the school, children's home background was viewed as a key factor in their acquisition of reading.

The Influence of Home Background on Reading Acquisition

The nature of children's home backgrounds was seen by classroom teachers as a factor of equal or greater importance to what was taught with regard to children's acquisition of reading. The following comments by teachers clearly illustrate their perceptions of the influence of home background:

Mrs F: Home and school together, without two sides pulling together, the teacher finds she has a much harder problem in teaching reading. Children who come from a home where books are well known seem to catch the habit rather than have to work at it. Some children never learn.

Mrs K: Some children, usually from homes where books have been important, catch reading like a cold.

Mrs S: I'd like them to get enjoyment from reading, but nowadays they have TV on at home all the time, they don't need to use their imagination.

Mr L: I must say, home background is the most important factor. If parents read and encourage reading, if it's a linguistically deprived home, whether they have a 'restricted' or 'elaborated' code. Children can often read fluently but they haven't learnt to enjoy books and I don't feel the fault lies with the school. Home has more to answer for, they teach them how to react to books. The difference lies in if they see their parents reading for pleasure or just watching TV. Television and video games stop children reading, you shouldn't expect too much from children in reading and enjoying books considering what their home background is.

Two messages appear to be contained in these comments. Firstly, children who come from homes where books had been given importance are seen as needing little assistance in learning to read; they were the 'natural readers'. Secondly, children who came from homes where television and magazines were believed to take precedence over reading seem to be seen as, to some extent, beyond the help of teachers in terms of their ability to learn to enjoy books and thus read effectively. In the comment by Mr L this notion is extended when he refers to the early ideas of Bernstein (1961) of 'restricted' and 'elaborated' language codes. These he interprets as being that the language of some children was essentially inferior and, therefore, such children were bound to do less well.

What the comments appeared to be giving was an explanation of children's failure to learn to read, and, of why teachers could have lower expectations of certain children. The teachers seemed to be apportioning the blame for why children did not want to read and placing it in the child's home and environment. In this way they seemed to be exonerating themselves from the responsibility of seeing that all children learned to read effectively. It could be suggested that this was a contradiction of their initial purpose in teaching reading which was that children should develop the ability to enjoy reading. What appeared to be said in this instance was that accessing children to that side of reading was beyond teachers' control. The above notion is further illustrated when teachers' responses to children who came from homes which were not considered to provide the stimulation and yet learned to be keen volitional readers is explored. These children were viewed as 'oddities'. An example of this was a child in the Y3 class; she was the only 'free reader' and considered to be the 'best' reader in the class. The child, Lucy, came from a home where her parent was, apparently, illiterate. This was made evident when I asked if she would mind undertaking a taped interview. She said:

> It's good for me to use the tape because I have to make some story tapes for my mummy, because she can't read very well.

Lucy said of reading:

> I like reading to myself; it's exciting and you can do things and make mysteries in them (the stories), you can get much more out of it and be happy about it.

This child was enjoying reading and appeared to be becoming deeply involved in the stories she read. Her teacher said of her:

> *Mrs F:* She's a special case, it's incredible that from time to time in spite of all good reasons you get the odd child who does this. Probably something in them discovers books. In Lucy's case she has no trouble with reading, she just takes to it. She finds it pleasurable and knows how to use it to escape. She was lucky to be born with that skill. It didn't come from home.

This comment seems to indicate that children who came from homes where there was little involvement in reading were not expected to be able to enjoy books. Sharp and Green (1984) refer to the situation where, 'some children take on a reified identity and are categorised as abnormal, "really" peculiar', because they do not come within the 'parameters of teachers' background expectations' (p. 125). They discussed this with regard to children who were failing to learn because teacher approaches did not work for them. However, it would appear to apply equally to those children who go beyond what teachers expect their approaches to achieve when considering children's circumstances. It is interesting to note that, rather than saying that the child's interest in books has been stimulated in school, it was viewed as something innate. This would seem to underline the notion that teachers accepted neither the credit nor the blame for children's success in reading. In the light of this, those children who succeed could be seen as doing so largely by fulfilling their own needs.

It could be suggested that the teachers perpetuated the differences which existed between the children; firstly, by typifying them in the manner described above as 'natural readers' or otherwise from the time they entered school; and secondly, by saying that you could not expect very much of the children because of their home backgrounds. As Sharp and Green (1984) suggested, teachers seemed to hold the view that ' . . . most children achieve normally for "this sort of child" most of the time' (p. 126). In this way the problems do not lie with the teacher but with the child. It is also possible that the emphasis on parental involvement in children's reading 'practice', particularly in the early years, where the children took home their reading books to practice in order to be prepared for reading in school would further enhance the difference between the children. It would seem reasonable to submit that those parents who had been involved in encouraging reading from the outset would generally be those who continued to do so when the children entered school, and that these children would be offered a greater chance of success within a system which was, to some extent, dependent on parental input.

Conclusion

The key influence on the approaches that the teachers adopted seemed to be the constraints under which they worked. These related, for the most part, to pressures of classroom organization, such as working with large numbers of children, and to a perceived scarcity of time. The evidence indicated that, in order to accommodate these pressures, teachers had to adopt approaches which were apparently non-commensurate with their initial intentions, thus relying almost entirely on the mechanism of the reading scheme for the teaching of reading. An implication of this was that in order to become effective readers in the eyes of teachers children had to acquire an understanding of reading beyond that which was provided in school. This meant that they had to see the purposes and possibilities of reading beyond the scheme; to be able to choose and discuss books; and to have the ability to use the library and reference materials. My research indicated that many children failed to do this. As one teacher said, 'They are not reading failures, they are just not readers'.

The advent of the Programmes of Study for the core subjects of the National Curriculum and English Attainment Target 2: Reading requires that children are provided with learning experiences designed to help them to develop wider reading-related abilities. The subsequent need for these teachers and others, who may share their perspectives, to move from 'situational' to 'global' approaches seems likely to prove very difficult and threatening. It indicates an immediate need for in-service training and additional support for teachers in an established area of the primary curriculum where, on the surface, this may not appear necessary. Such training might include assisting teachers to become familiar and confident with alternative approaches to learning which have the potential to facilitate more varied reading activities and to free teachers to give more attention to the reading needs of individual children. In order to implement the National Curriculum, headteachers who, like the one in the study, believe that changing teachers' practices is best achieved through personal example seem likely to find themselves not only having to devise additional strategies to bring about change, but also having to find extra resources in order to support teachers through the multiple changes that may be considered necessary. Given time, the careful management of change, adequate resources and support, teachers, such as those in the study, may come closer to achieving their initial intentions in the teaching of reading.

References

ADELMAN, C. (1985) 'Some problems of ethnographer culture', in BURGESS, R. G. (Ed.) *Field Methods in the Study of Education*, Lewes, Falmer Press.

BECKER, H. S. (1984) 'Social class variations in the teacher-pupil relationship', in HARGREAVES, A. and WOODS, P. (Eds.) *Classrooms and Staffrooms*, Milton Keynes, Open University Press.

BERNSTEIN, B. (1961) *Class Codes and Control*, Vol. 1, London, Routledge and Kegan Paul.

BURGESS, R. G. (1984) *In the Field: An Introduction to Field Research*, London, Allen and Unwin.

CORRIGAN, P. (1979) *Schooling the Smash Street Kids*, Basingstoke, Macmillan.

COX, B. (1985) *The Law of Special Educational Needs: A Guide to the Education Act 1981*, London, Croom Helm.

GALTON, M., SIMON, B. and CROLL, P. (1980) *Inside the Primary Classroom*, London, Routledge and Kegan Paul.

GALTON, M. and WILLCOCKS, J. (Eds.) (1983) *Moving from the Primary Classroom*, London, Routledge and Kegan Paul.

HARGREAVES, A. (1984) 'The significance of classroom coping strategies', in HARGREAVES, A. and WOODS, P. (Eds.) *Classrooms and Staffrooms: The Sociology of Teachers and Teaching*, Milton Keynes, Open University Press.

MEEK, M. (1984) 'Children's literature: Mainstream text or optional extra?', in EAGLESON, R. D. (Ed.) *English in the Eighties*, Sydney, Australian Association for the Teaching of English.

MURRAY, W. (1962/74) *Ladybird Keyword Reading Scheme*, Leicester, Wills and Hepworth.

NIAS, J. (1980) 'Leadership styles and job satisfaction in primary schools', in BUSH, T., GLASIER, R., GOODEY, J. and RICHES, C. (Eds.) *Approaches to School Management*, New York, Harper and Row.

POLLARD, A. (1985) *The Social World of the Primary School*, London, Holt, Rinehart and Winston.

REED, B. and HORBURY, A. (1988) 'A Threat to Quality', *The Times Educational Supplement*, 29 December.

SHARP, R. and GREEN, A. (1984) 'Social stratification in the classroom', in HARGREAVES, A. and WOODS, P. (Eds.) *Classrooms and Staffrooms: The Sociology of Teachers and Teaching*, Milton Keynes, Open University Press.

WELLS, G. (1986) *The Meaning Makers*, London, Heinemann.

Chapter four

Writing in the Infant Classroom

Linda Russell

I first became interested in the area of children's writing when, whilst taking a top infant class for the first time, I found that the children's written language bore little resemblance to their spoken language. The former seemed static and formal, whereas the latter was so dynamic. I began to realize the tremendous problems faced by the children when they were asked to write. For example, motor control, handwriting, spelling, letter formation, and even the left to right convention, are all technical factors that children have to contend with at the same time as they are searching for ideas and for the words to express them.

It was a matter of gaining insights and hopefully, a greater understanding of the task a child faces when asked to write, that was to be my starting point in the research. I felt that by investigating writing from the children's point of view, instead, as is often the case, from the teacher's perspective, I would be able to develop the kind of constructive and consistent interventions in the children's writing necessary to improve its quality. As Smith (1982) says:

> Writing is fostered rather than taught, and what teachers require is not . . . advice about 'methods' of writing instruction, but an understanding of the task a child faces in learning to write. (p. 200)

In formulating my research I began, not with a specific question to which I needed an answer, but with the feeling that my classroom practice might be improved by a greater knowledge of the processes by which a child becomes a writer.

Data Collection

Case-study research enabled me to draw on a variety of data-collection techniques such as observation, tape recording and interviews. In the initial stages, it was important that a great deal of time was spent simply observing the children writing. As observing the behaviour of a class of twenty-four children would have produced an unmanageable volume of data, I decided to look at just twelve children who worked in two groups of six. The children, seven girls and five boys, were randomly selected in order to avoid the inevitable bias that my knowledge of the children and their abilities would have produced. The groups were observed, one at a time, over a period of six months, in the classroom, as part of the whole class and when the rest of the children were doing PE with the headteacher.

Initially, the best method for observing the children proved to be noting down as much as possible of the detail of the session from a general, overall viewpoint. Backed up by notes written after the sessions and tape transactions, it was then possible to focus in on certain points that seemed to occur frequently, and patterns began to emerge.

Observation of the children was something I had experienced before on a language course run by the Local Education Authority. The course was concerned with listening to children talking and analyzing this in terms of the guidelines set down by Tough (1977) in her work on children's oral language. I had also made use of observational techniques during the MA course which led to the research now under discussion. When observing the children in the home-bay castle that we had created for a research assignment, I made use of an 'invisible cloak'. It was simply a matter of telling the children that I was putting a cloak on, and miming the action, and that the cloak made me 'invisible'. This proved to be more successful than asking the children not to disturb me for a few minutes when I had my notebook in my hand:

Clair: Where's Mrs Russell?
Lindsay: She's in here (the castle), but you can't ask her anything 'cos she's got her invisible cloak on.
Clair: Oh, ok.

It appealed to the children in my class at that time who quickly saw the funny side and were content to play along with me in this respect.

I felt that my presence in the classroom when the small groups of children were writing may have contributed to the quiet atmosphere in the room that was generally present. Although the groups of children often finished their tasks before the rest of the class returned, those who did not manage to do so carried on with their work in the same manner. I was able to record a great deal of detail about the children's behaviour during these writing sessions. The problem of trying to get it all down when the whole class was in the room was tackled by making timed observations of one or two particular children during a session. This I did using a five-minute schedule. I looked up from what I was doing and made a simple note of what the children I was observing were doing at the time. This behaviour could be looked for specifically in the small-group sessions that we had regularly. In this way I was able to see for myself that I did affect the children's behaviour by putting them into a small group, because in class sessions they were often engaged in non-writing activities such as tickling each other, looking at a toy, or combing hair. These behaviours were not observed in the sessions where I was able to observe them more closely.

I told the children that I was going to tape writing sessions, interviews and discussions. I also told them why I would be doing this, stressing the importance that I placed upon their opinions and feelings. I also stressed the fact that nobody else in the school would be given the information that they provided me with. They were also able to listen to the tapes afterwards and I noted down any immediate response that occurred when they were listening to the recording so that I could discuss it with them later on.

Initially, the tape recorder did disturb or interfere with the children's interactions, which were markedly different when I was just observing. When being taped writing, the children became very quiet and industrious. Gradually, over the next few sessions, it was obvious that the novelty and restriction of the tape recorder had worn off and the children were behaving as naturally as possible under the circumstances. It is interesting to actually listen to what the children say. On one occasion, I had positioned the tape at the beginning of a writing session and had left the room for a few minutes to see what would happen during my absence. I wondered if the tape would stop the children from behaving as they would have done in a similar situation. I also felt that my presence may have had some effect on the subjects the children chose to talk about. When I came to transcribe the tape later on, I found that the children certainly seemed to know a lot about their class teacher and her reactions. On transcribing one particular tape, I found that a swear word had been used by one of the boys:

Girl: Oh, you'll get done when she hears that!
Boy: No I won't . . . she'll just laugh.

And I did.

The transcribing of the tapes was extremely time consuming, but it was very necessary as it recorded all the talk going on at the table. I was not always in a position to make detailed notes of the conversation that was going on. One problem with this method of data collection is the background noise that you pick up in a classroom. During the period when it was only the writing group in the room, it was comparatively easy to transcribe the tapes. However, it became increasingly difficult once the rest of the class returned to pick out the children under observation from the rest.

I felt that by asking the children questions I would be able to gather more information about matters arising from other methods of data collection I had been using during the research. It was one very direct method of collecting information. I interviewed the children in the two observation groups and individually. Two of the children did not react well to the individual or group sessions. One of these two children is fairly quiet anyway, but the other child appears extremely confident in the classroom. In the group interviews, however, she was extremely quiet and when I tried to draw her into the discussion she replied with short answers or gestures which could have been due to my lack of experience as an interviewer:

Teacher: What about you, Sarah? Why did you write about that?
Sarah: (No answer. She shrugs her shoulders.)
Teacher: Was it something already in your mind?
Sarah: I don't know.
Paul: I wrote about aeroplanes 'cos I like them.

Talk

Talk is the basic form in which language is manifested. Reading and writing both have their basis in talk, and ways of using language must first be established through talk. The demands of writing, both on the child's physical skills and on the available time, set limits on what he can communicate in writing. Not until the later years of the primary school are reading and writing so well established that they can become an alternative means of communicating. (Tough, 1977, p. 7)

In a session where the drawing came before the writing, the children in the second group sought to obtain comment on their work or commented on each other's work. This had not been a feature of the observation of the usual writing sessions:

(Simon takes his picture of an aeroplane to show his friend Kirsty.)

Kirsty: Where's the writing?
(Simon does not answer. Returns to his seat. Adds more detail to the picture, specifically another bomb dropping from the aeroplane, then he starts to write.)
Geoff: I like your picture.
Simon: Why don't you do some more to your picture?
(He then draws something on Geoff's work.)

This interaction did not feature in the work of the first group. The children in this group gave help with words more frequently than the other, but they did not participate in the kind of comment observed in the second. The second group had children in from all the social groups in the class. They were not with any of their usual friends. The composition of the first group was different in that it had one child from outside the friendship group, two girls who played together in the playground and the three boys who were part of a larger, very strong friendship group. Perhaps the children in the first group were more at ease with each other and did not need to seek approval. It could also be that the children in this group were more confident in the situation in which they were placed.

One particular child, Simon, spent a lot of his time talking to himself whilst writing and drawing. He tended to sit alone for many of the writing sessions that I observed:

(Simon is drawing his picture prior to writing. Talking aloud about what he is doing, but in a quiet voice.)
Simon: I'll put a propeller on 'cos it's not Concorde. There, that looks alright. I'll put some bombs on here. Oh, it looks like a whale. (Smiles.)
(He then starts to write, saying each word as he writes it.)

When I asked him about his behaviour in an interview, he confirmed that he did this quite a lot. I wondered if he knew why:

Simon: I can think about what I'm going to do next when I'm drawing. The words for writing help me remember what I've said . . . where I am.

Simon was not a good reader and this may account for his need to say the words aloud. However, other children with the same problem did not exhibit this behaviour.

A great deal of talk was observed between the children about the technical side of writing; they were talking about their writing together, helping and advising when I was not helping them with any spellings they required:

(Three children observed discussing the zoo. Only one of them writing about the zoo at this stage.)

Paul: No such things as pigs in a zoo, they'd get eaten up.

Lee: Some pigs have horns from the mouth in Flamingo Land. Well it looks like a pig, but it's something else.

Paul: Mucky pigs . . . they smell.

Peter: They'd rip your skin open.

Lee: Yeah. They've got horns.

Paul: You could put bird, I know how to spell that, I'm not sure about pig.

Peter: Ok, I'll put bird then.

I wondered if the children had any preferences as to the work environment from a noise point of view. All the children in my class I spoke to during the course of the research project said that they were distracted by people talking at the table:

Ann: It's hard to carry on because you can't think properly.

The general noise level in the room was also commented on when the children were asked how they preferred working:

Question: What about you, Geoff? How do you like the room to be when you are writing?

Geoff: Quiet . . . because you can think what you're doing and when it's noisy, you can't.

Although objecting to a noisy classroom, one child had a wonderful suggestion to make, but none of the others liked his idea:

Simon: I'd like to listen to a music tape and not people talking.

In one session, where the drawing aspect of the task came before the writing, Karen decided to move from the table where she was working. When I asked her why she had moved, it was because of the noise. She could not concentrate, but she only moved when she wanted to start her written part of the task. Although the noise had been a constant factor at the table, she had told the others to be quiet when drawing, but the move had come when she wanted to write.

Reasons for Writing

I wondered if the children had any thoughts about the reasons for writing. One of the children said he wrote because he enjoyed it:

> *Geoff*: I like writing because I like making stories up. At home I write a
> lot because it is fun.

However, the overwhelming reason given by the children was that the
teacher had told them to do it:

> *Kirsty*: Why do you write? Because the teacher says get that writing
> done!
> *Sarah*: I write because the teacher said.

The children were confident of their facts here. They wrote because I told
them to do so. With this in mind, I asked them what they thought I was
looking for in the work that they did for me:

> *Peter*:   You look at the work to see if we've done it right.
> *Question*: What do you mean by that?
> *Peter*:   To see if all the words are right.
> *Paul*:   You look and see if you like the stories we've written.

Peter believes that I am concerned with the technicalities of the written
work, but Paul mentions the content. However, he was the only child that
did. I went on to ask the children how they felt when they were asked to write
something. The responses were equally split: half the children in the group
liked writing and the other half did not. Those children who did not like to
write gave several reasons for this:

> *Lee*: I don't like writing because it is hard and because the other
> children copy me.

I did not find any evidence to back up his statement.

> *Paula*: I don't like writing because it's hard to find the words.

She is talking about looking them up in a dictionary.

> *Peter*: I don't like writing because I have to make up stories and it is
> boring.

Those children who said they did like writing sessions also gave various
reasons for this:

> *Paul*: I like writing because you learn more things.
> *Sarah*: I like writing because it is work. It is easy because you only have
> to think.

I was interested in the type of writing task the children preferred. Four
of the six children in the first group said that they preferred me to provide
them with a subject to write about either using a story beginning, a book we

had read or just a title:

> *Paula*: You can copy a story out of a book.

The second group said that they preferred it when I said they could write about anything they liked because the other writing tasks were more difficult. It is possible that they might not have had any immediately obvious or easily recollected previous experience to draw upon:

> *Question*: What about if I said to you write a story about something, a shipwreck, for instance?
> *Karen*: That's hard.
> *Ann*: It's hard because you get loads of thinking to do.

I wondered if any insights could be gathered from looking at the length of the child's written output when I had been the instigator of the writing task, or whether, when left to their own devices, the children produced work that had a greater length. Seven of the twelve children wrote more when given a teacher-directed task, but only Geoff and Jenny wrote considerably more during these tasks. Interestingly, it was the second group who said they preferred a free choice when writing. Three children in this group wrote more when this was the option, Geoff and Ann writing less. The majority of the children in the first group said during interviews that they preferred to write when given a topic to start from, and four of them wrote slightly more on these occasions. It is possible that the children wrote more when they had something particular they wanted to write about, or when the teacher-directed task set them off on something where they could draw on previous knowledge or their own experience.

One response I personally made to the comments the children were expressing about the difficulty of finding ideas was the introduction of class writing themes. These were much more heavily teacher-directed than had been the case previously in my teaching. The class would come together for the initial discussion of the theme and an introduction to the task being set. The work took varying forms including storyboard, menu-planning, imaginative writing, and re-telling part of the story in the children's own words. Each task was called a chapter and built up into a book over a period of ten days. During these periods of work, the children would all be engaged in writing their particular response to the task set. Because they were all beginning from the same starting point, the discussions which arose were about the plots they were conceiving, the task set and the characters involved. The buzz in the room was extremely exciting — for example, when the children became very animated by the thought of an alien spaceship landing in the local wood:

(I have just set the scene for the opening chapter of a space story. Each child has been asked to write their discovery of the spaceship in the wood).

Lee: I'm going to find it on my way to school this morning.

Paul: It flew right over my head and I fell over!

Karen: You didn't really see a spaceship this morning did you, Lee?

Lee: Yes I did. It was all silver and it crashed in the woods over there (points to the window).

(The whole group of four look towards the window.)

Choice of Content

When given a free choice to write, what did the children choose to write about? Furthermore, how many of these pieces of work were about actual events the children had experienced? In this context, a story means something they had invented for themselves and an adapted story means the idea has been given to them by either something they had seen on television or had read in a book.

The first group wrote about:

Paul: Going to nan, seeing Concorde, relations.

Peter: Hijack (story), going to the park, the zoo (story).

Sarah: Auntie, swans (story), Superman (adapted story).

Kirsty: TV, football match (adapted story), seasons (story).

Jane: Scarborough, grandma, the zoo (story).

Lee: Supermarket shopping, the park, the fair.

In total there were eleven actual events written about and eight invented stories.

The second group wrote about:

Karen: The seaside, the little girl (story), the zoo (story).

Simon: A model he'd made, a squirrel (story), space (story).

Ann: The woods (story), a sick boy (story), a ball (story).

Paula: Cat up a tree (twice, directly copied from a book, word for word), a witch (story).

Geoff: A boy and wolf (adapted story), hijack (story), playing snooker.

Jenny: Visiting dad, a boy in the tree (adapted story), space (story).

In total, there were four actual events written about and twelve invented stories. The two groups together give fifteen actual events and twenty invented stories.

The Plowden Report (1967) noted:

> It is becoming less usual for personal writing to take the form of an invented 'story'. Save for exceptional children who have a story-telling gift . . . this type of writing tends to be second rate and derivative from poorish material. (DES p. 219)

However, the children in the study often chose to write in this mode and very successfully too. The degree of invention for Plowden seems to be the main criteria. However, being able to put together a sequence of events and give appropriate emphasis within the sequence are other criteria. As Smith (1982) says: 'Children have a natural interest in stories. They create imaginative worlds' (p. 193).

Three of the six children in the second group said that they got many of their ideas for writing from books:

Question: Where do your ideas come from?
Karen: Books that I've read at home and school.
Paula: You can copy ideas out of books you've read.

In the case of Paula, she had literally copied the story from a book on two occasions. She had not attempted to enter the story herself. Ann had utilized the ball scene from the story of Cinderella, but she had been involved in dressing up in a 'beautiful ballgown'. The other three children in that group said that their ideas for writing came out of their heads. In the other group, two children said the television gave them ideas for their writing at school. One child said ideas came from out of her head. The other two children said that books were an important source of ideas. In one of his stories, Geoff had used the story of Peter and the Wolf we had been reading in class as the basis for his own encounter with a wolf. Two of the other children in the group, Ann and Jane, had collaborated on a story that was turned into a book for the library corner in school. They had used one of the 'Flightpath To Reading' long books about 'Tim and the People of the Moonlight' as the basis for their own adventure with Tim.

Sarah, Simon, Paula and Kirsty felt that their ideas for writing came from inside:

Sarah: My ideas comes from my head.
Simon: The ideas come from out of your brains.
Paula: My ideas are in my head.
Kirsty: Ideas are in your brain.

However, it was not possible to penetrate for deeper explanations beyond this level with the children in the two groups.

Although two of the children said that they got ideas for writing from the television, very little of the work done during the periods of observation showed traces of being influenced by what was on the screen. The story about Superman was written after watching the video of the film, and two pieces of writing were on the theme of a hijack (one in each of the groups). In both cases the writing was done in the week when this topic appeared on the news programmes. I was surprised by the fact that television-based plots in stories had not appeared as much as they had done in the general work of the class, Jaws the shark being a particularly common theme in the writing the children produced in the classroom. Television appears to have an important part in the play in which the children participate both in and out of the classroom. For example, the children are often engaged in games where they take on the name of a particular character from their favourite programme. The lack of writing about characters from television could be accounted for by the fact that the children may have watched a great deal of television: 'Children find it easier to recall programmes if they have seen a smaller number of them' (Cullingford, 1984, p. 94).

Collaborative Writing

The most direct and relevant way for a teacher to demonstrate to a child the power of writing is to write with the child. (Smith, 1982, p. 201)

The writing as a partner with the child, collaborative writing, can enable the teacher to show that writing can be a shared activity. I tried this approach with the children in my class. The children with whom I wrote asked to do so; they were not selected by me for the task. It became a task that the children wanted to do. They asked if they could work with me. The closeness and exclusiveness of these sessions appealed to a number of the participants:

Simon: I like being the only person at the table.

However, this approach was not universally popular. It was regarded a little suspiciously by one of the children:

Geoff: If you write with me, then it isn't my work 'cos I didn't really write it.
Me: I only wrote what you wanted to say.
Geoff: But I didn't write it myself . . . it's cheating.
Me: Why?
Geoff: Writing you have to do yourself.

Here, Geoff is expressing his belief that the term 'writing' only refers to work which he has physically carried out himself. He places the emphasis very firmly on the physical activity, not the mental activity involved. It is also possible that Geoff feels he has lost the ownership of the ideas he is expressing when he filters them through his teacher.

The use of a microcomputer for this collaborative writing did produce some work of greater coherence. This was particularly so in the case of Peter. He was excited and highly motivated by having work produced in this way, eager to try it again. The use of a printer to bring the work off the screen was an added factor:

> *Peter*: How does it do that? . . . It looks really good. Can I take a copy home?

This was a common finding when working with the computer. The children were freed from the necessity of physically producing their work, and consequently the work gained enormously: 'Children, shown that writing is fun, are motivated to achieve high standards of work' (McLeod, 1988, p. 33). Word-processing packages, such as Writer and Folio, are both very simple for the children to use. In each of these programs, the text is keyed in and appears on the screen as if it were being typed onto paper. The enormous difference is that the text can be altered very easily, and therefore slips of the finger and incorrect spellings can be corrected. These word-processing packages can take over some of the tedious chores that writing does involve, leaving the child free to concentrate on the ideas, content and organization:

> Word processors give young writers control over wayward ideas and over technical problems like spelling and editing. They can then get on with the important aspect of writing — producing something interesting. (Smith quoted in Obrist, 1983, p. 56)

The work looks very professional when it comes from the printer. The appearance of the final product looks as good for every child. I was surprised at the easy transition which the children made between the writing of words using lower-case letters and the need to type from a keyboard using only upper-case (although the text does appear in lower-case). I had been prepared to add self-adhesive lower-case letters to the keyboard if the children had found it problematical, but the necessity did not arise.

The Appearance of the Writing

I noticed during the initial observation period that much of the time during a writing session was spent by the children either hunting for a rubber or hunting for words. During successive observation sessions I noted the amount of times each child got up from the table to either sharpen a pencil, get a rubber or a word. In all the cases I observed of the children getting up from their tables to find a word, sharpen a pencil or use a rubber, none of them used it as an opportunity to have a look at what the others were doing or have a chat with a friend. I had expected this to happen and I think the constraints of the small group being withdrawn from the whole class played a part in this particular finding. I could have easily noticed someone who was frequently getting up from the table and, although I was not in a position to comment on this at the time as I did not want to influence the behaviour of the group I was observing, the children were perhaps more conscious of my presence in the room than is normally the case in a busy classroom. I had observed Sarah during other writing sessions, when the whole class was in the room, getting up to look for a word from the wall dictionary, going the longest way round the room that was possible and dangling her hand in the water tray in the process.

I asked the children in both groups why they used a rubber and all the children said because they wanted the work to look neat and tidy:

Paul: I think it's more better rubbing out than putting a line across.

The children were very concerned about the appearance of their work. They saw it as a matter of getting words right and wrong which determined the quality of a piece of writing. Children's attitudes to school activities are formed early and condition the way they learn. Some research carried out in Scotland with older children (top juniors) found that children in the research group saw the secretarial skills as being more valued and important than the compositional ones; the superficial appearance of the writing as being more important than a grasp of compositional skills (Michael, 1985). The children in my research group were working to similar criteria, even though they were considerably younger (four years younger). The children in the study were influenced by the notion that appearance is very important in the assessment of a piece of written work:

Me: What do you think is the most important thing to remember when you are writing?
Geoff: To get it neat.
Me: Why do you say that?

Geoff: In case someone looks at it.

Me: What's the most important thing to remember when you are writing?

Sarah: To get it neat.

Me: Why?

Sarah: So it doesn't look a mess.

Me: Why is that important, do you think?

Sarah: Well, my mum . . . em . . . parents might look at it.

As the class teacher I was always, in my opinion, stressing the structure of a piece and the need for a rounded story. Perhaps I had not been doing this vigorously enough for these children. Somehow these aspects of writing, such as spelling and neatness, could be hampering the children's composition:

Question: Is it important to get the words spelt right?

Chorus: Yeah.

Question: Why?

Peter: Because you might say a different word that you wanted to say or the teacher might not be able to read it.

Paul: You might write it all your life.

Peter is, by expressing the need for correct spelling, showing his awareness that the writing he does is being written for an audience. It is not something he does purely for himself. It is important that others (peers, teacher, parent) can read what you have written.

A number of dictionaries of varying degrees of difficulty were available in the classroom. These have been part of the equipment in the room from the beginning. Also, a system of word cards to act as a resource bank for commonly occurring requests was available. These cards have the individual letters of the alphabet on and the children select the appropriate card for the word they want to write. If it has not been written on already, they come to me and I write it. I wondered what use the children made of these facilities. In interviews, all the children claimed to look in a dictionary for an unknown spelling:

Me: What do you use if you can't spell a word?

Simon: I get a dictionary.

Chorus: So do I.

Me: Does anyone look at the word cards first?

Lee: I do sometimes, but then I get a dictionary.

Yet only three children were observed actually consulting one of the dictionaries available in the room. All the children realized what a dictionary was for, but it was only the children with the highest reading age who had used a dictionary to obtain the spelling of a word.

Other children relied on the word cards for words they did not know how to spell. They would scan the word card to see if the word they wanted was there. Some of the children often asked for a word which had previously been written on the card. The more able readers amongst the group of children also did this occasionally. It was particularly true of Peter who had the lowest score on the reading test (unable to answer any of the questions), and who said 'spelling' when he was asked about problems he had with writing. It was the word cards that the children turned to readily for unknown words. This is much less demanding for them than looking through a dictionary. It is also a speedier process which enables the word to be completed more quickly. The time spent wandering round the room in search of words may have had an effect on the writing produced. I asked the children the following session to write without any help from me from a spelling point of view. There was a noticeable increase in the volume of sound. The children were asking each other for help with spellings. Peter actually obtained help from one of the children at the table he was working on when he was searching for the correct word card. Geoff helped Simon spell a word and then later helped him with the construction of a sentence.

After the session where I was not available for help with spelling, there was the following observation:

Me: Did anyone ask someone at their table for help with words?
Kirsty: No. I can do it on my own.
Lee: I asked Sarah.
Karen: I asked Ann.
Paula: I asked anyone if they knew what it was and if they didn't I left it out.

This comment, along with the Flamingoland Pig episode, could suggest that what the children write about is sometimes conditioned by the words which they or their friends know how to spell. It appeared that the removal of the constraint of correct spelling improved the children's concentration and motivation. A marked difference in time was noted when the children had to be self-sufficient in finding words. All the children finished more quickly than during other sessions that had been observed.

The work done by the children in the observed sessions, when they could ask me for spellings, showed no evidence of invented spellings at all. In the session where I was not available for help, the children produced a number of invented spellings:

invented	*correct*
enuf	enough
meet	meat
kodnt	couldn't
fluw	flew

In all the cases of invented spellings I understood what the child wanted to convey. In fact, all these errors show the children spelling the words as they speak.

I asked the children to comment on six pieces of work from members of the class. Most of the children felt that the best piece of writing was the one that went to the bottom of the page:

Sarah: Once I wrote a lot of pages.

Sarah obviously feels that this is one criterion when attempting to assess the writing which the children produce. The children rejected another long piece of writing because, although it went to the bottom of the page, the writing was 'scruffy' and 'not very neat'. Two of the children chose the piece of work about cats because they liked the picture. The children looked at the appearance of the piece; its length and quality of handwriting were their major concerns. Not one of the children chose to discuss the content of the pieces.

The choice of the well-illustrated piece of work by two of the children led me to discuss with the two groups of children the part played by the illustration of a piece of writing with a picture. Usually, the children are asked to write and then to draw the picture and this was the format used in the writing sessions observed for this study. One session was deliberately reversed, with the picture coming before the writing. I felt that it was important to see if there was any difference in the way the children approached the writing task. I also wondered if the illustration first would help some of the children to clarify their thoughts and thereby increase the coherence of the finished piece of work. All the children said they found drawing the picture first, then writing, easier than the usual way they were asked to work:

Question: Why do you find that easier?
Paul: Because you can draw your picture and it's more easier and then you can do your work after you've drawn your picture.
Peter: You can explain it more.

The ability to describe more through the medium of a picture was also something the children were very clear about:

Question: Why do you think that is?
Peter: Because you can draw more of it or less of it.

The use of a picture to enable the writer to develop ideas for writing purposes was brought out by the children:

Kirsty: The picture tells you more about what you are going to write.

The children used the picture to refer to whilst they were writing. It helped to maintain their train of thought. Through drawing, the child can learn to hold the writing tool correctly, to concentrate for longer by adding fine detail, and to become accustomed to the idea that you can add to or modify a piece of work later. The majority of the children did take longer over the task when it was a case of drawing first and they all completed the task to their own satisfaction.

Conclusion

When I started my research into children's attitudes to writing, I could not be certain what would emerge from the work I was doing or where it would lead. I was aware that the beginnings of writing were a very under-researched area, as evidenced by the paucity of information I was able to collect on this specific theme. However, since completing my research the publications of the National Writing Project have provided insights and advice on a range of writing issues (see, for example, Czerniewska *et al.*, 1987).

The problems children may have with writing from the physical point of view, as outlined by Smith (1982), were something I had not sufficiently recognized. During the day, the children are asked to write for a variety of purposes. It could be that I am asking too much of them to always be writing for themselves, especially the children in my class who are at the elementary stages of the process. The difference between the child's oral output and the teacher writing or using the microcomputer, compared to what they produce when transcribing for themselves, was illustrated by the children in the two groups. This has led me to use the techniques of shared writing and word processing much more in the classroom.

Children need to be given a real purpose for writing. It was a salutory lesson for me when the children believed that the only reason for this activity was to satisfy me. Perhaps I need to develop meaningful contexts and reasons for the tasks I set in the classroom, such as writing for other classes to read, writing letters to local papers about issues that concern the children and developing pen-pal links with schools in other areas. It could be that the chore of writing what you did at the weekend every Monday morning gives rise to the children's belief that there can be only one reason for doing that — because the teacher asks you. I also need to develop alternative places for writing, other than in a book, which can be shared with a wider audience to overcome this feeling. Here again it is the microcomputer which can offer facilities for multiple copies, and writing which looks extremely professional that everyone can read with ease.

The part played by drawing, as an aid to telling the story, was not one I had previously considered as being that important. The writing generally always precedes the picture, apart from in the reception class, and is often requested in order to keep the child busy for a few minutes longer. Some children prefer to draw before they add the writing. It does not seem to affect the time they spend on either aspect of the work and, therefore, I now offer the children the choice of work method.

The experience of doing the research into an aspect of the curriculum that I am offering the children has certainly taught me more about the children in my class. By asking them, I feel I have given their views and opinions a chance to be heard. Using their comments, I have been able to try out different methods of working with other children in the class. It has been a case of me learning from them and it was this aspect of the research that I found so stimulating. Certainly, the keeping of a diary of observations forced me to look more closely at myself, the children and how we interacted. This has now become a regular part of my school day. I feel that these notes may give me the opportunity to learn more about the reasons behind both the successes and failures in language work that go on in my classroom. By observing the children and talking with them about the writing tasks in which they were involved, I feel I have been able to highlight certain areas where I and other teachers could possibly intervene more purposefully to aid the writing process.

The actual collecting of data was quite manageable in the classroom. However, the same cannot be said for the sorting out of the volume of material I collected, even with a relatively small sample of twelve children. This was the most difficult part of the whole exercise. Trying to handle the material from the research project and keeping up with the commitments in the classroom is a real difficulty for the teacher who is also attempting to be a researcher. There is constant conflict between allocation time for the preparation of materials for the class and for research work. Yet I feel that the insights the children have given me into the writing process far outweigh the difficulties which I encountered. I think it is only by continually looking at your teaching in a fairly systematic way that you can keep it relevant and fresh for the children in your care.

References

CULLINGFORD, C. (1984) *Children and Television*, London, Gower.

CZERNIEWSKA, P. *et al.* (1987) *Writing Development in the Early Years*, Occasional Paper Six, The National Writing Project, London, SCDC.

DES (1967) *Children and Their Primary Schools* (The Plowden Report), London, HMSO.

McLEOD, R. (1988) 'Better writing from wordprocessing', *New Educational Computing*, June 1988, pp. 31–3.

MICHAEL, B. (1985) 'Foundations of writing', *Child Education*, May 1985, pp. 8–11.

OBRIST, A.J. (1983) *The Microcomputer and the Primary School*, London, Hodder and Stoughton.

SMITH, F. (1982) *Writing and the Writer*, London, Heinemann.

TOUGH, J. (1977) *The Development of Meaning*, London, Allen and Unwin.

Chapter five

Information Gathering in Topic Work: The Pupil Experience

Rosemary Webb

My personal interest in topic work, which arose from my experience as a class-teacher, led to my undertaking doctoral research in this area. When I began a literature search, I found books on topic work (see, for example, Gunning, Gunning and Wilson, 1982; Hoare, 1971; Rance, 1968) which provide suggestions as to content and activities and several teachers' accounts of ambitious topics successfully accomplished, such as Brinton and Shaw (1984) and Bloom (1985). However, these give minimum insights into the processes of managing learning and little access to pupil perspectives and experiences. I soon came to share Dadds' (1988) view that 'what we lack, in general, are well-researched and well-documented examples of the variety and wealth of valuable learning emanating from subject-centred and child-centred topic work' (p. 53). Consequently, I decided to carry out an in-depth examination of the problems and possibilities encountered by both teachers and pupils engaged in topic work.

Case study in the CARE tradition (Simons, 1980; Stenhouse, 1982) was selected as the most appropriate research method and case studies were subsequently carried out in two middle schools and a middle and combined school. The research was made possible by my obtaining a DES Information Science Studentship which was administered by the British Library Research and Development Department. To make the research proposal on topic work attractive to my sponsors I focused on the development of information skills. Information skills were broadly defined as those skills involved in the retrieval, evaluation, analysis, presentation and dissemination of inform-ation. For a review of the literature on information skills, a critique of the term, its diverse interpretations and their associated implications see Webb (1987).

Topic work is often referred to by other terms, such as integrated, thematic and project work, and exists both as a distinct activity on the timetable and as an approach within specific subjects. Consequently, it is difficult to determine the extent of topic work in British primary schools from existing research. However, the ORACLE study reported that 15 per cent of pupil's curriculum time was spent on topic work (Galton, Simon and Croll, 1980, p. 162). More recently Long's (1988) survey of current practice in topic work within thirty-four 8–12 middle schools in one local education authority (LEA) revealed that 'between 25 and 50 per cent of the week was devoted to the myriad forms of topic work' (p. 174).

Over the last decade there has been much criticism of topic work for fundamental weaknesses such as lack of purpose, structure, assessment and recordkeeping (see, for example, Avann, 1982; DES, 1978; Leith, 1981; Tann, 1988). HMI have continually drawn attention to the fact that 'although sometimes of high quality, topic work more often than not lacks continuity and progression, or any serious attempt to ensure that adequate time and attention are given to the elements said to comprise the topic' (DES, 1989, p. 7).

From the literature it appears that books are either the only, or the major, source of information for children to use to carry out topic tasks (see, for example, Avann, 1983; DES, 1985; Griffin, 1983; Heather, 1984). The Bullock Report (DES, 1975) and the survey of primary education (DES, 1978) drew attention to the amount of time children spent copying from books in topic lessons. During the last decade topic work has continued to incur similar criticisms for the ways in which children gather information:

> I have also sat in as a participant observer at one school looking at topic work as it developed one afternoon a week for five weeks in a top junior class. The children had chosen topics approved by the teacher and she attempted to direct their enquiries by posing questions for each, based on the subject. On the whole I saw little evidence that any child was doing anything but copying in an un-systematic way from the book or two to hand. (Avann, 1982, p. 19)

However, because, at its best, topic work facilitates the development of skills and understanding across a wide curricular range and as its potential for pupil learning is highly valued by teachers (Kerry, Eggleston and Bradley, 1983) it continues to be the medium through which many aspects of the primary curriculum are taught — especially history, geography, language development and some elements of science.

Initially, the notion of a subject-based National Curriculum was perceived by many educationalists as a straitjacket which would remove from schools decisions about curriculum organization. Forms of cross-curricular work and integrated approaches such as topic work were viewed as under threat. However, the recommendations of the subject working groups and the requirements of the statutory orders reveal many common elements between the core subjects such as collaboration, communication, problem-solving, the use of IT and the development of information skills. Also, as the number of Attainment Targets (ATs) grows, as those for each new subject are formulated, it becomes increasingly apparent that schemes of work need to contain activities which combine aspects of the Programmes of Study (PoS) and ATs from two or more subjects. However, there is widespread recognition that if topic work is to meet the requirements of the National Curriculum it must be planned, implemented and monitored in a more systematic and rigorous way. Consequently, schools, LEAs and subject associations are engaging in the analysis, modification and extension of existing topics and the planning of new topics based on the PoS and ATs of the National Curriculum subjects (see, for example, Association for Science Education, *et al.*, 1989; The Early Years Curriculum Group, 1989).

As mentioned above one of the common elements threading through the National Curriculum for the core subjects is the need for pupils to develop information skills. The National Curriculum for English stresses the importance of reading for information. Opportunities must be provided to:

> refer to information books, dictionaries, word books or simple data on computers as a matter of course. Pupils should be encouraged to formulate first the questions they need to answer by using such sources, so that they use them effectively and do not simply copy verbatim. (PoS Reading; DES, 1989, p. 16)

Strategies for discouraging copying are to be devised, although as illustrated in the above quote from Avann helping the children to formulate questions to direct their enquiries is only a partial solution. The role of discussion with adults and other children in order to gain information and ideas and to clarify and evaluate these is also emphasized. It is intended that pupils should:

> talk about the content of information texts. (PoS Reading; DES, 1989, p. 16)
> [work] with other children and adults — involving discussion with others; listening to, and giving weight to, the opinions of others; perceiving the relevance of contributions; timing contributions; adjusting and adapting to views expressed; (PoS for Speaking and Listening; DES, 1989, p. 13)

The programmes of study for science and mathematics also draw on these general information skills as well as those that are subject specific. In science, pupils at Key Stage 1 and 2 are required to report their work and develop and exchange their ideas through discussion with adults and their peers. Both first-hand experience gained through participating in visits, investigations and experiments and secondary sources are to be used for gaining information which is to be presented in a variety of ways (such as talking in groups, drawings, simple tables, bar charts, line graphs and prose) to a range of audiences. In mathematics — particularly in relation to ATs 1 and 9 on 'Using and applying mathematics' and ATs 12 and 13 on 'Handling data' — there is a similar emphasis on the importance of pupils locating the information needed for the task in hand, explaining their work to others, recording results systematically in a variety of ways and presenting them to others in oral, written or visual form. It is these general information skills involved in the process of information gathering that form the subject of this chapter. It portrays the problems and possibilities pupils experienced in collecting information from sources such as visits, television, books and museum exhibits. The purposes and contexts which gave rise to the inform- ation-gathering activities are examined for their effects on pupil learning.

The research data for this chapter are drawn from the study of two topics: a farming topic and a topic based on a television programme for schools entitled 'How We Used To Live 1936–53'. The term's topic on farming was studied by the three second year classes at Greenmeadows, a rural 8–12 middle school. The history topic, which lasted one and a half terms, was studied by the two second year classes at Heath Street Middle School, an 8–12 middle school situated on the outskirts of a large market town. Data were collected through participant observation, unstructured or semi-structured interviews and analysis of school documentation and pupils' work. The schools, teachers and pupils were promised anonymity when the research was negotiated. Consequently, pseudonyms are used throughout this chapter.

Collecting Pupil Data

Delamont (1981), who acknowledges that all researchers have problems getting beyond the 'everydayness' of school and classroom life feels that this is especially true of:

> the experienced teacher who all too often has little research training and no background in social science . . . The teacher- observer may not be bored, or see 'nothing', but will see the inter- action through the eyes of a teacher or an educationalist rather

than those of a social scientist. Here the familiarity brings into play common-sense interpretations of events rather than formal socio-logical ones. (p. 71)

When I began my fieldwork I was a relative novice at conducting research. I was aware that my early observations were descriptive accounts of what the teacher was teaching and what was there to be seen. I felt like one of the researchers of whom Becker (1971) wrote 'I have talked to a couple of teams of research people who have sat around in classrooms trying to observe and it is like pulling teeth to get them to see or write anything beyond what "everyone" knows' (p. 10).

Delamont extolls the virtues of reading, and certainly I read a number of methodological texts and the case studies of primary schooling written by Jackson (1968), King (1978), Nash (1973) and Sharp and Green (1975) before beginning my fieldwork. However, in the early stages I was wary of having my perceptions pre-determined by the work of others. My allegiance to the notion of pedagogic research, which was present from the beginning, although not fully articulated, made me reluctant to turn to the disciplines for assistance. I wanted to be able to make the familiar strange but to do so from the standpoint of an educationalist, not a social scientist as re-commended by Delamont. Consequently, I strove to make 'the familiar problematic by self-conscious strategies' (Delamont, 1981, p. 74).

The strategies that I used were two-fold. Firstly, I conceptualized everything that was happening in terms of information-handling (Labbett, 1985). In lessons I would pose myself questions such as what information was being handled, by whom and in what ways? What were the range of purposes for which the information was being handled and who determined what these should be? These questions served as initial categories for organizing and analyzing the data generated from research on different topic lessons. As the fieldwork progressed a number of other themes were identified which were common to several lessons and more than one case-study school, such as the concept of 'proper' and 'real' information which is discussed later in this chapter. Secondly, I compared my account of events and the inferences I drew from them with those of the research participants. For example, in the case study of a museum lesson, I collected perspectives on the event from the class who attended it, the museum teacher who gave the lesson, the Director of the Museums' Education Service and the class-teacher. I then compared these to my own observations at the time and my further reflections on reading the lesson transcript. This triangulation strategy (Adelman, 1981), together with the triangulation of different data sources on particular events (Patton, 1980), also contributed to the validity of my case studies.

As the research progressed I became increasingly interested in collecting pupils' perspectives and experiences as these provided me with new and challenging insights into classroom life. Also, although I was not researching my own practice, I was aware that in many respects it resembled that which I was observing and my findings posed a number of very disconcerting questions about aspects of my teaching. For example, the findings on note-making reported here made me aware of the complexity of the process and the unnecessary and pointless demands that I had sometimes made of pupils.

I tape recorded the more formal aspects of lessons and visits when the whole class was being given information or the teacher was leading an activity such as a question and answer session. This allowed me to concentrate on writing observations of the behaviour of a particular pupil, a group or the teacher. However, early on in the fieldwork I concluded that my tape recordings of groupwork were so inaudible owing to background noise that little could be learned from them. Therefore during lessons, when the children were working on tasks, I usually moved around the classroom sitting with individuals and groups and asking them to tell me about what they were doing. These conversations caused minimal disturbance to the rest of the class and were very informative probably because the children had something immediate or tangible about which to talk. I took down their comments in a series of small notebooks which formed my research diary, some extracts of which are drawn on in the chapter.

When I interviewed children outside the classroom, I always worked with pairs or groups of up to six pupils. During a pilot study that I conducted in another school prior to embarking on the main research, I found children rather self-conscious and tongue-tied if they were asked to talk to me on their own, and like Burgess I came to the conclusion:

> that in a group situation pupils would have the potential power to redefine the topics of conversation. Furthermore, it allowed spontaneity so that pupils could enter into debate and discussion with their friends. In these circumstances, they could take the conversation in directions that were meaningful to them and develop a story about their lives in school. (1984, p. 107)

I told the pupils what I was doing, asked them if they were willing to be interviewed and explained that I would like to tape the interviews in order to have a detailed record of their views. Taping did not appear to constrain conversation, probably because they knew why I was doing it and they grew increasingly accustomed to the fact that I always had my cassette recorder with me. After an interview, usually, I let them rewind some of the tape and listen to it as they liked to hear the sound of their voices and to revisit some of our discussion.

I always found pupils extremely enthusiastic to put their points of view to someone who had the time to listen, and obviously valued what they had to say. I promised them anonymity and, unlike Burgess (1984), my experience was that the pupils considered this extremely important. They seemed quite aware that in telling me about their topic work they were constantly making evaluative judgments about their learning experiences and the teaching that they received. They were concerned about what effect this might have on their relationships with their classteacher. Although I shared my data with the teachers to enable me to gain their interpretations of it and to enable them to learn from it, I was always careful to preserve that anonymity. Occasionally, this actually led me to discard some data, such as that supplied by two girls who considered themselves to be victimized by their teacher's assessment procedures. To have shared this with the teacher would have identified the pupils concerned and betrayed their trust, even though it would have allowed me to have gained the teacher's perceptions.

First-Hand Experience as an Information Source

A key feature of the Farming Topic at Greenmeadows was the programme of outside visits: three trips to local farms, a museum visit and two country walks. The purpose of the visits was to increase the children's store of personal experience of farming, enable them to tap people as an information source, use and evaluate oral information and work cooperatively across classes. Each child went on two visits. For the purpose of the visits the children were grouped according to which house they were in. One group went out while two remained at school, which ensured that information on every visit would be part of the experience of each class, and legitimated the activity of reporting back. Reporting back took the form of teacher-directed class discussions, short talks by pupils on aspects of the visits that interested them and sessions where the participants in a visit made up a brainstrust panel and answered questions put to them by members of their class.

During the farm visits the children obtained much information through asking the farmers a great many questions. These questions both demonstrated their desire to make sense of what they saw and to clarify their understanding about what they were being told:

Extract from the transcript of the visit to Broomsby Manor Dairy Farm, Tuesday afternoon, 15 May.

[We were standing in a large hangar divided into cow stalls and Mr Roberts was explaining the ways in which cows were fed during the Winter and the Summer.]

Girl 1:   What sort of cows are they?

Mr Roberts: Friesians. Gosh, yes, I'm sorry, I'm bad aren't I? I don't start at the basics do I? Yeah, all Friesians.

Girl 1:   Do you prefer Friesians?

Mr Roberts: Yes, I prefer Friesians because they will produce more milk than any other breed. A Jersey will produce 8–900 gallons while a Friesian will produce 14–1500 gallons, but Jerseys give creamier milk of course.

Boy 1:   Were the cows ever affected by foot and mouth disease?

Mr Roberts: No.

Boy 1:   Have they ever had mastitus?

Mr Roberts: No.

            [The previous week the children had been working on a comprehension sheet on cattle diseases, which was what I assumed had prompted the boy's questions. I wondered if Mr Roberts' reaction, which made the questions appear as if they were inappropriate, made the boy think that his school knowledge of farming had little connection with reality.]

Girl 2:   Why have the cows got numbers on?

Mr Roberts: The numbers are how we know the cow. They haven't got names except on their record sheets, but we can't remember one hundred and forty cows' names and so we know them by numbers.

Boy 2:   Why are there two sets of numbers, one on their behind and one on their ear?

Mr Roberts: A lot of the new ones, the latest ones, they're the same on the ear and on the backside, but the earlier cows — I had to change my numbering system because of the computer and so the one in the ear is the one put on the computer — but as we do them now the one in the ear and the one which is freeze branded is the same.

Boy 3:   What's freeze branded?

            [Mr Roberts begins to explain.]

The children's model of questioning appeared to be derived from outside school, as it did not conform to the pattern they experienced with their teachers. To give an example, the teachers, who were concerned to spread their attention among the class, directed a question first at one child then another. They seldom followed up a child's answer with a number of increasingly probing questions in the way that the children did, when they were questioning the farmers. The influence of the media was also in evidence. One boy, who taped an interview that he conducted with a farmer on a later farm visit, was careful to capture the farmyard sounds and the noise of footsteps made by him and the farmer. He explained that this was to make it resemble the 'proper' interviews that he had heard on the radio.

The three second year teachers all felt that the activity of reporting back the information obtained had considerably improved the quality of the children's oral responses, and developed their self-confidence. Reporting back also alerted the children to the difference between fact and opinion, and made them critical of suspect or extraordinary information. When the teachers were listening to reports of the visits that they had not accompanied, they found evaluating and clarifying the information given a problem. This was particularly the case after the visit to a mushroom farm which gave rise to a host of queries and conflicting information on all stages of the production process. Collecting information was hindered by the noise of piped music and the machinery which obscured what the guide was saying. Also, as some of the sheds were in darkness note-making was difficult. After a session run by the group from her class Gail Brooks, the year leader, commented:

> It turned out the children didn't realize mushrooms were spread by spores. Jason wasn't the only one who thought they grew in the ground; several of them thought they were dug up. Someone said they were put in half an inch apart; someone else said they were planted in rows. Fortunately Charlotte was very interested and most coherent. She remembered nearly everything and she said that they put the spores in wheat, but she didn't seem to know what they did with the wheat, and I didn't know that either; so I left it. (Gail Brooks, Second Year Meeting)

Gail was no longer in control of the information exchange in the sense that she could neither supply the missing information about mushroom production, nor evaluate the children's suggestions in the light of their experiences during the visit. Responsibility for the information that was reported rested with the children. Bearing in mind Avann's (1983) criticisms of topic work 'for its disturbing lack of accuracy' (p. 57), for me this raised an interesting issue about the criteria to be used to assess the written work on the mushroom farm. In such situations any assessment must surely focus on the processes involved in reaching an end product, rather than on the quality of the end product itself. Can information-gathering opportunities which give rise to incorrect accounts be viewed positively, if as in the above case they enable the children to recognize conflicting and partial information as problematic?

Central to the history topic of the second year children at Heath Street was the opportunity to look around a museum with their teacher and to go to a museum lesson entitled 'When the Sirens Wailed' which was offered by the Museums' Education Service to support the television series. The lesson took the form of a talk given by the museum teacher during which the numerous objects that featured in the talk were passed along the rows of children for them to handle and examine. My observations of the lesson suggested that most of the children looked at the objects very closely. I watched one boy spend nearly five minutes examining a firebomb. He ran his hands over the outside of it to feel the texture and he looked closely at an inscription. He moved the firebomb across from one hand to the other as though testing out its weight. He unscrewed one end and sniffed inside. He shook it and discovered that it rattled. He held the firebomb and tried to look through some holes in the other end, which, after a while, he also managed to undo. He took a loose piece of brass out of the inside and studied it carefully. Then he put the firebomb back together again and copied the inscription off the side before passing it on.

When they returned to school after the visit the children talked enthusiastically about the objects and supported the view held by Bob Bryant, the museum teacher, that 'ultimately the real learning experience is in seeing and handling the objects'. In the interviews the children constantly referred to what they had found out and a few actually said that they valued the opportunity to examine the objects:

James: It's much better going to the museum because you can see the things more than just when you look at a programme. Then you can't really see 'em. You don't feel 'em or what they are made of and everything. You can do that when you go to a museum.

Vicky: And when he passed the gas masks round, 'cos on 'How We Used to Live' they didn't have the little red one, or the one they put the baby in, you didn't see the other one neither [the soldier's gas mask], so you didn't know what they looked like. (Group C, Interview)

> *Darren*: I quite liked it when I was handling things where I could actually get a good look at them. The ration books, he handed them round for us to look at them and the gasmasks and everything.
>
> *Tim*: I'd seen a ration book before but I hadn't really looked at it and turned the pages. (Group B, Interview)

However, the curiosity which some of the objects aroused had to remain unsatisfied:

> *Jane*: I wondered if we could have opened that tin of cream margarine and seen what it was like. It was probably all mouldy. (Group A, Interview)

In contrast to the farm visits the formal setting of the museum lesson together with the museum teacher's awareness of the classteacher's expectation that the children were there to gain information created a situation where the children asked few questions. Most of these, such as 'Is it called a blackout?', were volunteered as tentative answers to Bob's questions. The few 'real' questions asked for amplification of something that he had said. For example, early on in the lesson, when he told the class that the name of the owner of the gasmask was written on its container, a boy asked him if it was anyone that he knew. Bob said 'No', and went on with his talk. This might have given the impression that he wished to discourage questions in general or served to convey that only 'proper' questions deserved more than a one word response. I asked the children for their views on why he wasn't asked more questions:

> *Jane*: He never said we could have a question time did he? We would have liked to ask some questions, but nobody dared put their hand up in case he said there's no time for questions. We've got to move on.
>
> *Ann*: We were already about five or ten minutes late finishing in that group weren't we?
>
> *Gail*: Someone kept opening the door [a member of the next school group waiting to have a lesson].
> (Group A, Interview)

The message was that there was much information to be passed on and insufficient time to do it, and this was picked up by the children. Bob kept looking at his watch, and several times he referred to the need to move onto a new topic as there was only a limited amount of lesson time left. When I raised this with him he admitted that lack of time was a constant problem and that he frequently found himself rushing through his material. He also said that given the time constraints, too many questions could be perceived as a problem, particularly by the teachers, as the questions interrupted the flow of the lesson and led to digressions:

> Sometimes you get the persistent questioners. I had one this morning. He was quite a bright little lad and he kept wanting to ask things and the teachers were signalling to him to stop it. (Bob Bryant, Interview)

Apart from a few 'persistent questioners', in situations such as the museum lesson most children appear to have learned to ration their questions and to recognize which ones it is 'proper' to ask. In the museum lesson the children could be seen to be conspiring with the teachers to maintain the agenda and form of the lesson.

Gaining Information through Vicarious Experience

Television was extremely important for enabling children to obtain information through vicarious experience as was certainly the case in the 'How We Used to Live' topic. The national survey of primary schools (DES, 1978) found that 'television programmes provided the basis for work in history in about a quarter of the 7-year-old classes and two-fifths of the 11-year-old classes' (p. 73). However, unlike the situation at Heath Street, only occasionally did the programmes form 'an integral part of a well planned scheme of work with careful preparation before viewing and follow-up afterwards' (p. 73). The Director of the Museums' Education Service certainly felt that schools often abused the use of television by 'sitting the children in front of the TV and assuming that they will automatically imbibe information'. She said that she and the two museum teachers often found themselves working with children who, although they were following a television series, had little idea of the subject or content of the programmes. She considered that the 'How We Used to Live' series created particular problems of this nature:

> It is based on the story of a family and the kids get totally involved in the life of the family. They can tell you who has just had a baby, but they miss all the general historical points. Unless the teacher draws these out they seem to pass by the children, which is a terrible shame as it's such a good resource, but it's likely to get wasted. (Director of the Museums Education Service, Interview)

The children from Heath Street Middle School certainly were involved in following the lives of the characters and these concerns predominated in their written accounts of the programme. However, they also appeared interested in the historical context and told me how the programme combined the fictional element and the historical background:

Darren: It showed you what life would probably be like, not exactly what it would — what it could have been like.

Donna: It showed you how — if we were um in them days — it showed you how we would have lived.

Darren: It might not be exact but that's just how they thought it would be.

Tim: It was very interesting.

Donna: And in 'How We Used to Live' it's coloured and after a time it goes black and white and tells about how things were.

Wendy: About the new look.

Darren: And proper things what did happen like the Jarrow March and everything.

(Group B, Interview)

Each week, following the programme, their classteacher Mrs Bond reiterated the 'important events' that were portrayed in the programme. Darren had obviously come to recognize that the 'proper' sorts of information for study in history topics are 'the general historical points' and 'the important events'. Pupil involvement in the personal lives of the characters, which added realism to the 'proper' history, was viewed by the Director as a waste of the programme's potential as a resource.

Anecdotes provided another way in which historical information could be personalized and made realistic and meaningful. During the interviews at Heath Street the children told me a number of facts and events that they had learned about from listening to the recollections of their relatives and neighbours. The following extracts from the interview transcripts illustrate how some of the children related the facts given in the museum lesson to information gained at home and at school. A can of powdered egg was passed around during the lesson and Tim remembered Mrs Barnes, another teacher, had told him about it. The first extract also shows how in the children's enthusiasm to convey information to me, although they wait for a turn to speak, they each try to pursue their own conversation. However, Darren who has picked up Tina's mistake is determined to correct it. She appreciates that during the war the children had few sweets and obviously she feels that she would have found such rationing hard to cope with, but she has no concept of the relative weights or amounts involved in pounds and ounces of sweets:

Tim: Mrs Barnes was telling us what the food was like, about the egg powder.

Wendy: My mum was born just after the war.

Tina: Fancy only having two pounds of sweets a week.

Penny: My dad was born in Germany during the war.

Darren: Two ounces.

Penny: In 1940.

Tim: Mrs Barnes said it was horrible. The only thing you could do with it really was make cakes and have scrambled eggs.

Tina: Think, only two pounds of sweets a week.

Darren: Two ounces.

Tina: Oh two ounces then.
           (Group B, Interview)

The second extract shows how the children got excited about an anecdote which they wanted to relate to me. Initially they all talked over the top of one another but then they cooperated to try to reconstruct the story as faithfully as possible. The way in which they do so demonstrates the possibilities of group discussion as an aid to the recall of and the critical reflection on information:

Donna: Mrs Smith told us about them — cos her house — she had two, one at the back and one at the . . .

Tim: Oh yeh. She had a fire in her house.
           [They all begin telling the story together.]

Darren: . . . a fire bomb came down in front of her house and it was set on fire. Then one came through the extension, through the glass or something and set fire to the back. They couldn't have gone in the Andersen shelter 'cos it was flooded. It was flooded twelve inches, so they hid in this cupboard under the — 'stairs'
           [supply the others in chorus.]

Donna: The stairs were quite . . .

Darren: [interrupting] Then this air warden came along and later he got some other men to help. He couldn't, you couldn't just shove water over the fire, 'cos the chemicals ud- ud-.

Donna: They'd spread everywhere.

Tim: So they had to put sand and mud over it.

Darren: They dug a hole in the soil.
           (Group B, Interview)

The use of anecdotes clearly has inherent problems of accuracy and reliability. The information gets changed as events are continually recounted and embroidered. However, anecdotes can be entertaining and therefore contribute to the enjoyment of learning and they also appear to enable children to experience vicariously historical events through access to personal histories. By combining the 'real' and the 'proper', anecdotes appear to provide children with strategies for interacting with information and increasing their understanding of history.

At one point in the lesson Bob made use of role play to illustrate the role of the homeguard. This role play, which involved a homeguard checking the identity of a girl on her way home from school, was a memorable one for the children. It was mentioned in all the interviews and featured in some of the follow-up writing and drawing produced after the visit. Clearly, it brought the information alive for the class even though the two children selected were very self-conscious and inhibited. This was probably due to the fact that they had been chosen by Bob who prescribed exactly how they should act. However, the class obviously enjoyed that aspect of the lesson and other children wished that there had been an opportunity for volunteers to repeat it, or try to act out some other events:

Tim: I think it was — it's quite interesting if you get the children to demonstrate like they did with the identity card.

Darren: I would have liked to do a little acting with the gas masks and everything, walking and showing the things a bit more, 'cos only two people came out.

Wendy: Last time we went a load of people went out to try things on.

Donna: Julia Thorneycroft, our friend, she showed off because she had — she was called up to put a hat on and some spectacles.

Darren: Yes, but even then, most of the others are just sitting there listening because I wanted to go out and do something.
          (Group B, Interview)

Darren expressed the frustration that he had felt when he had to sit and watch other class members doing an activity in which he wanted to participate. Insufficient time and being one of a crowd recurrently had an adverse effect on the quality of pupil experience during the museum visit and imposed a constraint on learning.

Note-Making

In both schools children were expected to write an account of the films and television programmes that they had watched and most of the visits that they made; in which case they were advised to take notes. These accounts were nearly always global narratives requiring all the information that the children were exposed to be treated equally. Most children regarded the ideal note-taking strategy as being able to take down everything and a few of them managed to write at fantastic pace, recording almost verbatim complete chunks of films or videos. This meant sustaining intense concentration and manual effort for fifteen minutes to an hour. The children at Greenmeadows that I spoke to within the context of the farming topic all experienced difficulty with some aspect of note-making:

> It's difficult trying to listen and write notes. Most people talk so quick, don't they?
> When I'm watching TV I get interested and I miss it. I suddenly think I better make some notes.
> In the dark I wrote on my hand the other day, I missed my notebook.
> Mr Woods told us how to do it in a different way and not to write it all out. He says just jot down the main words. But when I try to write it out from my notes I forget what things go with the words and I have to go round asking people.
> He [Mr Stone] puts milk, udder and pipes but a few days later I don't know what that means so I always write in sentences.
> You need to write up quickly to remember what it's about.

These views were echoed by the children involved in the topic on 'How We Used to Live'. When telling me about their experiences taking notes during the television programmes, they were most concerned about the physical problems incurred by trying to write in semi-darkness, balancing a notepad on their knees and coping with remarks from the teacher such as 'Lift your head up you're not watching the television', when they were trying to write. The majority found it impossible simultaneously to watch a film or video and understand, memorize and record a continual outpouring of facts. Consequently, they often abandoned the task after the first five or ten minutes.

The children at Heath Street Middle School knew that following the museum visit they would be expected to write about it. Consequently, from the moment they arrived in the museum they were concerned to collect as much information as possible. Their criteria for judging effective note-making was solely quantitative:

Fieldnotes, Feb. 27th, 10.40am

Five boys are gathered around a plaque busily making an exact copy of the information on it. Two girls near me are comparing their notes. 'I've only done half a page.' 'I've done two and a bit.' 'Let's have a look.' 'This is more than I've ever done before, last time [a previous museum visit], I hardly got down the names of anything'.

The children's notes on this part of the visit were predominantly excerpts from the plaques and other notices. This was perhaps because such copying appeared the easiest way of recording some information, especially given the time constraints. However, it could also be interpreted from their actions that they attached more importance to the printed word than their teacher's commentary on the exhibits or their own observations.

The main problem from the children's point of view that was posed by note-making while looking around the museum was not a cognitive one but the physical difficulty of the process, as is demonstrated by the following conversation:

Darren: When you're trying to find out something, there's people squashing everywhere. If you move away and try to write it on the board you've got to rest it on the floor, 'cos you're not allowed to rest it on the furniture. There's people blocking your way so you can't see, and if you try and hold it up like that [he demonstrates what he means by holding a book horizontally in front of him, with his arm under the book to support it and his hand clasped along the edge], I can't write very well. It comes out all scribbled because the board keeps wobbling.

During the museum lesson I noticed several children making notes while looking at the artefacts. Some of them, like the boy I observed examining the firebomb, were clearly copying information off the actual objects. I therefore asked the children:

RW: What sort of things did you write about the objects that you looked at?

Ann: Well, I looked at some things, and say there was a date on there, I'd sort of put what it was and put the date next to it.

Gail: Yeh, so did I, and when it was made.

Gill: I wrote all the numbers on them [the objects].

RW: What were the numbers?

Gill: Don't know.

Ann: They were like 976.384.

RW: What do you think they were for?

Ann: I don't know.

Gail: A code — we think — if they got stolen they'd know the code, so if there were other people in the country with them, you could make sure it was yours before you took it back. They were modern numbers because they were in white airfix paint.

Gill: I just put them down. I didn't write them in my book [topic exercise book].

Ann: I put down all the — um — initials of the things he was talking about.

Emma: There was this identity, identification card, and some people wrote down the name on it in case it was needed.

(Group A, Interview)

It appeared that most of the children were indiscriminately gathering any information that could readily be collected from the objects. This paralleled their behaviour in the museum rooms where they copied information off the plaques.

Some of the children also attempted to make notes on what the museum teacher was saying. As with the television programmes the children attempted to write down as near verbatim as possible everything that Bob was saying which, not surprisingly, proved an impossible task:

Penny: When you're writing some notes, and when he goes on to another thing and you're writing something, you forget what he said. Then you have to miss it out, don't you?

Darren: I would like it if he'd give you a little space, just between things, to let us write it down. I started something about the gasmasks and before I knew where I was, he was on about something else.

Wendy: Yeh, clothes.

Darren: If you are trying to listen to him, then you can't write at the same time.

Wendy: And you've gotta go quickly like that [pretends to scribble frantically].

(Group B, Interview)

Taking notes during a talk can be a difficult process for students at any level of education. This would seem to be particularly the case, if the person taking the notes does not have a personal or imposed agenda to guide the selection of what is relevant or practice in possible methods of recording it. In such a context note-making could be regarded as a form of alienated labour, in that it was not an end in itself and so gave the pupils no intrinsic satisfaction. Also it was required of them as a necessary part of the production of an end product over which they had little control.

The Director of the Museums' Education Service thought that note-making in such circumstances was too advanced for most primary age children and prevented them from fully participating in the lesson in the way intended. Consequently, when she took lessons she asked the children not to do it. The museum teacher, who favoured children making notes in lessons, also thought that most children found note-making difficult. However, he considered that this was largely because only a minority of schools actually tried to teach them the relevant skills:

> Very few schools can make notes. I would say about one in ten. The children are not sufficiently able to do it, without it getting in the way. For those who can make notes I think it is worthwhile. Note-making is an important skill and a museum lesson is a very good opportunity to practise that skill. (Bob Bryant, Interview)

He also observed that very few teachers acted as models by taking notes themselves. He felt that this was regrettable because the teachers' lack of notes probably limited the scope of later class discussion and they had missed an opportunity to demonstrate to children the process and value of note-making.

Note-making is a complex skill which draws on a number of different and yet interdependent abilities such as identifying the main points, deciding on headings and abbreviations, writing rapidly and legibly. Difficulties with any of these jeopardizes the whole process. The skill can be taught out of context which allows for it to be broken down into its component parts in order that each part can be taught and practised separately. This was the approach adopted by Gail Brooks in her role as English coordinator at Greenmeadows when, once a week, she taught note-making to the third year children as an English lesson. However, Svensson (1984), an advocate of the *gestalt* approach to skill psychology, argues that training in individual study techniques such as note-making may be viewed as superficial and meaningless if divorced from the general framework of content, task and educational setting that the student is working within. As research into the teaching and learning of library skills has shown (see, for example, Brake, 1980; Lunzer and Gardner, 1979), children have difficulty transferring learning through practice exercises to 'real' situations. Consequently, skills such as note-making seem likely to be developed more readily when introduced in connection with subject matter with which the children are already familiar, and/or regard as important.

The problem with introducing note-making in a genuine context where its relevance can be appreciated is that children are required to grapple simultaneously with new content and new ways of handling it. The girl quoted earlier expressed her interest in the television programmes she was watching, and precisely because of this she forgot to take notes. Making notes while watching television is an 'unreal' activity for children. This problem was recognized by the first year leader at Greenmeadows, who considered that just as the children 'haven't learn't there are two sorts of reading, reading for entertainment and reading for information, so they don't know there are two sorts of viewing, viewing for enjoyment and viewing for learning, and that is something else we need to teach in a structured kind of way'. Viewing for information involves particular processes which need to be taught, of which making notes on specified aspects of the programme might be one.

The second year teachers at Greenmeadows stressed that notes were personal aids to memory. This meant that it was acceptable for notes to be scruffy and incorporate 'homemade' shorthand. However, the children found this difficult to accept as it went contrary to the usual emphasis placed on neatness, and instructions to 'write in complete sentences' and 'fill up the lines'. The teachers also offered advice on note-making strategies. For example, on four occasions Gail suggested labelled columns in which to note information, such as when through the use of the farming slides she was encouraging her class to recognize the advantages and disadvantages of modern farming methods and those used fifty years ago. She thought that the children found this simple method useful, as when they carried out a study of a local hedgerow, without prompting from her, a number of the children began drawing columns to record the various categories of wildlife. On three other occasions in relation to the production of cornflakes, mushrooms and milk she encouraged the children to try to record the most important parts of the production process in the form of a flow diagram.

John Stone, one of the second year teachers, used a master apprentice model of teaching to assist his class with note-making, which was the kind of approach that Bob Bryant recommended. John copied onto the blackboard the notes that he had taken during one of the farm visits and explained how and why the notes were in the form that they were, and suggested to his class that they might try a similar approach. In its traditional form this model is concerned with passing on the manual techniques necessary to achieve a particular end product. However, it has the potential to be extended, thereby enabling children to increase their understanding of the cognitive aspects of gathering and recording information. This would involve teachers as senior learners giving children access to their thought processes in order 'to release a comparable process from the centre of the other' (Abbs, 1981,

p. 10). By gaining insights into the learning of their teachers, children might come to reflect on and thereby understand more about their own learning and so be empowered to take control of it.

Using Books and Magazines

During the farming topic each second year teacher tried to spend time, at least once a fortnight, to do some vocabulary work based on new words introduced during the topic lessons. Referred to as 'doing meanings' by the children, vocabulary work involved asking the class either to write the new words in sentences which demonstrated their meaning, or to compose paragraphs which explained them. In order to do this the children used their dictionaries, material in their folders and the year-group collection of library books on farming from the School Library Service and the school library. I observed several such lessons and while the children were working, I moved around the classroom to talk to them and find out how they tackled the task. As is illustrated in the following two extracts from my fieldnotes, these observations raised questions both about the children's use of text and the quality of that text:

> Gareth is engrossed in one of the library books when I sit down beside him. He is reading about sheep-shearing competitions in Australia. He says that he finds the work easy as some of the words they have had to explain he already knew before doing the topic; others he has learnt through watching the films, or Mr Stone has mentioned them. He tells me that all of these he can write about without using any books. He only uses books with an index and complains that a number of the school library books do not have one. He says that he really enjoys doing meanings because it enables him to flick through the books, look at the pictures and read any sections that appear interesting. As he resumes reading I have a look at the previous week's work. It consists of neat, competently written definitions. (Research Diary)

Vocabulary work was readily accomplished by Gareth and could be viewed as insufficiently demanding. However, he enjoyed it because it allowed him to pursue his own agenda. His evaluation of the school library books appeared valid. I found that a number of the reference books that were written for younger children were designed to be read continuously rather than dipped into for information. Consequently, they had neither an index nor section headings to facilitate access to their contents. Both Avann

(1983) and Gregson, in Chapter 2 in this book, comment on the inadequacy of reference books written for children both in terms of their unhelpful structure and for their lack of detailed, in-depth information.

Like Gareth, Jeremy only used books with an index:

> He takes one of the books, shows me the index and starts looking for the words on the board, searching for them in the order that they are written up. He finds a reference under threshing machine and turns to it. There is a picture and a small amount of writing. 'It's enough', he says. 'I read the information then put the book down and try to write in my own words.' 'Do you find that difficult?', I ask. 'Sometimes', he says. 'Then I just have to have several looks at it.' (Research Diary)

Jeremy's interpretation of writing information in his own words actually involved trying to write out small pieces of text from memory. Although he did not perceive it as so, what he was doing was actually a more sophisticated and exacting form of copying. John Stone encouraged the children to adopt this strategy for processing information taken from books. He anticipated that the children would read and internalize the meaning of a short passage, and having done so would be able to convey that meaning in their own terms. However, Jeremy's use of the strategy to reproduce the structure and content of the text did not necessarily involve him in engaging with its meaning. This approach to introducing children to expressing text in their own words is often employed in primary schools. Jeremy's experience raises the question of how often it is interpreted and practised in the way envisaged by the teacher.

Hayley knew how to look for terms in an index, but she did not understand its relationship to the contents of the book. John had reminded the children how to use reference books at the beginning of the farming topic, but this had taken the form of a quick demonstration to the whole class:

> Hayley says that she dislikes doing vocabulary work because 'it's too hard' and she cannot find the information that she needs. She recounts how last week she had 'the best book in the pile', thus evaluated because it was the largest, and was therefore assumed to contain the most information. 'But I still couldn't find the words I wanted in the index. Then I hunted through the book page by page looking for the words and I couldn't find them. It took ages, but not dairy farm, that was easy.' She tells me how eventually she got so 'fed up' she asked Nicky, one of her friends in the third year, to help her. 'Nicky knows a lot about farms and she was able to do them for me.' (Research Diary)

Hayley asked her friend Nicky to supply the information she needed rather than help her to develop the skills she needed to find it for herself. There were numerous examples within the farming topic of children using their peers as information sources to help them cope with the demands of set tasks.

Within the farming topic the children were given the opportunity to complete personal studies on any aspect of farming that interested them. While some children found that their personal interests were catered for by the year-group resource collection, or they were able to obtain additional information from the local library, the subjects chosen by others were often pragmatically determined by the resources available:

> *Zoe*: We might do poultry because we just looked through a couple of books and poultry was the longest. We also found quite a bit on markets which wasn't on the sheets. I'd like to do something different from the sheets [comprehension sheets]. We could go to a market as well. I prefer doing my own topic.

The large collection of farming journals, which were provided by the teachers and those children with farming connections, were the most popular of the printed resources. Although the language in the journals was technical and rather difficult, they were colourful and contained advertisements that amused or intrigued the children. Often they were able to find illustrations of things that they had actually encountered during the farm visits, and so make a direct link between the literature of farming and personal experience. One girl, for example, was very excited when she found a tiny black and white picture of a milk cooler like the one that she had seen on the visit to a dairy farm. Also, as there was a large pile of journals, the children could collect several containing relevant information from which to work, whereas with the books, they tended to be limited to one or two. This prevented them from comparing and synthesizing information. Apart from one occasion when Gareth and some friends were comparing the tractors advertised in the journal with some outdated models in one of the older library books, I was not aware of the two sources being used to complement one another.

The children enjoyed browsing through the journals and some of them complained that the time allowed for this was inadequate. John Stone explained:

> I think sitting reading is very worthwhile but you can misjudge it if you don't see any end result . . . If you don't get a written or drawn end product you tend to think nothing's going on. (Interview)

John's comment with its tacit notion of productivity emphasizes the practical at the expense of the cognitive. It provides an illustration of the need felt by teachers for reassurance, in the form of observable activities and assessable end products, that learning was taking place.

Conclusion

The detailed observations of children working on topic tasks together with their views on how these fostered or constrained their learning raised many questions about the teaching of topic work. In this chapter I have portrayed the experiences of children gathering information from a variety of sources. To conclude I shall draw out the main lessons learned and their implications for classroom practice.

The children's abilities to gather, organize and evaluate information appeared to be best demonstrated and further developed in those situations where they gathered information through firsthand experience. The farm visits gave children direct access to information about farming both through their observations and their questioning of the farmers. Their questioning strategies revealed considerable competence in clarifying and expanding on the information given. Through pupils comparing the information that they had each gained personally and subjecting that information to the evaluation of their peers and their teachers, they were introduced to the difference between fact and opinion, the problem of partial and conflicting information and the need to question the reliability of personal recollections. On the museum visit the firsthand experience of the artefacts was much valued by the children for the further insights into life on the Home-Front that it gave them. This experience also allowed them to demonstrate and to benefit from the skills of observation and deduction that they already possessed.

The research data and the conversations and interviews that I carried out with the children greatly increased my respect for the information skills that they already possessed and the ways in which they could critically reflect on their experience. As a teacher, I felt that often I had underestimated what children could achieve and had not presented them with sufficient opportunities to demonstrate their abilities. Within the framework of any topic, situations need to be created to allow pupils to make decisions about what information they want and frame questions or plan investigations to obtain it. Activities need both to value and to build on children's natural curiosity and existing skills and to extend them. Pupils' perceptions of topic activities are likely to be very valuable in evaluating and improving a topic as well as helping them to develop their powers of self-evaluation. Apart from conversations with individuals, their views could be gained through taped small-group discussions, simple class questionnaires and pupil topic diaries. In the diaries apart from recording progress through the topic they might write about their likes and dislikes, which tasks they found easy or difficult and why, try to identify what they felt that they had learned and suggest any additional activities that they would like included.

Mrs Bond, the classteacher, and Jan, the Director of the Museums' Education Service, separated 'proper' information on historical events from the biographical information about people's lives, which made these events become real for the children. The notion that 'real' information was of less value than 'proper' information was conveyed to the children through the teachers' attitudes to the 'How We Used to Live' series, their reponse to the children's questions and the information considered appropriate content for written work. This had the effect of limiting the contexts for learning. King (1988), who is particularly concerned to promote the use of the historical novel as a resource, views fiction as a powerful medium for developing pupils' understanding and sensitivity to the past. While he stresses the need to ensure 'artistic faithfulness' to the period in question, he believes that fiction can 'excite an interest in the past and bring periods vividly alive, evoking the feel of the time' (p. 26).

The farm visits also indirectly posed questions about the interrelationship between school knowledge and the reality of farm life. School library books and the comprehension sheets on farming provided little information which could be directly related to the firsthand experience of farms. The journal articles brought in by those with farming connections best served to make the links between the school and the 'real' world. The research raised questions about the usefulness of the kinds of books often found in school libraries to resource pupils' enquiries and the need for teachers to check that they can serve their intended purpose. It also suggested that retrieving, organizing and presenting information from books is a demanding process for many pupils who, if they are to cope successfully, will need considerable help.

The ritual of note-making was much practised and mainly used to record 'proper' information. A message continually coming through the research was the vast amount of information with which the children were required to interact and the amount of information that was reproduced in prose form. This placed an explicit or implicit emphasis on knowledge acquisition rather than the development of the skills and attitudes needed to obtain and use that knowledge. Lack of a specified purpose and focus to guide information gathering meant that children collected indiscriminantly the most readily available information. The resultant disparate pieces of factual information contained in the pupils' notes were generally not of the kind that they could draw on to write their global accounts or to inform subsequent topic tasks. Consequently, on occasions such as the museum visit, note-making functioned predominantly as a device for maintaining social control through keeping children busy.

From the research it appears that situations when note-making is required should be carefully selected in order to prevent it becoming a distraction or a pointless chore. Specific times for concentrating on making notes could be agreed rather than there being an expectation that it should continue throughout an entire lesson, television programme or visit. The purpose for which pupils are to collect information — whether their own or the teacher's — could be clearly defined beforehand and the particular sorts of information required and possible key words identified. The ways in which the information is to be presented, such as personal writing, improvisations, models, paintings and posters could be discussed in relation to the effect this has on the information to be gathered. Different note-making strategies for recording the information might be introduced gradually for pupils to experiment with and discuss with their peers afterwards, in order to find the one that suits them best.

The children's enjoyment and understanding of the information needed for their topic work was shown to be considerably enhanced by the imaginative and abstract forms of learning provided by anecdotes and role play. Through vicarious experience they developed empathy with people of another period and an understanding of cause and effect in human terms. Jones, who writes about the local history project on the school community (1902–26) which won the Yorkshire TV 'How We Used to Live' Competition (1985–6), values greatly the information that pupils obtained by interviewing relatives, friends and neighbours:

> It becomes vital and significant history requiring all the accepted research procedures and disciplines. It gives to the extended family an interest and a focal point for discussion and contact, and relatives talk to one another with purpose, interest, sympathy and developing awareness. History becomes a living involvement. (1988, p. 29)

She describes how through cross-referencing the accounts pupils came to appreciate the problem of reliability in oral history and the difficulties of making claims that were generalizable beyond their own community. Some schools have also begun to build up a tape library of the recollections of elderly members of the community (see, for example, Evans, 1989). While the pupils using these tapes have not experienced the challenge of interacting with people to gather the information, such tapes can serve as a useful additional resource and a way of ensuring that information about past events in the locality is not lost.

The value of drama is increasingly being recognized for its potential to both aid the understanding of historical information and generate questions which motivate pupils to search for evidence in documentary sources. For example, for one month of the year Kentwell Hall in Long Melford, Suffolk, engages a large number of volunteer specialists to recreate the life of the Tudor period. Children are invited to come dressed in appropriate costume and participate in the crafts, cooking and language of the times. However, May and Williams (1987), who argue that drama is under-used as a teaching strategy, suggest that such sophisticated projects 'may have the unwanted effect of discouraging teachers from making the effort in their own classrooms' because teachers may feel that they cannot tackle drama activities for history teaching unless they possess 'the combined talents of Elizabeth and A.J.P. Taylor' (p. 11). However, as was shown in the museum lesson (see p. 110), very simple classroom role play or dramatic activities can substantially contribute to pupil motivation and understanding.

An initial concern when the National Curriculum was on the horizon was that it would be heavily content oriented and therefore would lead to pupils being required to assimilate vast amounts of knowledge. However, as is discussed in the introduction to this chapter, the programmes of study for the core subjects emphasize the important role in the curriculum of learning processes including information skills. While the National Curriculum for Science has 16 ATs devoted to the acquisition of scientific knowledge, together they assume no greater importance than AT1: Exploration of Science. Also, as stressed in the Non-Statutory Guidance for Science (NSG) pupils should arrive at knowledge and understanding through engaging in investigative work — see, for example, the group activities on making and investigating a windmill suggested in the NSG for Science (NCC, 1989, C6–C16). As well as being part of the programmes of study, information skills including those involved in the gathering of information are embodied in the statements of attainment — see, for example, Science AT1 Level 4: 'raise questions in a form which can be investigated, draw conclusions from experimental results and describe investigations in the form of ordered prose, using a limited technical vocabulary' (DES, 1989, p. 4). Since pupils are now entitled to opportunities to achieve the process-based statements of attainment, and individual progress through these will be monitored, the National Curriculum legitimates pupils spending time on learning activities which do not give rise to immediately tangible end products, thus reducing the kinds of anxieties expressed by John Stone (see p. 118).

The implementation of the National Curriculum is posing a challenge to those who wish to teach it through topic work. However, it also provides the means by which topic work can be strengthened in relation to the development of information skills and in other areas where it has continually incurred criticisms for lack of planning, structure, continuity, progression, criteria and procedures for assessment. Topic work now has the potential to be rigorous and systematic while maintaining the diversity, creativity and spontaneity that have made it popular with both pupils and teachers.

References

ABBS, P. (1981) 'Promoting new first principles', *Times Higher Educational Supplement*, **21** August, 1981, p. 10.

ADELMAN, C. (1981) 'On first hearing', in ADELMAN, C. (Ed.) *Uttering, Muttering*, London, Grant McIntyre.

Association for Science Education, Association for Teachers of Mathematics and National Association for the Teaching of English (1989) *The National Curriculum — Making it work for the Primary School*, Hatfield, Association for Science Education.

AVANN, P. (1982) 'Information skills teaching in primary schools: Progress report on a Coventry survey', *Education Libraries Bulletin*, **25**, pp. 15–23.

AVANN, P. (1983) 'Information Skills in Primary Schools', Unpublished M.Phil. thesis, University of Loughborough.

BECKER, H. (1971) Footnote to Wax, M. and Wax, R., 'Great tradition, little tradition, and formal education', in WAX, M. and WAX, R. (Eds.) *Anthropological Perspectives on Education*, New York, Basic Books.

BLOOM, W. (1985) 'Information skills through project work', in AVANN, P. (Ed.) *Teaching Information Skills in the Primary School*, London, Edward Arnold.

BRAKE, T. (1980) 'Education for access into the information culture', *Education Libraries Bulletin*, **23**, pp. 1–14.

BRINTON, P. and SHAW, C. (1984) 'Case study 3: The Victorians', in WRAY, D. (Ed.) *Teaching Information Skills Through Project Work*, Sevenoaks, Hodder and Stoughton.

BURGESS, R. G. (1984) *In the Field: An Introduction to Field Research*, London, Allen and Unwin.

DADDS, M. (1988) ' "Whose learning is it anyway?" Concerns about continuity and control in topic work', in CONNER, C. (Ed.) *Topic and Thematic Work in the Primary and Middle Years*, Cambridge, Cambridge Institute of Education.

DELAMONT, S. (1981) 'All too familiar? A decade of classroom research', *Educational Analysis*, **3**, pp. 69–83.

DEPARTMENT OF EDUCATION AND SCIENCE (1975) *A Language for Life*, Committee of Inquiry into Reading and the Use of English, Chairperson Sir Alan Bullock, London, HMSO.

DEPARTMENT OF EDUCATION AND SCIENCE (1978) *Primary Education in England: A Survey by HM Inspectors of Schools*, London, HMSO.

DEPARTMENT OF EDUCATION AND SCIENCE (1985) *Education 8–12 in Combined and Middle Schools: An HMI Survey*, London, HMSO.

DEPARTMENT OF EDUCATION AND SCIENCE (1989) *Standards in Education 1987–88 The Annual Report of HM Senior Chief Inspector of Schools based on the work of HMI in England*, London, HMSO.

DEPARTMENT OF EDUCATION AND SCIENCE AND THE WELSH OFFICE (1989) *English in the National Curriculum*, London, HMSO.

DEPARTMENT OF EDUCATION AND SCIENCE AND THE WELSH OFFICE (1989) *Science in the National Curriculum*, London, HMSO.

EARLY YEARS CURRICULUM GROUP (1989) *Early Childhood Education, The Early Years Curriculum and the National Curriculum*, EYCG.

EVANS, D. M. (1989) 'A small oral history project in four rural Cumbrian primary schools', *Teaching History*, 57, October, pp. 25–7.

GALTON, M., SIMON, B. and CROLL, P. (1980) *Inside the Primary Classroom*, London, Routledge and Kegan Paul.

GRIFFIN, M. (1983) *Study and Information Skills in the Primary School*, Slough, NFER.

GUNNING, S., GUNNING, D. and WILSON, J. (1982) *Topic Teaching in the Primary School*, London, Croom Helm.

HEATHER, P. (1984) *A Study of the Use of Books and Libraries by Children in Primary Schools*, CRUS Occasional Paper No 11, Centre for Research on User Studies, University of Sheffield.

HOARE, R. J. (1971) *Topic Work With Books*, London, Geoffrey Chapman.

JACKSON, P. (1968) *Life in Classrooms*, Eastbourne, Holt, Rinehart and Winston.

JONES, J. (1988) 'Research work in the primary school', *Teaching History*, 50, Jan. pp. 27–9.

KERRY, T., EGGLESTON, J. F. and BRADLEY, H. W. (1983) 'Developing pupils' thinking through topic work', in MALLEY, I. (Compiler) *Information Skills: An Introductory Pack for Teachers*, London, British Library Board.

KING, C. (1988) 'The historical novel: An under-used resource', *Teaching History*, 51, April, pp. 24–6.

KING, R. A. (1978) *All Things Bright and Beautiful? A Sociological Study of Infants' Classrooms*, Chichester, Wiley.

LABBETT, B. (1985) 'Creating the classroom space to handle information', *Cambridge Journal of Education*, 15, pp. 88–92.

LEITH, S. (1981) 'Project work: An enigma', in SIMON, B. and WILLCOCKS, J. (Eds.) *Research and Practice in the Primary Classroom*, London, Routledge and Kegan Paul.

LONG, S. (1988) 'Supporting teachers and children in topic work,' in TANN, C. S. (Ed.) *Developing Topic Work in the Primary School*, Lewes, Falmer Press.

LUNZER, E. and GARDNER, K. (Eds.) (1979) *The Effective Use of Reading*, London, Heinemann.

MAY, T. and WILLIAMS, S. (1987) 'Empathy — A case of apathy?', Teaching History, 49, October, pp. 11–16.

NASH, R. (1973) *Classrooms Observed*, London, Routledge and Kegan Paul.

NATIONAL CURRICULUM COUNCIL (1989) *Science Non-Statutory Guidance*, York, NCC.

PATTON, M. (1980) *Qualitative Evaluation Methods*, London, Sage Publications.

RANCE, P. (1968) *Teaching by Topics*, London, Ward Lock Educational.

SHARP, R. and GREEN, A. (1975) *Education and Social Control*, London, Routledge and Kegan Paul.

SIMONS, H. (Ed.) (1980) *Towards a Science of the Singular*, Norwich, CARE, University of East Anglia.

STENHOUSE, L. (1982) 'Experimental design and research in classrooms — an example', in RUDDUCK, J. and HOPKINS, D. (1985) *Research as a Basis for Teaching: Readings from the work of Lawrence Stenhouse*, London, Heinemann Educational Books.

SVENSSON, L. (1984) 'Skill in learning', in MARTON, F., HOUNSELL, D. and ENTWISTLE, N. (Eds.) *The Experience of Learning*, Edinburgh, Scottish Academic Press.

TANN, C. S. (1988) 'The practice of topic work', in TANN, C. S. (Ed.) *Developing Topic Work in the Primary School*, Lewes, Falmer Press.

WEBB, R. (1987) 'Developing Information Skills in the Middle Years of Schooling', Unpublished Ph.D., University of East Anglia.

Chapter six

Language Counts in the Teaching of Mathematics

Susan Wright

Introduction

'You should say what you mean,' the March Hare went on.
'I do,' Alice hastily replied: 'at least — at least I mean what I say —
that's the same thing you know.'
'Not the same thing a bit!' said the Hatter.

(Lewis Carroll)

The research described in this chapter is concerned with meaning, understanding and concept development in the area of mathematics, referring specifically to middle infant children. As Lewis Carroll, himself a mathematician shows, the relationship between language, meaning and understanding is a far from straightforward one.

The Cockroft Report (DES, 1982) asserted that:

Language plays an essential part in the formulation and expression of mathematical ideas. (p. 89, para. 306)

It was with the intention of investigating some of the issues involving various aspects of language in the teaching and learning of primary school maths that two colleagues and myself undertook the research as part of the University of York Outstation MA in Applied Educational Studies. The course is unusual in that it is organized on a team basis. The members of each team do their research in linked areas with a common theme. My particular concern was to carry out a closely focused case study of six middle infant children, considering their language, my language and the language of the Nuffield Infant Maths Scheme.

The school in which the research took place was a maintained group 4 primary school with junior and infant departments. There were approximately 160 children on roll, arranged in five classes, two infant and three junior. All the classes consisted of split year groups. In order that maths could be in taught year groups rather than class groups, my job as the part-time member of staff was to withdraw both the second year juniors and the middle infants from their respective classes for five sessions a week each. The former were taught in the hall, the latter in the corridor alongside the hall. The six children involved in the study were half of this group of middle infants. Two factors affected the choice of the particular six selected. Firstly, there were only two girls in the year group, and therefore both had to be included to give the best possible balance between the sexes. Secondly, these two girls and four of the boys had been studied the previous year by another member of the team, and so it seemed a good idea to use the same group again, thus enabling comparisons to be made between his work and mine. I adopted his pseudonyms for the children: Charles, Faye, Kirsty, Ian, Ned and Simon.

The Research Questions

The origin of the research was embedded in a growing awareness of some children's difficulties in coping with the language of maths lessons. These difficulties seemed to relate not only to specifically mathematical language, although they included that, but to wider areas of confusion. By considering in some detail the three topic areas of Time, Length and Weighing it was hoped that these problem areas could be identified and some suggestions made for remedying them. The specific questions fell into the following four groups:

Questioning	— What kind of questions do I ask?
	— What kind of questions do the children ask me?
	— What kind of questions do the children ask each other?
	— What kind of questions are asked on the worksheets?
	— What kind of response do the various questions elicit?
Word Usage	— Which words do the children actually use?
	— How does this compare with the words in the Nuffield lists?
	— Are there any mathematical words which cause particular difficulty?
	— Which words do the children use wrongly?
	— Does my language have any bearing on this?

Shared meanings and misunderstandings
  — Is there any discernible pattern in the areas of mis-
  understanding?
  — In which areas is there little or no confusion shown
  by any of the six children?
  — Can I as a teacher learn anything from this?
Non-linguistic evidence of understanding
  — What factors other than language indicate
  comprehension?

As the analysis progressed these original questions assumed greater or lesser importance. Data relating to each general area but answering questions other than those originally posed were also included where appropriate. The progressive focusing, which is characteristic of case study, meant that certain aspects (for example, the Nuffield Worksheets) assumed proportionately greater importance in the analysis than anticipated.

Data Collection

Adelman *et al.* (1980) indicate several advantages of case study as a method for educational researchers. They suggest it is 'strong in reality' and 'a step to action', originating in and contributing to a world of action. The action in this case was the development of the maths curriculum within the school.

Data were collected over a six-month period during normal maths teaching sessions and covered the topics of Time, Length and Weighing. The data consisted of tape recordings, an observation diary and the children's written materials, namely completed worksheets and individual notebooks. Although the collection of the data was topic-based, the analysis was issue-based. Some comment on the techniques of data collection is appropriate because problems arising from these techniques influenced the findings. The problems were associated particularly with tape recording and observation which I will briefly consider in turn.

Tape Recording

Using a corridor as a teaching area has obvious drawbacks, and trying to tape record at the same time raised more problems. There were limitations which would not occur in a classroom. For example, the only accessible power point was situated in the hall, behind my desk. It was thus feasible to record children working as a group around my desk, or alternatively to arrange the tape recorder in the doorway, in order to pick up what was going on in the corridor. However, because it picked up well, it also recorded the sound of the television from the library, the telephone ringing in the office and the conversation of anyone passing in the corridor. This meant that it was virtually useless just leaving it on to record all the classroom interaction, but it was quite satisfactory in a more structured situation where children were called on to speak in turn. This of course affected the data collection and I found as I analyzed the early tapes that I had very few examples of children talking to each other. I therefore modified the technique for the third period of data collection, the Weighing topic, and arranged for groups of children to work on their own at my desk in the hall with the recorder on, while I worked with the others in the corridor. This gave a considerable amount of important additional material.

Observation

Field-notes or a research diary are invaluable both as back-up material, in the case of tape failure, and as part of the triangulation process. If what is observed confirms what is heard on the tape, it adds extra weight to the evidence. The problems arise firstly from the inherent tension in the situation which Walker (1985) describes as:

> fundamental differences between the nature of research and the nature of teaching as intellectual and social processes. (p. 5)

One requires detachment, the other involvement. The second problem is the difficulty, verging on impossibility, of trying to observe in one's own classroom (or corridor) whilst teaching. There is the further complication of trying to get down on paper as accurate a record as possible as soon after the lesson as possible. As Ball (1984) points out:

> For everything that is noticed, a multitude of other things go unseen, for everything that is written a multitude of things are forgotten. (p. 75)

This is particularly true when working with infants, where the demands on one's attention are almost continuous. In addition, the educational needs of the members of the group who were not included in the study had to be considered just as much as those of the chosen six.

Four issues emerged from the data: Questions and Responses; Vocabulary and Word Usage; Misunderstandings and Confusions;

Understanding and Shared Meanings. These were similar to but not identical with the groups of research questions given above. Because of the constraints imposed by the length of a single chapter, I have concentrated on those findings which I consider have the greatest implications for practice. A fuller account may be found in the MA thesis (Wright, 1987).

My Questions

All the questions in the data from each of the three topic areas were identified. They were subdivided into my questions, the children's questions and the questions direct or implicit in the Nuffield material. Within each subdivision, categories were devised, their possible significance considered and tentative conclusions drawn or hypotheses suggested. The additional material from the Weighing topic obtained from groups of children working on their own provided one further category of the children's questions.

The transcripts contained over 750 of my questions. They seemed to fall into four categories:

Factual Knowledge Questions

Just over half of my questions fell into this category. They varied from relatively open questions where a variety of answers were acceptable, such as: 'What else might be wide?', when asking for examples which would show whether the children understood the meaning of width, to closed ones where only one answer was acceptable. An example of the latter would be 'When is your birthday?', asked during work on the months of the year in the Time topic.

Personal Questions

These were questions which only the individual child could answer. They were usually invitations to children to explain their work, such as 'How are you getting on?' or 'What are you going to try next?'.

Prompting Questions

These were of two kinds. The first were aimed at encouraging children to enlarge on their answers to a previous question. They often involved repetition of part of a child's previous statement, as in the following example taken from the work on things which move quickly or slowly. Simon was telling me about his picture:

Simon: It's a worm.
SW: That's a worm is it!
Simon: Yes, and I saw one on the grass near our caravan.

The second kind of prompting question was an expression of doubt on my part, where the question was used instead of a negative statement. The intention was to encourage the children to think more carefully about what they had said. For example, Faye and Kirsty were completing a worksheet where they had to decide from looking at a picture which of two items on the scales was the lighter. As they had done the final item wrong, I asked: 'Is the paintbrush lighter than the button?'.

Reasoning or Hypothetical Questions

This category reveals most about children's concept development and is also valuable in encouraging their ability to predict, an important feature of the National Curriculum. The DES document *Mathematics in the National Curriculum* (1989) gives as one of the statements of attainment for level one (the level at which most children of this age are likely to be working) 'make predictions based on experience'.

In order to answer questions in this category, the child has to be able to consider at least two items of knowledge or information, work out their inter-relationship and come to a conclusion. For example, to answer my question, asked in the context of revising the distinction between night and day: 'Why do we have fireworks at night, rather than during the day?', a consideration of the following or similar statements was required:

1   It is dark at night.
2   It is light during the day.
3   Fireworks are bright.
4   Bright things are more visible at night.

Ian in fact offered an answer showing this sort of understanding:

If they were in the day, you wouldn't see them very clearly because the day's light and they're light.

Less than 10 per cent of the questions from time and length fell into this category and of those nearly a third occurred during a session when I worked with Ned and Kirsty on their own because they had been absent earlier in the week. In that session, the reasoning required was the drawing of conclusions from observations and measurements. If one child's shoe was nine cubes long and the other child's was eleven cubes long, then the latter must be longer. This requires a deductive style of thinking not needed to draw the same conclusion from direct comparison of the shoes. In comparing the length of my desk and that of a cupboard, measured in pencil lengths, the replies to my question: 'How do you know it's longer?' were:

Kirsty: Because it's eight.
Ned: 'Cos it's — 'cos we measured it.

Both children appeared to understand, but neither said explicitly that the cupboard was longer because more pencils were needed to equal its length.

Perhaps because of my growing awareness of their importance, there were as many reasoning questions from the topic on Weighing as from the other two topics put together. There was also rather more recorded material overall on this topic and so some increase could be expected. It is interesting that when asked to explain beforehand how we would know which was the heavier or heaviest of two or three objects, having weighed them separately, only Ian could do so. However, as we proceeded and completed the weighing, the others were then able to answer the question:

SW: . . . which is heavier, the orange or the apple?
    Yes, Faye?
Faye: The orange.
SW: How do you know it is!
Faye: Because it's — because it's got the highest number.

Questions in this category give a lot more insight into a child's thinking and understanding than those which demand factual recall or direct observation. Perhaps it is significant that in the two earlier topics more of them occurred in the session with only two children. In a larger group, the temptation is to ask as many individual children as possible a question, which while superficially fairer makes it more difficult to investigate the thinking of the individual child. Edwards and Westgate (1987) comment on their observation of teacher questioning:

The evidence produced from such observation indicated that most of the questions were factual, their sheer number eliciting mainly brief recalls of already provided information because the pace of interrogation left little or no room for thinking aloud. (p. 97)

An awareness of the importance of hypothetical and reasoning questions both for assisting and assessing concept development, can lead to a deliberate policy of asking more such questions and encouraging the children to be more explicit in their way of answering.

The Children's Questions

Even though 'it is a normal feature of classroom discourse that teachers ask a great many questions, and consequently that pupils do a great deal of answering' (Atkinson, 1981, p. 109) nonetheless, the most striking thing on analyzing the transcripts was the comparative infrequency of the children's questions. The topics of Time and Length contained only thirty-four children's questions as opposed to about five hundred of mine. However, the Weighing topic with the extended recording, produced eighty-five children's questions, forty-three of which were addressed to me and forty-two to other children. The fact that variation in data-collection techniques can influence results so dramatically makes one hesitant to draw any firm conclusions from the number of questions asked.

Analysis of the questions produced four categories initially:

1 Checking up questions.
2 Tentative answers.
3 Requests for information.
4 Miscellaneous questions.

A further category (5) came from the additional tape-recorded material and consisted of those questions from one child to another which did not fall into the previous four categories.

Checking-up Questions

These were mainly directed to me although the Weighing topic included three from one child to another. They involved the children checking up on their understanding of what they had to do. An example would be Simon's question 'Do I count?', asked when he was given the task of turning over the one minute sand timer each time it finished in order to work out the duration of an unmarked timer. Sometimes the children were wanting confirmation of their theoretical understanding, as when Charles asked: 'Even one could just do it, couldn't it?'. This was in the context of measuring with repeated units. He had remembered that the previous day I had shown them that a large number of pencils or rubbers was not really necessary for measuring. It was possible to do it with only one or two as long as a mark was made where one finished and they did not lose count as they measured again from the mark.

Tentative Answers

There were sixteen of these, including two from one child to another. They were replies to questions where the child's tone of voice showed a lack of confidence in the answer being offered. For example, in response to my question as to which month comes after August, Ian replied: 'October?'.

When Ned and Charles were working together finding things lighter than a jug, Charles played the leading role:

Charles:	Now we need one more thing.	
Ned:	What? Um . . . what can we use?	(5)
Charles:	I know, I know, what they're called — matchsticks (actually a packet of spills). Right, cross out something in your picture.	
Ned:	A rubber?	(2)
Charles:	No.	
Ned:	A stone?	(2)
Charles:	Yeh.	

A characteristic of these tentative answers, labelled (2) in the transcript, is that greater knowledge is assumed in the person to whom they are addressed, whether teacher or other pupil.

Requests for Information

These were directed in more or less equal proportions to me or to other children. They were all work related and the information required was usually to enable the questioner to complete the task in hand or proceed to the next one. The former include Ian's question when doing a work card:

'What are cubits? I've forgotten.' The latter include: 'What do I do now?' as one task was completed.

Miscellaneous

These were not necessarily related to the work in hand. Some of them seem to be thinking aloud and not really expecting an answer. The transcripts contain frequent examples of Ian wondering where his pencil is.

Pupils' Open Questions

These were questions from one child to another of an essentially open nature in that either positive or negative responses seemed to be accepted by the questioner. They seemed to be suggestions offered to someone equal in status, and were usually work related. An example was Kirsty's question to Faye when they were working together on a weighing worksheet finding three things lighter than a ball:

Kirsty: Shall we get a pencil sharpener to be light?
Faye: If you want.

The categories of the children's questions seem to have little in common with the categories of my questions. One basic difference is that my questions were generally aimed at finding out what the children knew, and presupposed my knowledge of the answer. The children's questions on the other hand assumed that knowledge lay with the person receiving rather than the person asking the question. Category 5 questions were the exception to this where the conversation was essentially between equals.

Worksheet Questions

The worksheets contained very few direct questions. Such examples as there were included factual questions about a weather chart and reasoning questions requiring deductive thinking about comparative lengths. Several of the Weighing worksheets had a direct question at the top of the page for the child to complete. Other worksheets were entirely of the sentence completion type. I would maintain that in order to do many of the sentence completion tasks the child has to answer implied questions. For example, one worksheet shows a picture of a family with sentences to complete concerning their relative height. In order to complete the sentence: '_____ is the tallest', the child has to answer the implied question: 'Who is the tallest?'.

Similarly, but with greater complexity, another worksheet starts with the direct question: 'Who is quicker you or your friend?', but at this stage does not give indication marks for an answer. It gives instructions for the task of making towers of five cubes high while sand runs through a timer, and then gives three sentences to complete:

I made _____ towers.
_____ made _____ towers.
_____ was quicker than _____.

The first two sentences imply factual questions. The third sentence is much more complex. It not only asks an implied reasoning question: 'Who is quicker?', requiring deductive thinking about the relationship between speed and the number of towers built, but provides the opportunity for much confusion over pronouns. 'I' was needed if the first person was quicker, but 'me' following 'than' if the first person was slower. Not surprisingly, all the children found difficulty in the writing required, but when asked the direct question posed at the beginning of the section, gave the answer without hesitation.

Including the implied questions and using the same criteria as before to analyze them, I found nearly five times as many factual as reasoning questions in the worksheets (57 factual, 12 reasoning). This reinforced the conclusion from the analysis of my own questions that ones requiring factual answers are asked a great deal more frequently than ones which require reasoning. Too rigid control of the child's learning by this kind of questioning can leave little opportunity for the 'thinking aloud' which Torbe (1982) considers 'the essence of learning'. Barnes (1976) refers to 'control by worksheet' and the implications of these findings apply to teaching materials as much as to teacher-language.

Vocabulary and Word Usage

The words itemized in *The Nuffield Teachers' Handbook 1* (Moore, 1979) as being important for each topic were used as the basis for a checklist, with others added as they occurred in the transcripts if they seemed relevant for the work. The checklist was used to investigate the extent to which the words were used by the children and by myself as teacher. Vocabulary can be seen as something both active (in use) and passive (in understanding). I therefore also considered whether there was evidence of words being understood by the children when used by me and as they occurred in the Nuffield worksheets. Considering the completed checklists for the topics, and the transcripts generally, three things became apparent: firstly, the only person to use all but one or two of the words listed was myself; secondly, the variation in usage between children; thirdly, the variation between topics regarding the proportion of listed words used.

Given that, as the *Bullock Report* (DES, 1975) suggests, 'on average the teacher talks for three-quarters of the time in the usual teacher–class situation' (p. 142), and that the tape recorder is not on all the time, there is statistically a far greater chance of any particular word being picked up when used by me. Children may be ready to use the word but not be called upon to give the answer; they may use the word while working in the corridor or on a day when the tape recorder is not on. That the children were generally able to understand the various items of vocabulary is shown by their usually successful completion of the Nuffield worksheets. However, this only establishes what I would call passive vocabulary. There remains the possibility that, in addition to the alternatives suggested above concerning the somewhat arbitrary nature of tape-recorded evidence, some children may understand particular words but choose to use different ones themselves. For example, no-one other than myself is recorded as using the word 'tall', though my questions containing it were correctly answered. 'Big' was often used instead of 'tall' and 'small' in preference to 'short'. Any comment on variations in word usage between children has to be prefaced by the caveat above.

From the evidence available Ian was the child who used the greater number of words from the lists. A boy with wide general knowledge offered the Statue of Liberty as an example of something taller than himself. In the context of work on 'fast' and 'slow', his association of speed and energy was interesting as was his vivid description:

SW: Right, Ian, tell me about your picture.
Ian: It's a cheetah.
SW: It's a cheetah?
Ian: Yes.
SW: What's a cheetah like — what's it do that makes it so fast?
Ian: Er — because it's got a lot of energy.
SW: Got a lot of energy — right. What does it look like when it's going very fast?
Ian: Er — it looks like a big blob of yellow with black, black with black fire coming out of it.

Simon too used graphic vocabulary in the same context of drawing a picture of something fast:

> *SW*:　　Right Simon, tell me about yours. What have you done?
> *Simon*: That's a roller coaster and it's going speeding down.

Ned, who used the second highest number of Nuffield words (21; Ian used 23) was the only one of the group who seemed to have problems with everyday vocabulary. On at least two occasions he did not know the names of objects with which the rest of the group were familiar. He was finding three things heavier than a domino:

> *SW*: Right, Ned, just come here and tell me what you've put.
> *Ned*: Sharpener.
> *SW*: Right. The sharpener's heavier than the domino.
> 　　　And the second one?
> *Ned*: I don't know what you call that stuff in there —
> *SW*: Rice, wasn't it?
> *Ned*: Yeh.

On the same worksheet finding three things heavier than a shoe, he had problems with his third item:

> *SW*: What was your first one Ned? Peas are heavier than a shoe, dominoes — it's a box of dominoes isn't it? — right, take the dominoes out. What are you going to use for the third one? Well, there's something here that I can see.
> *Ned*: Yes, I can — this.
> *SW*: Well, try it and see. Is it heavier?
> *Ned*: Yes.
> *SW*: Right — what is it, Ned?
> *Ned*: Um — a click-box.
> *SW*: It's a stapler.
> *Ned*: Stapler.
> *SW*: Yes.
> *Ned*: s — t —

The two girls, Faye and Kirsty, were the children recorded as using fewest words from the lists, 12 and 14 respectively. Half of Kirsty's words from the list on length were recorded when she was working on her own with me, after having been absent. Both girls, and particularly Kirsty, tended to be quiet in class and let the noisier boys dominate what was being said. They also had very soft voices which meant that some of what they did say was inaudible on tape. Although two girls from a group of six children is a very small sample and generalization would therefore be foolish, it is interesting that concern is expressed in the *Cockroft Report* (DES, 1982) about the mathematical underachievement of girls. Reference is made to the Fourth International Congress on Mathematical Education, where it was suggested that:

> Girls may have a greater need than boys to develop understanding through discussion . . . it seems likely that in classrooms where it is not practised sufficiently girls are likely to be especially disadvantaged. Even in classrooms in which there is plenty of discussion teachers may need to take steps to ensure that boys do not dominate the discussion and that girls are given opportunity to play their full part. (para. 212)

When asked direct questions, both girls usually answered correctly and Kirsty particularly had good mathematical understanding, an example of which is given later.

There were some words which caused particular difficulty. These fell into two categories. The first consisted of words which were familiar but which embodied concepts which the children found difficult. For example, the children knew the names of the seasons but found difficulty in describing their characteristics. They all knew what a 'birthday' was, but not all knew when their own birthday fell.

The second category consisted of words with which the children were evidently not familiar. Ned's difficulties with particular items of vocabulary have been considered already, but apart from this there were several words, all in the topic on Length, which had to be taught quite specifically. 'Wide' and 'narrow' were words the children did not seem to know, and perhaps less surprisingly, the names for limb measures such as cubit, span and pace were new to them. Even after some discussion on 'wide' and 'narrow', using the stripes on Simon's jumper as an example, there was initial reluctance to use the new vocabulary:

SW: The stripes are *narrow*. Who's got a ribbon in their hair? Yes — not in her hair, but Faye's got a ribbon (on her dress). Now it isn't a *wide* ribbon. Sometimes you can get very wide ribbons. Let's bring it round here and tie it in a bow.
Tell me what this ribbon's like, Ned?
Ned: Thin.

However, evidence was provided some time later that the vocabulary had in fact been assimilated. I had been taking pictures down from the wall, and noted in my observation diary that Charles asked what he should do with his. When I suggested that he keep it in his tray until hometime, he replied: 'I can't — it's too big. It's too long and too wide.'

Of the words for limb measures, 'span' and 'foot-print' seemed to be learned most easily, perhaps because they were familiar in other contexts and in the latter case easily definable. 'Cubit' caused some difficulty not only in learning and remembering but also in the physical operation of measuring. However, there were some instances of clear understanding in this. Ned must have found measuring of particular interest as he brought in a list of things he had measured in spans at home. Kirsty too not only understood what she was doing but was able to reason and compare:

> SW: If you're doing something in spans, and the *same thing* in cubits — you're doing your table in spans and your table in cubits, do you think it will be more spans or more cubits? Put your hand up when you've thought. Think carefully — well Kirsty?
>
> *Kirsty*: More spans.
> SW: Right — why do you think there'll be more spans?
> *Kirsty*: Because they're smaller.

Given then that the data provided evidence of my use of specific vocabulary and the children's understanding of much of it though not of their using it, and also their difficulties with certain new words, consideration can be given to the question posed by Torbe and Shuard (1982):

> Is it important to encourage the learner's use of language in mathematics, rather than simply to concentrate on teaching the mathematics as clearly as possible? (p. 15)

Both the *Bullock Report* (DES, 1975) and *Cockroft Report* (DES, 1982) comment on children's need to put into words for themselves the concepts and experiences they meet in school. This seems to me to involve not only encouraging them to use their own words but also teaching them the relevant vocabulary and encouraging them to use that as well. This is one of the areas to which I have paid particular attention since completing the research.

Confusions and Misunderstandings

These range from the relatively trivial and easily corrected to the more fundamental. The trivial included examples of my mishearing or misunderstanding what the children said and their misunderstanding of me because the language I had used was ambiguous. One particular ambiguity revealed by the tape recordings was my constant use of the word 'right'. Sometimes it meant 'that's right' but at other times it was used more loosely to mark a change of direction or even just indicate the next child's turn. It was certainly very irritating to listen to. These trivial misunderstandings are unlikely to be particular to this age group or subject area, but occur frequently in school and home life.

The more fundamental difficulties fell into two separate areas: the one involving concepts, and the other confusion arising from the format of the worksheets. There was at least one instance which could be included in both categories.

Concepts

The work on Time produced most examples of lack of understanding. The problems centred around the fact that although the children knew the names of the seasons, the days of the week and, more haphazardly, the months of the year, they were not consistently able to make appropriate associations. Fewest mistakes occurred with the days of the week. This is not surprising since the cycle is a frequently recurring pattern.

When we were making a block graph of birthday months all the children knew what a birthday was, but neither Ned nor Simon knew when theirs fell. Of the children who knew which month their birthday was in, only Faye and Ian were sure of the date. Ned, however, showed awareness of what we had been doing, after the specific work was finished. I noted in my observation diary on November 5th, nearly a month after we had made the birthday graph, that when I was writing the date in another child's book, he commented:

That's the month with no birthdays, isn't it?

When I looked puzzled, he pointed to the graph on the wall, showing that there were no birthdays in November.

Given that children of this age have only had five or six birthdays, and that their experience of things that happen in particular months is similarly limited, it is not surprising that they find annual and seasonal events a difficult concept. *The Nuffield Teacher Handbook 1* (Moore, 1979) comments:

Young children live almost exclusively in the present. One of the first words the young child learns is 'now'. In order to understand time words, children have to relate them to an actual event which was important or easily remembered for one reason or another — for example the name of the month in which their birthday falls, Christmas in December, Guy Fawkes in November, etc. (p. 131)

There was less evidence of failure to understand concepts in the work on Length and Weighing, perhaps because the work involved very practical activities rather than talking about, or drawing pictures of, things outside the immediate context. Sometimes, however, questioning revealed that a correct answer had been given for the wrong reason. One worksheet required the children to indicate from looking at a picture which item on the scales was lighter. Faye was showing me her completed work:

SW: Which is lighter on this one, Faye?
Faye: (inaudible)
SW: Is the paintbrush lighter than the button?
Faye: No.
SW: How do you know it's the button, Faye?
Faye: Because it's smaller.
SW: Well, is it just because it's smaller? What —
Faye: Up.
SW: Because it's up on the scales, right.

Ned too had problems with the same item:

SW: Now then, which is lighter in this bottom picture?
Ned: The paintbrush.
SW: Is it? Why is the paintbrush lighter?
Ned: 'Cos it's at that side.

On the previous picture the lighter object had been in the left hand pan of the scales and Ned evidently thought that the same must be true for this one also. Further questioning however elicited the response:

Ned: The light one's up.
SW: Right — well which one's up in the picture then?
Ned: The button.

In the practical work done later, both Faye and Ned coped well. Perhaps it was the reasoning required to deduce the correct answer from a picture which caused the difficulty, rather than a failure to understand in practice. The ability to deal with the abstraction of the picture of scales as opposed to working with actual scales could be seen as one rung higher up the developmental ladder.

The Nuffield Worksheets

Many confusions arose over the layout of the Nuffield worksheets. The children did not usually have problems in carrying out the tasks but got muddled over what they were to write and where to write it. Particular problems arose when the worksheets reversed comparisons half way through. This happened especially in Weighing. Sheets which changed from 'heavier than' to 'lighter than' half way through caused several children difficulty either because they did not read what was required properly or had forgotten the initial warnings given by me. An extract from the discussion with the two girls following their completion of one such sheet illustrates this point:

SW: How much was your paste brush, Faye?
Faye: Er — thirty-seven.
SW: Thirty-seven peas. And the cotton reel was how much, Kirsty?
Kirsty: (inaudible but she had written twenty-three on her sheet, and so presumably that was her reply).
SW: Right, so which was lighter, Faye?
Faye: The reel.
SW: Right, the cotton reel was lighter because it was less — you've done this the wrong way round.

The understanding is there; the confusion seems to arise from a question asking for 'lighter' following two questions asking for 'heavier'. Older children who are more fluent readers might check by re-reading the question, but that does not seem to be a strategy employed by children as young as this.

The sentence completion format of many of the worksheets has been discussed already in the context of implied questions. Another type of format which caused confusion was where several arrows led to one object of comparison. One example required the children to find three things heavier than a domino. When we discussed it, the children supplied several suitable suggestions, but when completing the sheets seemed to find the arrows confusing. This is perhaps not surprising since they are used in many different ways, sometimes on their own (e.g., $3 + 2 \rightarrow 5$), sometimes with written instructions for an operation (e.g., $7 \xrightarrow{\text{count back 2}} 5$). There seems little justification in using them in an additional descriptive way when three sentences would have been clearer. Shuard (1982) comments as follows on the arrow symbol:

Uncertainty seems to exist in the minds of some primary school children about that ubiquitous symbol, the arrow. This symbol takes its meaning entirely from the context. Often the words are written above the arrow when it is first used with a particular meaning . . . On other occasions, however, the children have to supply their own meaning for the arrow (p. 93).

She illustrates her point with several examples of children's confusions over the symbol, taken from various maths schemes, and therefore the criticism is not specific to Nuffield.

There was one area where it was difficult to decide how far the cause of the confusion lay in the format of the worksheet and how far the difficulties in completing the worksheet arose from an imperfect grasp of the necessary concepts. The questions, set out as sentences to complete, concerned the days of the week. There had been a lot of discussion and preparatory work earlier in the week about activities on various days. Everyone knew the current day and correctly identified 'tomorrow'. After an initial slip from Simon, who went back two days, they all managed 'yesterday was
_____'.

The next two questions however caused real problems:

SW:	Now then, think a bit more carefully for this one. 'Tuesday is the day after _____'. Which day does Tuesday come after? Look on the list, then put your hand up. Kirsty, how about you? What does Tuesday come after?
[No answer]	
	Well, Faye?
Faye:	Monday.
SW:	Monday. Tuesday comes after Monday, doesn't it Kirsty? There's Tuesday, there's Monday. Tuesday comes after Monday. Alright? Now then, 'Wednesday is the day before _____'. Look at Wednesday on your list. 'Wednesday is the day before _____'. What does Wednesday come before? Now think, make sure you get it the right way round. Charles?
Charles:	Tuesday.
SW:	No, Wednesday doesn't come *before* Tuesday does it? 'Wednesday comes before _____'.

Child not in group:	Thursday.
SW:	That's right.
Charles:	I thought you said it was one up.
SW:	You have to look at it carefully, whether it says 'after' or 'before' don't you?

Charles' rather enigmatic reference to 'one up' must refer, I think, to my pointing to the list of days, showing Kirsty that Monday was before (in fact above, since it was a vertical list) Tuesday. Again, the change to the opposite form of comparison, from 'before' to 'after' had caused confusion. An alternative explanation might be that the children did not in fact have a basic understanding of the concepts of sequence involved in 'before' and 'after', but there is no evidence from their other work to suggest this. Perhaps difficulties in spelling and reading contribute to the problem. The confusion seems to be particularly between Tuesday, with its initial 'ch' sound and Thursday, rather than over the order of the days. Certainly this was the case for Ned:

SW:	Look at the list it might help you.
	Look at your list here — Wednesday, what is it *just* before?
Ned:	Tuesday.
SW:	(laugh) Well, you're pointing to the right one, but it doesn't say *Tuesday* — now what does it say — ?
Ned:	Thursday.

Of the various types of misunderstanding considered, I feel little can be done about mishearing and that while ambiguity can be avoided in written materials, some degree of it is almost inevitable in conversation. There may well be examples of both which go unnoticed every day, but an awareness of the possibility does increase the chance of immediate correction and explanation. The confusions arising from half-formed concepts are more serious. In any group of children there are likely to be differences in degrees of understanding. If, however, the same areas of a maths scheme, or any other part of the curriculum, cause difficulty each year, then the question arises as to whether the material is being taught at an appropriate time. Reformulation of many of the worksheets would help clarify which confusions are conceptual and which are due to an unsuitable format.

Understanding and Shared Meanings

In the previous sections, areas of confusion and misunderstanding have been considered. The data do, of course, provide many examples of their opposite. If this were not the case, there would be serious cause for concern as to the suitability of the content, materials and methods of the school's infant maths curriculum. The data revealed patterns of common errors from which generalizations could be made and implications for my teaching identified. However, linguistic examples of understanding (as opposed to correctly completed worksheets) tended to be particular to the individual child. Barnes (1976) comments:

> Classroom learning can be best seen as an interaction between the teacher's meanings and those of his pupils, so that what they take away is partly shared and partly unique to each of them. (p. 22)

Since the research was on a case study of six particular children, it seems appropriate to consider each child in turn, give a few examples of their understanding from the various topics and indicate the kind of learning I derived from this. They are considered in alphabetical order of their pseudonyms.

Charles

Although he was the youngest of the group, having his sixth birthday in April, towards the end of the period of data collection, Charles showed considerable maturity of understanding. This was particularly apparent in the work on Time, which many of the children found difficult. In the activities using the sand timers, I noted in my diary that as he was making towers of ten blocks, Charles said, perhaps to himself, 'Keep watching the timer', thus indicating that he had made the necessary connection between speed in doing the activity and the observable passing of time.

Perhaps the best example of his understanding of the work on Time came from the sessions on the Seasons. In his workbook he drew a picture of a tree, to illustrate Summer. The caption reads:

> This is summer. The tree has grown.

His recorded comment, contrasting this with a Spring picture was:

> The tree's grown — last time it were there and I made it a bit up.

This explicit association of growth and development as the seasons progress seems to me remarkably mature for a 5-and-a-half-year-old. It is important to realize that even with a small group of children there can be wide variations in ability and the work provided must be sufficiently demanding for the most able. In terms of the National Curriculum, Charles would have been in the first year of the first key stage, but his depth of understanding was such that he could have been working at level two or even level three which the average child would not reach for another year or more.

Faye

Faye was rather quiet in class and not everything she said was audible on tape. Sometimes it was necessary to rely on non-verbal evidence of understanding. When the children were finding something in the hall higher than the radiator but not as high as the climbing frame, this was the case:

SW: Faye, what did you think of?
(Silence)

          Well, go and show me what it is, if you don't know what it's called. Well done, that's right. It's the gate to the climbing frame, isn't it?

Though she found difficulty in judging the relative mass of two objects by feeling them, she understood how the scales worked. We were comparing containers of polystyrene bits and of gravel:

SW: First of all, who thinks the polystyrene will be heavier? You do, Faye, do you? So if it's heavier, will the polystyrene side go up or down — if it's heavier?
Faye: Down.

When she was working alone with Kirsty, they were finding three things heavier than a shoe:

Faye: No — that isn't heavier. NO, that isn't.
Kirsty: The gravel — the gravel is though.

Faye seemed to trust what her eyes told her on the scales without being able to make confident judgments by feeling objects. Kirsty, as the example in her section shows reacted rather differently. This underlined the importance of the note in each section of the *Nuffield Teachers Handbook 1* (Moore, 1979):

> Worksheets should not be introduced until children have had plenty of practical experience and opportunity for discussion. (*passim*, e.g., pp. 6, 12, 19, 22, etc.)

'Plenty' required more in Faye's case than for some of the other children.

Ian

Ian was a very intelligent boy with a high reading age (9.0 Young's Test; Chronological Age 6.7) and a wide general knowledge. This was reflected in many of the comments he made about the work as we did it. In the context of Time, he chose to mime an aeroplane as an example of something fast, but when he came to draw a picture apparently preferred a cheetah. His vivid description of the cheetah has already been commented on, but he also made an interesting comparison:

Ian: That's my cheetah.
SW: That's your cheetah, Ian, is it? I like his spots. What can you tell me about a cheetah?
Ian: Er — he's got a lot of energy. He goes fast. He doesn't go as fast as an aeroplane though.

He was able to reverse comparisons easily, as this comment from the work on Length shows:

SW: Faye is taller than Kirsty. What would you say about Kirsty? Ian?
Ian: Smaller.

Ian's intelligence sometimes showed itself in the consideration of possibilities which did not occur to the other children. He, Simon and Charles were weighing in the hall:

SW: Now then, let's do the bean bag and the nails. Who's put the bean bag in? Right, Simon. How many nails, Charles? Put them in one at a time.
Ian: Maybe it's less than one.

The nails we were using were heavy six inch ones and so his comment was very perceptive. Perhaps, like Charles, he should have been given work of a more demanding nature and the advent of the National Curriculum will increase the possibility of such children being taught at a more appropriate level.

Kirsty

In a group, Kirsty showed great reluctance to volunteer answers, even though she knew them. Consequently, apart from the session with Ned and myself after they had been absent, there is less transcript data for her than for any of the others. Nonetheless, despite the lack of oral participation, her work showed evidence of a good understanding. An example of this has already been given in connection with the relative size of spans and cubits.

After general discussion about the Seasons, she was able to tell me about her picture:

SW: That's a nice picture. What's it about?
Jirsty: Autumn.
SW: This is Autumn, is it? What happens in Autumn?
Kirsty: The leaves fall down.

When asked what she would like to draw next, she replied:

Kirsty: Winter.
SW: Winter — what happens in Winter?
Kirsty: All the snow comes.

The work on Weighing provided a very interesting example of Kirsty's reaction when what she expected did not seem to be the case. She and Faye were finding things lighter than a ball:

Faye: We'll do the stone.
SW: Well, do you think the stone will be lighter than the ball?
Kirsty: No — yes.

She changed her answer because when they put the stone in the scale pan, it did not go down. The apparent evidence contradicted her expectation. However, her original supposition was the correct one:

SW: Wait a minute. You've got the bottom of the scales
                        stuck on the jug. Is it lighter?
Faye and Kirsty: NO.

Kirsty's understanding of the work we did in maths was good and certainly did not fit in with Whyte's (1983) reference to a study on children's mathematical learning in infant and primary school, where girls' good performance is explained as:

They only follow the rules, they don't have proper mathematical concepts. (Quoting from Walden and Walkerdene, 1982, p. 24.)

Ned

Ned had two short spells in hospital during the data collection period and because I was able to work with him on his own afterwards, recording the sessions, there is consequently more material relating to him than to the other children. Several examples quoting him have been given already.

During a lesson where he and Kirsty were working alone with me, I asked: 'Which way are we going to measure for deep then?'. Ned replied 'down' and then expanded his reply:

> *Ned*: I know that word, 'cos the river's deep and you can sink into the water. That's called deep.

In the work on Weighing, Ned showed that he not only had the concepts of lightness, heaviness and balance, but that when one object was already on the scale, he could make a correct inference about comparative mass when another object was put in the other side:

> *SW*: Now, what are you going to put in that side? You said a rubber. Put a rubber here and see . . . is the rubber lighter than the ball?
> *Ned*: Yes.
> *SW*: Right. How do you know it is?
> *Ned*: 'Cos it doesn't go down. It doesn't go down, Miss.

This seems to me to be one stage further than putting the objects on the scales simultaneously and deciding which is the lighter.

One characteristic of Ned's language, both when talking to me and when working with other children, was a constant checking that he was doing things correctly:

> Do I write it here, Miss?
> How do you write it then? (to Charles)
> Is that right? (to me)

Donaldson (1978) felt that:

> 'learning to ask' should be of direct value in itself, for it implies that the child has become conscious of his uncertainty over the interpretation of what the teacher says. Thus his self-awareness will grow. (p. 101)

It is important to have a classroom atmosphere where children feel able to ask questions and to express their uncertainties freely. I have been more aware since I did the research of children doing this, perhaps in response to my changed questioning techniques.

Simon

Although Simon often rushed through his work making careless mistakes, he did have a good basic understanding and occasional flashes of real insight. When we were looking at the sand timers, before I had started to talk about them at all, he looked at the ten minute one and said:

Simon: That goes slow 'cos it's got a little hole.

His lack of facility with words, but his clear comprehension, is shown again in the following extract. We had measured a paintbrush with cubes and then with dominoes:

Simon: I know why there's — er — less than the bigger because they're bigger than the them.

(I have double-checked the transcript with the tape: those were his exact words.)

SW: . . . Tell me what you just said, Simon.
Simon: Well, er. I know why that's less than them — because — er — they're bigger.
SW: The dominoes are bigger, so it doesn't take as many.
Simon: Yes.

Kerslake (1982) suggests that:

Teachers need to adjust to the natural language of the children in the classroom as well as expecting the children to adjust to the more formal language of mathematics. (p. 79)

Children like Simon need a lot of help and encouragement to express their understanding of concepts in a comprehensible way and to move towards 'the more formal language of mathematics'.

Conclusion

The findings of the research had implications for improvements in both practice and materials. There should be greater use of reasoning questions by the teacher and more opportunity for children to hypothesize about their work; children's active use of mathematical vocabulary should be encouraged together with an awareness of the need to extend the personal vocabulary of some children; some of the worksheets which caused confusion by their format rather than their conceptual content should be redesigned.

Two members of the original team are still working in the same school, one with reception children and myself with middle infants. The findings of our research overlapped to a certain extent, particularly with regard to the use of mathematical language. We have been consciously working towards implementing the recommendations we made, both in our own practice and in disseminating the results of our work among other infant staff.

In addition to these improvements, the experience of closely observing individual children and analyzing their work in so detailed a way, has been valuable preparation for the monitoring requirements of the National Curriculum. Identifying when children have reached attainment targets and providing work at an appropriate level are skills which improve with practice and experience. The opportunities afforded by this study provided both.

References

ADELMAN, C. *et al.* (1980) 'Rethinking case study: Notes from the second Cambridge conference', in SIMONS, H. (Ed.) *Towards a Science of the Singular*, CARE, University of East Anglia.

ATKINSON, P. (1981) 'Inspecting classroom talk', in ADELMAN, C. (Ed.) *Uttering, Muttering*, London, Grant McIntyre.

BALL, S.J. (1984) 'Beachside reconsidered', in BURGESS, R. (Ed.) *The Research Process in Educational Settings: Ten Case Studies*, London, Falmer Press.

BARNES, D. (1976) *From Communication to Curriculum*, Harmondsworth, Penguin Books.

CARROLL, L. (1961 edition) *Alice in Wonderland*, London, Dent.

DEPARTMENT OF EDUCATION AND SCIENCE (1975) *A Language for Life*, Report of the Committee of Inquiry Chaired by Sir Alan Bullock, London, HMSO.

DEPARTMENT OF EDUCATION AND SCIENCE (1982) *Mathematics Counts*, Report of the Committee of Inquiry Chaired by Dr W. H. Cockroft, London, HMSO.

DEPARTMENT OF EDUCATION AND SCIENCE AND THE WELSH OFFICE (1989) *Mathematics in the National Curriculum*, London, HMSO.

DONALDSON, M. (1978) *Children's Minds*, London, Fontana.

EDWARDS, A. and WESTGATE, D. (1987) *Investigating Classroom Talk*, Lewes, Falmer Press.

KERSLAKE, D. (1982) 'Talking about mathematics', in TORBE, M. (Ed.) *Language Teaching and Learning Vol. 6 Mathematics*, London, Ward Lock Educational.

MOORE, W. (1979) *Nuffield Maths 1. Teachers' Handbook*, Harlow, Longman.

SHUARD, H. (1982) 'Reading and learning in mathematics', in TORBE, M. (Ed.) *Language Teaching and Learning Vol. 6 Mathematics*, London, Ward Lock Educational.

TORBE, M. (Ed.) (1982) *Language Teaching and Learning Vol. 6 Mathematics*, London, Ward Lock Educational.

TORBE, M. and SHUARD, H. (1982) 'Mathematics and language', in TORBE, M. (Ed.) *Language Teaching and Learning Vol. 6 Mathematics*, London, Ward Lock Educational.

WALDEN, R. and WALKERDENE, W. (1982) *Girls and Mathematics: The Early Years*. Bedford Way Papers 8. University of London, Institute of Education.

WALKER, R. (1985) *Doing Research: A Handbook for Teachers*, London, Methuen.

WHYTE, J. (1983) *Beyond the Wendy House: Sex Role Stereotyping in Primary Schools*, Harlow, Longman for the Schools Council.

WRIGHT, S.J. (1987) 'Aspects of Language in Infant Mathematics: A Case Study'. Unpublished MA Thesis, University of York.

Chapter seven

A Process Approach to Science

Virginia Winter

The research reported here is concerned with the promotion of skills and processes in a middle school science curriculum and with the effect of such an approach on children's performance and the role of the teacher. For some years there has been a lively debate concerning the nature and style of science teaching most appropriate to the children in our schools. Much discussion has centred around the methods of science, the content versus process dichotomy, prescriptive versus open-ended approaches, and their effect on children's motivation, thinking, involvement and achievement. Such debates are indeed encouraged by government publications, whilst in an attempt to justify the place of science in the curriculum, Raper and Stringer (1987) state:

> Science is an ideal vehicle for acquiring skills, fostering attitudes and developing an understanding of a range of concepts relevant to everyday experiences. (p. 10)

Whilst there is no consensus amongst educationalists about the methods of science, there are some points of fairly general agreement. Millar (1988) states that:

> One of these is the now widely accepted view that science enquiry resembles . . . the practice as a 'craft': in deciding what to observe, in selecting what observations to pay attention to, in interpreting and drawing inferences, in drawing conclusions from experimental data . . . (p. 157)

However, as the Schools' Council Working Paper (1975) writes:

> There are so many things that could be done in school. There are so many things that are done. How are we to decide what should be done? (Ross *et al.*, 1975 p. 11)

Criticisms from the Department of Education and Science (DES), the Association for Science Education (ASE) and the Assessment of Performance Unit (APU) have suggested that the making of such decisions has led to an overload of content and that available process-based packages and approaches are under-used.

The HMI Report (1983) stated in its assessment of middle school work:

> Most of the schemes discussed the content to be covered in each year group but fewer drew attention to the skills, processes and general ideas children were to learn as they progressed through the school. (DES, p. 39)

The APU (1983) concluded that where there was an emphasis on process it tended to be on general skills fostered across the curriculum, rather than on science-specific skills such as the design and performance of investigations.

There have been countless attempts in the past to produce lists of processes and skills and reviews of existing lists can be found in Thier (1973), Martin (1983) and Harlen (1987). Problems do arise, however, when terms such as 'process', 'skill' and 'process skills' are used inconsistently by educationalists, but in the DES document (1985) priorities are clearly stated and the processes to which all children should be progressively introduced are listed (pp. 3–4, para. 11).

For the purposes of the research, I subscribed to the definition of 'science processes' proposed by Screen (1986):

> Science processes are: the sequence of events which are engaged when researchers take part in scientific investigations. (p. 14)

'Process skills' are succinctly described by Harlen (1987) as follows:

> Process skills are involved in connecting ideas with experience and attempting to make sense of the experience. They include the skills of:
> 1 Gathering information. (Observation)
> 2 Attempting to explain observations by applying existing ideas. (Hypothesizing)
> 3 Testing out ideas. (Raising questions, Devising investigations, Interpreting information)
> 4 Communication. (p. x).

As science co-ordinator in a four-form entry middle school of some 550 pupils, the important issues raised by such debates and reports seemed to demand more than subjective assessment and intuitive evaluation. The science work undertaken by the first and second years was essentially class-based, whilst the third and fourth years worked in the laboratory for one double lesson (1 hour 10 minutes) per week. All groups were of mixed ability, with average class sizes of thirty-four children.

In 1985 a group of teachers, whose interests encompassed all ages of children and areas of the curriculum, met periodically to discuss various issues and priorities within the school. The group had been disturbed by the HMI 9–13 Survey's criticism of middle school practice. In the survey, the DES (1983) stated:

> The middle schools provided a broad range of subjects for their pupils . . . The children applied themselves well to their tasks. They were taught a wide range of basic competencies but the schools often did not extend the work sufficiently to challenge their more able pupils, nor were children often observed to be finding their own way to the solution of problems posed, pursuing their own enquiries or making choices about the way in which work was to be tackled. (p. 5)

This extract was 'food for thought', as it could be argued that good science teaching surely presupposes an 'inherent' belief that science is a practical subject and should be taught at all stages in a way which emphasises practical, investigative and problem-solving activities. I began to feel the need to undertake a systematic appraisal of the science work offered within the school.

Although this study was undertaken from 1986–8 prior to the inception of the National Curriculum, its continuing relevance can be seen within the DES (1989) statutory orders which introduce Attainment Target 1 — Exploration of Science — as follows:

> Pupils should develop the intellectual and practical skills that allow them to explore the world of science and to develop a fuller understanding of scientific phenomena and the procedures of scientific exploration and investigation. (p. 3)

In addition, in the Non-Statutory Guidance (NCC, 1989) it is stressed that:

> Exploration of Science and Knowledge and Understanding [Attainment Targets 2–17] are interwoven into the science curriculum; they are not in any sense separable in the teaching programme. (D.5)

Role of Pilot Study

A pilot study, conducted in the Summer term of 1987, aimed at obtaining children's perceptions of science and their likes and dislikes in science lessons. Also, an attempt was made to assess the extent to which the development of science process skills was an integral part of the science work experienced by some of the children in a middle school. For the pilot study, purposive sampling resulted in selections being made according to certain criteria: both boys and girls, aged 11–12 years, from each of the four third year classes and encompassing all ability levels. The chosen sample of fourteen boys and fifteen girls all constituted various 'friendship groups' (Woods, 1986) and were generally regarded as communicating well with one another. For the main study similar considerations were made, with a resulting sample of thirty-six children comprising some twenty boys and sixteen girls. It should be recognized, however, that the sample may not be entirely representative of the year group as a whole, although an effort was made to achieve this representativeness.

The pilot study enabled my research techniques to be improved. Also it was regarded as contributing data to the main study and informing the development of the school science policy. From the pilot study, several conclusions were tentatively offered and further research questions raised which are worthy of brief consideration here because of their implications for the main research.

The children appeared to perceive their science lessons in a positive light, but did they perceive the experience as 'real' and 'valuable' and to what extent were activities regarded as challenging? The following comment from a child draws attention to this question:

SG: We learn about a new topic and then we do experiments about it.

I was reminded of Woolnough and Allsop (1985) who declare:

> Much practical work appears to be a succession of exercises with apparatus through which they [children] are led in the hope of solving an unasked question. (p. 2)

A resolution was made to ensure that future science work would not render activities to a series of 'meaningless' exercises. Where possible, children would be given or suggest for themselves, a problem in a scientific context, be encouraged to analyze the problem and decide on the relevant parameters. This would involve formulating ideas for testing and devising a range of possible lines of investigation prior to selecting the most appropriate. This would then lead to opportunities for executing plans and evaluating findings. In simple terms, it was resolved to ensure that children were offered opportunities for working as problem-solving scientists. When asked about specific activities undertaken, children tended to make vague references to concepts, which raised the question: Does practical work increase an understanding of underlying theory?

> *CH*: It's something to do with solutions and copper sulphate. We did an experiment but I don't really understand it now.

In the 1960s, the catch phrase, 'I hear and I forget, I see and I remember and I do and I understand' was widely quoted as a justification of practical work. However, findings of those who have researched into students' understanding of scientific ideas (see Osborne and Wittrock, 1983) would refute this suggestion, stating that very often children are left with slight, sometimes faulty understanding of underlying theory. Driver (1983) has written, not entirely flippantly, that 'I do and I understand' should perhaps be replaced by 'I do and I am even more confused' (p. 9). Indeed the APU (1984) concluded on the basis of research that:

> Despite the orientation of science courses to the teaching of content, the results from the tests of application of science concepts indicate that it is only a minority of 15-year-olds who are able to draw on and use some of the most basic scientific concepts. (p. 190)

The pilot study aimed at obtaining children's perceptions especially in relation to the processes of science. Findings revealed that certain fundamental process skills were not mentioned at all, most notable of which was 'observation'. One can speculate as to whether it seemed too obvious to mention, whether there was an unawareness of its importance or whether, and this is perhaps most likely, research methods failed to facilitate its mention. Lack of reference to 'inferring', 'evaluating' and 'application' was perhaps not so surprising since infrequent reference had been made to them in lessons. The APU (1983) warns 'that process skills can only be acquired if children are given opportunities to use them' (p. 31). However, this raised the question: Is current practice effectively developing process skills? The APU (1983) investigated performance in the practical skills of using apparatus and measuring instruments, using observation and designing and performing investigations, skills fundamental to the practice of being a scientist. Their results emphasized that it should not be assumed that these skills will be acquired *en passant* in science courses.

Following the pilot study it seemed most appropriate to embark upon some form of action research, defined by Kemmis and quoted in Hopkins (1985) as:

> Action research is trying out new ideas in practice with a view of improving or changing something, trying to have a real effect on the situation. (p. 34)

Action research is always a form of self-reflective enquiry, a pre-requisite for the examination of one's own practice. In addition it builds upon experience accumulated since it must involve action in the light of evidence collected and analyzed. As such it was my intention to take action in the light of evidence interpreted from the pilot study towards the successful development of a strong process element in the science work within school.

Choices had to be made regarding the kinds of data to be obtained, from whom and how, since these factors set limits on the quantity and quality of data eventually available for analysis. In order to make it rigorous, a number of different data collection techniques were employed, so enabling validity checks to take place through triangulation. The most important methods of this 'multiple strategy' approach (Burgess, 1984) were semi-structured interviews and participant observation, supplemented by documentary evidence in the form of solicited and unsolicited samples of children's work. Children were invited to keep a diary in which their 'truthful' thoughts about lessons could be recorded.

Observing and Interviewing Children

Experience gained in the pilot study showed that observing whilst teaching was likely to be problematic. In September 1987, intensive observational sessions of 15 minutes were decided upon for each group of children in the sample during full class lessons. I resolved to make impressionistic field-notes during each observed lesson to help re-create the picture later as well as more detailed entries in my research diary.

The research diary kept was based on the model outlined by Burgess (1984) and had been started during the pilot study. As Burgess says:

> If ethnographers are to provide detailed portraits of the situations they are observing then they require careful recording in the researcher's diary. (p. 199)

My research diary contained substantive (factual) accounts of events in lessons, methodological accounts giving biographical details and analytical (interpretive) accounts, in which ideas, hunches and questions were noted and anything else which might be of use in follow-up interviews.

The first observational sessions of the main research were not without their problems. Despite explaining the situation to each class there were inevitable interruptions. It was estimated that at least half the allotted observational time was spent in dealing with peripheral or matters irrelevant to the research; for example, a request for equipment from another member of staff, an 'indoor playtime' warning, and then there were the children who simply forgot about the observations in progress and wanted to talk to me or the members of the group under observation.

These problems were irksome and had a disruptive effect on observations. I deliberated whether to change the method of observing. Discussions with Outstation team members resulted in one colleague coming into the room as 'an extra pair of hands', when observations were scheduled to take place. His role was explained to the class and he helped with the routine matters while I interacted with and observed the children in the sample. This proved to be most helpful but could only be regarded as a short-term measure.

It would have been easier for observational purposes if the children not in the sample had been engaged in some non-practical activity. However, this would have created an 'unreal situation'. The children in the sample would have been made to look conspicuous and the situation would have threatened validity and reliability.

After the October half-term 1987 break, I decided that rather than continue with the pre-determined periods for observations (for example, 15 minutes in the middle of a lesson) I would observe on a 'little and often' basis. I made a point of being close to the children in the sample as often as I could and this enabled me to gather data from different parts of the lessons. As such, I was able to collect data ranging from initial group discussions, to the performances of investigations and to the closing stages of lessons. Observations became more focused (Spradley, 1979) and this I felt to be more successful. Rather than make general non-specific observations, the main concerns were classified into four major areas:

A Interest
B Acquisition of process skills
C Organization
D Social concerns

During each observation period I kept the following question in mind: What observable behaviour is there that informs me about each of the four areas? The schedule for progressive focusing has been summarized in figure 7.1.

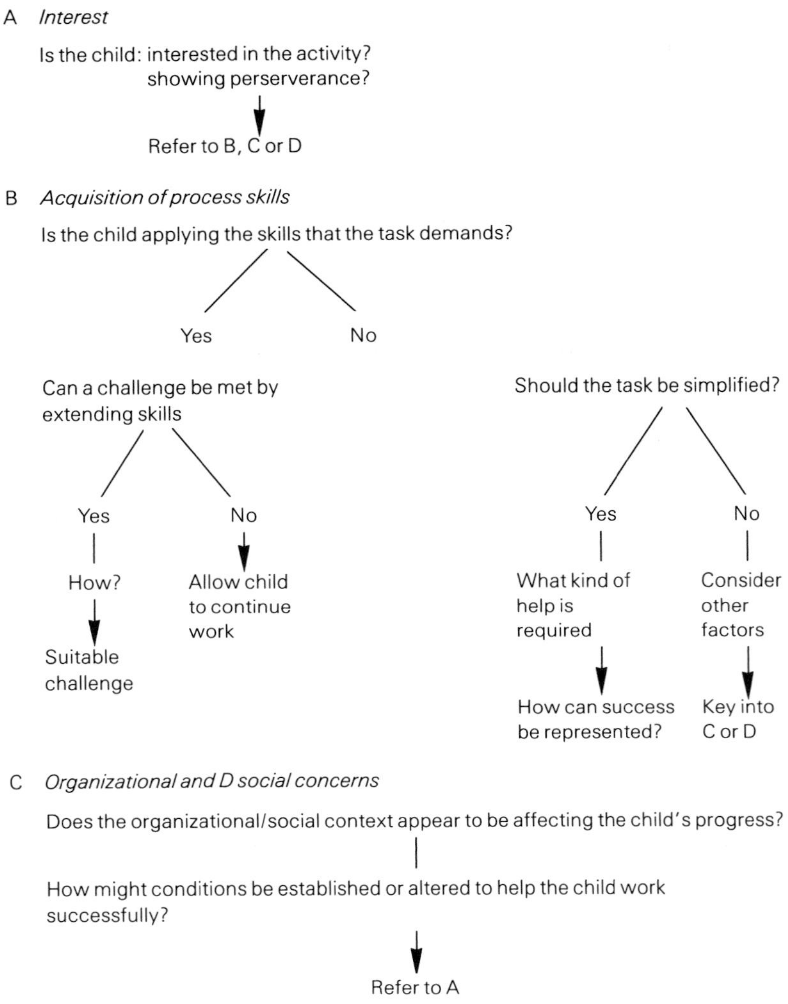

A *Interest*

Is the child: interested in the activity?
showing perserverance?

↓

Refer to B, C or D

B *Acquisition of process skills*

Is the child applying the skills that the task demands?

Yes   No

Can a challenge be met by
extending skills

Yes   No

How?   Allow child
            to continue
            work

Suitable
challenge

Should the task be simplified?

Yes   No

What kind of   Consider
help is   other
required   factors

How can success   Key into
be represented?   C or D

C *Organizational and D social concerns*

Does the organizational/social context appear to be affecting the child's progress?

How might conditions be established or altered to help the child work
successfully?

↓

Refer to A

Figure 7.1   Schedule for progressive focusing

At the beginning of January 1988, having given further thought to the
whole matter of observation, I decided to try leaving a small cassette recorder
in front of the children in lessons where movement around the classroom was
limited. The children reacted positively and were eager to hear themselves
'working hard' afterwards. This seemed most useful in recapturing those
children's conversations I might otherwise have missed. The data enabled
me to further supplement my observations and were particularly useful
when drawing up interview schedules. The tapes were transcribed selectively

as most were approximately 45 minutes long, making complete transcriptions too time consuming. Because of this, synopses were later presented to the children for validation and also to provide them with some feedback. Patton (1980) states: 'the giving of feedback can be a major part in the verification process in fieldwork' (p. 186).

For interviews, the cassette recorder, which became increasingly familiar to the children, was situated where audio-visual equipment was normally housed. The children seemed less affected by its presence than I was, in my attempt to acquire a measure of detachment and achieve 'anthropological strangeness' (Woods, 1986), guarding against 'going native' or reverting to the role of teacher. Despite having been piloted on colleagues, the initial interviews with children in this main research yielded responses which were vague. The children were generally keen to talk, but in general terms and often in an anecdotal way. I felt that references to process skills were being engineered by me and that the interviews had achieved very little in terms of spontaneity and useful data. The key questions available for reference had not prevented irrelevancies creeping in and so some drastic modification seemed to be called for.

Discussions with team members, who were able to view the problem in a more detached, 'objective' manner, produced some helpful advice. So, in the light of discussions, modifications were made to the design of the interviews. Key questions assumed a more vital role in determining the direction in which the interviews were progressing and in maintaining control. Different kinds of questions were included: 'descriptive' and 'structural' ones (Burgess, 1984) to enable children to talk about their science lessons and how they were organized and 'contrast' questions to enable comparisons to be made. When answers indicated that children were unclear, the questions were posed again using the children's own words to achieve clarification in their terms not mine. 'Why?' questions were avoided and instead children were encouraged to elaborate upon their statements (for a thorough exposition of question types, see Patton, 1980, pp. 207–40).

I also found that if interviewees seemed to be floundering and unsure of what to say, I unwittingly began to ask multiple questions, which only seemed to create more tension and confusion. For example:

Teacher: In what situations do you think the worksheets helped?
DT: Well sometimes they do.
Teacher: Yes . . .
DT: Well sometimes they don't.
Teacher: Can you think of any example when they did help? — or — perhaps a worksheet or banda that wasn't really needed? What do you think? [sic]:

This final question, predictably rendered the child and the entire group to silence! Of course, the actual wording of the question and its effect were not obvious to me at the time of the interview. Only whilst transcribing did the 'damage' done by such a question become apparent. In subsequent interviews I always made a conscious effort to try to include clear, simple questions with probing where necessary.

The pupils' views and experiences will now be discussed by drawing upon information which emerged during the analysis of data.

Perceptions of Science

I wondered how the children perceived scientists and whether they regarded themselves as 'young scientists'. They were asked to visualize a scientist and

Figure 7.2   A 'typical' scientist

then asked to draw their scientist at work, an adaptation of the Chambers (1983) 'Draw a scientist test'. Some children in the sample performed the test early in September 1987 while a second group did so about three months into the project. The pictures of the first group almost exclusively showed bald, bespectacled men working with chemicals to produce explosives (see Figure 7.2). These pictures would seem to support the findings of researchers like Chambers (1983) who found that children developed stereotyped images of scientists by the age of eight, possibly influenced by the media — 'I've seen 'em on the Tefal advert'.

The children in the second group were invited to practise 'working like a scientist' whilst engaging in activities with the exhibition, observing, collecting and interpreting information. They were exposed to large photographs of 'real' scientists at work and some listened to tape recordings relating the achievements of scientists notably those of women!

Figure 7.3   Scientist

The drawings produced by these children in November 1987 showed notable differences from the previous group's. Several girls (but no boys) drew female scientists, though they still mostly wore white 'lab' coats. However, nearly all pictures more closely resembled 'normal people' than the fantasy figures depicted in the media and featured in the September drawings (see Figure 7.3).

Developing Observational Skills

In an attempt to focus children's attention upon the observations they made, and to encourage the development of observational skills, an exhibition of some fifty natural and commercially produced objects was introduced to the 'new' third year children in September 1987. The observation of the various materials on the exhibition was seen as a priority, though not mutually exclusive of other process skills, since the exhibits could be named, investigated, discussed and recorded in some form. Children at work with the exhibits provided a good opportunity for collecting data not only on whether they were observing or not but also as to the level at which they were observing.

Analysis of data indicated a positive reaction to the exhibits which were not seen as a series of experiments to be completed in a set time. The children talked about their work enthusiastically:

> *SS*: We've been going round the exhibition looking at the objects and things. It's been really good. We've been finding out what we can about them, it's good.
>
> *LB*: It's like learning in a different way.

The same enthusiasm for observing the materials was reflected in extracts from the children's diaries (with the original spelling and punctuation preserved throughout):

> *CR*: I did a lot of good looking at the exhibition and thinking.

Most children viewed their activities as valuable though some doubts were expressed as seen in this child's diary extract:

> *AM*: It was quite good but I don't really see any point in looking at objects around the room its not learning us anything I mostly enjoyed it and I would like to carry on with it next week.

Some children began to make references to their observations after experience of working with them:

DW: We've been observing, like looking very carefully at the Garter snakes.

HP: You need to look carefully at things to get the information you need — observing — you observe things.

At first many observations were superficial, but when encouraged to do so, children used all their senses in making further observations, as revealed in the following diary extracts:

JP: We were all doing something different, looking and listening with our senses.

PD: The best bit was feeling them and smelling them.

Questions written boldly on card and placed strategically around the room acted as reminders and invitations to observe:

Does it have a special
    smell? — placed by a large piece of coal
What does it feel like? — placed by a wasps' 'paper palace'

Children's references to these questions revealed them as useful aids to observation and not at all interrogative:

KH: The questions give us clues what to do.

SS: Yes, they help us to work things out.

KH: Yes, if you put the answers together, you get a object, . . . sort of.

Later comments indicated that children felt that their observational skills had improved:

JH: We've learned how to observe better not just from books.

LB: I can observe better now, with care! You don't just have a quick look, a glance, you look properly and think. You use your senses but usually not taste, [laughs] — in case it's poisonous. You can find out more things by looking carefully.

The opportunity to assess the developing process skills arose when children were engaged in activities arising initially from the exhibition. Sometimes verbalizing questions on display seemed instrumental in encouraging the development of observational skills. For example, I asked 'Have you noticed any special features?' of one child seen watching stick insects on the bench. She later recorded:

SP: . . . I didn't know but they have not got any wings so they cannt fly. That is why they are walking on the bench.

Perhaps her previous observations had been hampered by a fear that the insects would fly away.

Games to encourage the identification of differences between exhibits were devised. They seemed popular, sharpened awareness and were not generally regarded as 'work':

> *SP*: We didn't do any work. We were playing games, odd man out and things like that.

The APU (1983) reported that children were less competent at observing similarities than differences. Experiences, which involved observing similarities were therefore incorporated into activities leading to attempts at pattern statementing:

> *Extract from classbook. October 1987*
>
> *LB*: All the exhibits were the same *because they were all parts of animals.*
> Most of these *were animals from the seaside.*
> A few of then *were big.*

This child had shown an ability to observe selectively using only some of the information available, albeit in simple form.

Some children were invited to sort out or classify the exhibits in the best way they could:

> *EH*: We put them into groups I did heavy, light, medium but it didn't work very well.
> *SM*: I did rough and smooth.

Some children found this a frustrating activity:

> *LP*: Sometimes it was a bit confusing knowing which 'fingy' to put it in.
> *Teacher*: 'Fingy?'
> *LP*: Group, category, you had to decide.

Other children were more confident:

> *SW*: We were sorting out the exhibition into groups. We made our own group up. I was putting once alive, never alive and alive. It worked OK. You can sort in different ways but our way was good.

This child could see that different groupings were produced by giving attention to different features.

The exhibition appeared successful in offering a variety of materials for manipulation and observation. Observational skills continued to be monitored in all subsequent topics using the schedule for progressive focusing already outlined.

There was much evidence to suggest that what children observe and how they interpret their observations in the context of most scientific activities depends largely upon the ideas they bring with them to their lessons. During the promotion of observation as a process skill, when children were working with the exhibition, some tried to identify those exhibits that were 'parts of animals'. This seemingly simple task raised all sorts of problems because of the ideas children already had about the concept 'animal' — 'Course we know what animals are, we did it in Middle Two'.

Typical ideas are illustrated by these extracts from children's recording:

AM: An animal is a two or four legged living creature.

HP: An animal is a creature that isn't human and has less than six legs, most animals have fur.

JH: Some people think insects are animals but their not and I don't know why, they all have a nose, and some have ears, some have tails and they all have a mouth.

The children's ideas of what constituted 'animalness' was restricted largely to land animals. Worms and spiders were regarded as insects but not thought to be animals, and neither were people. Perhaps the common use of animal statements (for example, 'no animals allowed') have had a narrowing effect on children's thinking.

Their old ideas appeared to obstruct their observational skills and experience was needed to re-assess their idea of the concept 'animal'. I felt it was important that the children's existing ideas were treated with respect and not scorned. The sorting and classifying activities not only served to develop process skills but also to enable the children to modify and adapt their original ideas, so as to give them more explanatory power. Further opportunity to work with the exhibits, reinforced by reference materials, enabled new emerging evidence to become personalized. Old ideas were modified and the children demonstrated a greater understanding of the concept animal.

Promoting Questioning

In promoting 'questioning' as a process skill the aim was to encourage children to raise their own questions of the kind that would lead to investigation. The pilot study had indicated children's questions in science were likely to be closely related to the way in which questions were handled by the teacher. They expressed a dislike of question and answer sessions:

CC: I don't like putting my hand up and answering questions. I don't like getting them wrong.

SG: You feel ashamed sometimes.

CC: I don't like putting my hand up even when I know most of the answers.

LH: You go red.

CC: People laugh at you.

LH: I don't like it when you 'pounce' on us.

An analysis of teacher-questions in one lesson was enlightening and quite disturbing. A table summarizing the analysis is shown in Figure 7.4. Of the seventeen questions asked, ten were either organization or management related and five required wordy answers relying on recall. All drew away from scientific problem-solving and none were invitations to investigate. The two which have been classified as 'productive' unintentionally sounded threatening rather than inviting.

Question Type	Number asked	Example
Organizational	7	Who are you working with?
Management	3	Why haven't you done your homework?
Recall	5	What did we say carbon was like?
'Productive'	2	Go have a look! What do they have in common?

Figure 7.4   Analysis of teacher-questions during one lesson

This analysis must not be regarded as truly representative of all lessons at that time, but did result in an increased awareness of questioning procedures. Subsequently a more conscious effort was made to stimulate productive activity and also to encourage children to raise all kinds of questions for themselves. A 'Let's see what we can do to understand it more' approach was attempted. The teaching skill involved is the ability to 'turn' the questions. As a result the need to establish an atmosphere of curiosity conducive to question-raising was highlighted and created initially through the exhibition.

As discussed earlier, questions accompanied the display hopefully to focus observations and to raise children's own questions.

These questions were of several kinds:

1 Those to *focus attention*:
  Did you notice . . . ?
  What happens if . . . ?
2 *Comparison* questions to encourage patterning statements:
  In how many ways are the exhibits similar?
3 Those involving counting or *measuring*:
  How many . . . ?
  Which is the heaviest . . . ?

Children's comments indicated they found the questions useful:

BW: The questions help you to look more.
SS: Sometimes they help you to think up your own questions.

However not everyone was impressed:

NS: Today we had to answer lots of hard questions.

Some activities were contrived to encourage children's questions of all kinds as this extract from a child's diary shows:
Diary Extract 4 October 1987

MB   Today we had to close our eyes and miss took round an object [teasel] for us to touch. You had to think of a question about it. KH asked what it was and so I asked if it was used for anything. In the end everybody asked a different question nearly.

Analysis of questions asked revealed that although some could be answered by direct observation and were factual:

Is it alive?
What colour is it?
Has it got teeth?

Others required reference to books:

What is it?
Is it a plant or an animal?

Some could lead to investigational work. Questions such as:

Is it as light as it feels?
Why is it light?

could be re-arranged into testable form.

At a later date questions were introduced to promote activity.

What happens if . . . ?

These questions seemed to be popular. They involved experimentation and always produced a result — for example, 'What happens if you drop a 1p coin into a trough full of water?'. This question caused great interest and enabled predictions to be made:

> *GH:*   It took 77 coins to make the water spill. J＿＿＿ was the nearest (14) but not much.

The activity raised spontaneous questions and suggestions for further experimentation:

> Why does it [water] bulge?
> What stops it spilling?
> Try £1 coins
> Drop it from higher
> Do it with the bath [tin bath in room]
> — a beaker!

These suggestions indicated that some children were beginning to see the relationships involved. Some went on to investigate surface area and surface tension.

Predictions were turned into questions to encourage the development of process skills. For example, 'Can you find ways to make the razor blade sink without touching it once it's floating?' (later amended to — without spilling the water!) produced floods initially and then purposeful work:

> *JH:*   . . . We thought it was easy. We dropped R＿＿＿'s pencil case on it. It worked and everything got wet and Miss was cross.
>
> *BW:*   We dropped some water on it with a pipette but it didn't always sink. When we put some Dreem [school detergent] on, it sank to the bottom and the skin got broken.

Learning through Discussion

Opportunities were provided where children had a chance to talk, argue and clarify their own ideas whilst trying to explain them to others:

> *DC:*   When we talked about it, it made our work make sense.

Some children argued in a negative way when given the opportunity to discuss. Others complained that no one listened to them and so strategies for encouraging a more positive atmosphere for discussion were devised, where listening and tolerance were applauded. The value of discussion became apparent to children and talking seemed to help create a flow of ideas and clarify thought:

> *RJ:*   It's better when you talk about it 'cos you sort out your ideas.
>
> *LB:*   Everyone has their own different opinions. Unless you discuss nobody else knows what you think.

During and after investigations groups exchanged ideas in 'reporting back' sessions. Some children found them helpful:

> *Teacher:*   Why did you change your mind?
>
> *AT:*   It was listening to everyone else giving their reports.
>
> *Teacher:*   How did that help?
>
> *NS:*   It helped you to think about what you were doing and if it was wrong.

Some however found these interactions distracting when taking place during investigations:

> *LB:*   What I don't like is sometimes we just get started and we know what we're doing and then you say, 'Everybody stop' and we have to stop and listen to what's going on. It gets on my nerves when we just want to get on.

It seemed more care was required in selecting appropriate times for these exchanges of ideas.

Whole class discussions were initially regarded as a motivating factor prior to investigations and as an aid to evaluation at the end of an investigation. The views of some children supported this intention:

> *KH:*   You can share your ideas.
>
> *JH:*   You can compare what you've got with others.

But discussions were not universally popular:

> *GN:*   You feel shamed if you're saying what you think and nobody agrees with you.
>
> *MB:*   It's the same people who do all the talking like R_____ and D_____ I just let 'em get on with it.
>
> *GH:*   I don't like having to say in front of all the class. If you sit at the back you've got to shout.

In order to foster participation, children were sometimes brought to one part of the room, usually near the front, but this was not always favoured:

> *KW*: I don't like it when you bring us round the front to discuss what we've done. You feel squashed and the boys don't sit still.

It seemed that such class discussions did not always kindle new interests and invite the testing of fresh ideas by opening up other avenues of discovery and exploration.

A few children saw talking as a possible alternative to writing, as revealed in these diary extracts:

> *CC*: I was glad we talked about it because we didn't have much time to write afterwards.
> *MD*: I have enjoyed it. We had a lot to do and we could talk. It was better than writing.

Other children who had difficulty in writing made their feelings known in their diaries:

> *SP*: Am not good at writing but we haven't done that much.
> *DW*: I don't lick riting I just lick ansering cwestons and torking about animals.

The pilot study showed that the children in that sample saw writing as the most frequently occurring method of recording activities. Little enthusiasm for writing was displayed and contradictions were apparent:

> *PT*: We do loads of writing after an experiment [pause]. Well, we don't do a lot really.
> *AB*: We have to do loads of writing; it's pretty obvious we have to.
> *JN*: We have to write it up or there'd be no point in doing the experiment.

Classbooks were not seen as useful instruments for recording and in some cases were regarded almost as a trap to 'catch children out'.

> *LG*: You mark what we've done and say what we've got wrong.

In the light of this, writing during the period of the main research was kept to a minimum, to avoid the tedium of 'writing up'. Wherever possible, other methods of recording, thought to be more appealing to children, were encouraged.

Throughout the analysis the importance of discussion in promoting the development of process skills was evident. Children's conversations, arguments and more formalized discussions seemed to play a vital role in helping to organize thoughts, recognize patterns and encourage further action.

The stages involved in planning an investigation are illustrated in the extracts from taped lessons below, where children were trying to find the hardest biscuit:

RM: . . . lay the biscuit on the table one at a time and 'whack' it with 'summat' and see how many 'whacks' it takes to break it.

The initial plan had been articulated briefly but no attention had been given to detail. Further thought resulted in the formulation of a general plan:

RM: We'll get some scrap paper on top of our best books and put the biscuit on top. We'll stand in the same position and 'whack' it.
TS: We'll 'whack' it with our lab books.
RM: The one that takes the most 'whacks' 'll be the hardest biscuit.

Here the children were beginning to give attention to detail. They had identified the variables to be changed and controlled but quantitative values had not been decided upon.

It seems to be worth planning at a general level, as it helps children to keep their problem in mind and to see how the separate parts of what they are doing relate to the whole investigation. Planning at a specific level resulted in the identification of biscuits to be tested and exactly how the tests would be administered:

CT: You do Ginger R_____, I'll do Rich Tea and T_____ you do Digestive.
RM: Hang on, we'll practice how hard we're going to 'whack' it. Right, go on then, do it!
CT: Shall I hold it [the book] like this or like this? [demonstrates]
RM/   Like this . . . [in agreement]
TS:

Other children who had been dropping their biscuits also debated the specifics:

AT: We change the biscuits to compare them and the height if we've got to. Start at 50 cm.
MA: Then if it doesn't work go up to 65, 70, 71, 72 up to 100.
AT: What? You need to keep going up the same.
MA: Yes.
AT: You can't do one from 50 and one from 70. The method's got to be the same.

Communication in the form of discussion was vital to this group's preparation. They had previously agreed on a general plan but not all members of the group had fully appreciated what was involved.

The idea of fair testing was also in evidence and of repeating tests for confirmation of results:

RM: Right, we'll do a fair test and we'll make it fairer this time — T_____ .

TS: We'll try it again and I'll keep my book flat. It went like that [demonstrates] and kind of stumbled over.

CT: We've all got to be the same if it's fair.

Some children who had begun their investigation without any prior planning then realized its value:

Teacher How did having a plan help?

AT: Because before we didn't think about the heights we just did it. We didn't really know what we were doing.

Some children were able to make judgments about what they had done:

AM: It was a reasonable plan. But we couldn't really make any decisions about the crumbs.

SP: We didn't know whether to count them or not.

AM: We tried to make it fair.

SP: But we didn't count 'em.

The following group changed tactics after a trial run indicated flaws in their plan:

SB: We thought we'd snap the biscuits to see which was hardest but it wasn't a good idea when we tried it.

MB: We snapped them and that was it. We didn't know what to do next.

SB: Now we're dropping the weight on these biscuits.

Teacher: How's the investigation going this time?

SB: It's better this time.

Later, the children were able to evaluate their work in a more systematic way. Children talked to each other constantly throughout investigations. Some discussions led to consideration of recordings:

JP: We didn't know how to write it down, 'cos if you said — so many pieces it could be any size and a pile of crumbs. So we decided to draw pictures. It's clearer.

Analysis of the children's talk showed that they included the notion of fair testing, fitness for purpose, objectivity, accuracy of recording and presenting, in their discussions and evaluations.

Practical Work and the Understanding of Theory

Many educators hold the view that practical experiences enhance and consolidate children's learning (see Isaacs, 1958; McLelland, 1970). The Cockcroft Report (DES, 1982) places great emphasis on children's practical involvement in mathematical problem solving, whilst the DES Report (1985) concerning science teaching states that:

> Science education should . . . give opportunities through practical work and otherwise for the acquisition of knowledge and understanding. (p. 4)

Such sentiments are also endorsed in the science statutory orders (DES, 1989). These are noble statements which tend to imply that practical work will inevitably result in increased knowledge and understanding. In the introduction to this chapter the question of whether practical work elucidates theory was raised and it was suggested that this cannot automatically be assumed. During the children's planning, execution and discussion of work on 'change of state' evidence was gained which seemed to support the suggestion that practical work does not necessarily elucidate theory:

Extract from Research Diary 22.3.88   9.55am

Activity — Can you find the fastest and safest way of changing water from its solid state to its liquid state? At what temperature does it seem to start changing?
Children are working very well in their groups. Lots of ideas are being explored. They seem to be using thermometers accurately. My assistance is hardly required.

It could have been assumed that this practical experience was enabling concepts relating to 'change in state' to be understood. However, the above extract shows how easily the teacher can be fooled into assuming that all is well if standing back from the situation. In fact the children were experiencing unknown problems which did not come to light until I engaged in conversations with groups and listened to their ideas in reporting back sessions. This example from a taped conversation is typical:

CW: The ice is melting at 47°C.
Teacher: Is that the temperature the ice starts to melt?
CW: Yes.
Teacher: Why do you think it's 47°C?

CW:	We put the ice cubes in this little beaker and stood it in hot water and it warmed up to 47°C.
Teacher:	Do you think ice won't melt until the temperature is 47°C?
CW:	It won't.
Teacher:	Go find out the air temperature in the playground and tell me if you think the playground should be covered with ice . . .

This conversation took place with another group engaged in a similar activity:

ST:	We've put ice cubes in our hands and blown on it and collected the drips as it melted.
Teacher:	What temperature does the ice cube start to melt?
ST:	We didn't do that bit.
DW:	We'll do it now.
Teacher:	How will you do it?
SL:	We'll see what temperature the water is.
CW:	And how hot my hands are.
Teacher:	Are they likely to be the same?
CW:	Yes 'cos our hands melted the ice cubes.

The children, of course, had experience of water and ice and wintry weather conditions but were not drawing upon these ideas to help them interpret their findings. They were not building upon their existing ideas, but were being misled by their observations and were misinterpreting the evidence. They needed to be guided carefully towards repeating and checking observations and measurements and to considering their interpretations.

In the follow-up activity where the children were challenged to change water from its liquid state to its gaseous state, some evidence obtained this time indicated that previous ideas 'blocked' observations rather like with the 'animal' work described earlier:

DM:	The water evaporates by steam.
MC:	We were boiling water. I already knew it evaporates. It goes to nothing, it disappears.
MB:	Water vapour is when cold water goes to boiling water.

Their observations were selective, being used only to reinforce existing ideas. Once this had been 'spotted' during ongoing analysis of fieldwork, it enabled provision to be made for ideas about water vapour and steam to be further explored.

Collaborative Work

The importance of communication as a means of fostering collaborative work, developing positive attitudes, improving the learning process and enabling teachers to monitor pupil progress is a common thread throughout the National Curriculum core subjects. This is illustrated by such DES (1989) statements as:

> Their learning is supported and extended throughout discussion with peers and adults. Through talk and informal writing they are able to make their ideas clearer to themselves as well as making them available for reflection, discussion and checking. (p. A.8)

The children had been encouraged to exchange ideas in a group situation from the beginning of their third year, in an attempt to promote communication skills. However, as mentioned, this was not without its unexpected problems. I had expected the children to welcome the opportunity of working with friends but at first working in friendship groups did not necessarily mean this would produce an ideal working situation. During September and October it was continually noted that some children in the sample simply could not or would not listen to the views of others. Their behaviour seemed reminiscent of the egocentric behaviour normally associated with much younger children (see Newson and Newson, 1976). They argued and contradicted each other in a hostile way and there was little evidence of teamwork. They paid 'lip service' to my pleas for them to show consideration to others:

> KW: I still don't think they're listening. They're quiet when you [I] talk and then when you stop they all start shouting their own idea, it's hopeless.

This child was right. Certain social skills, prerequisites for this kind of group work, seemed to be decidedly lacking. It seemed most important that all children were encouraged to take an active part in all aspects of group work in order that each child was involved in the necessary thinking, talking and doing and not assuming one role within the group.

I negotiated a plan of action with all the third year children. The guidelines were simple and given to each child on a printed sheet. They seemed to respond well to the formalization of the plan for group work which can be found on Figure 7.5. Several children made favourable comments, for example, 'Miss, this is a really good idea', from the girl who had previously declared group discussion as hopeless. Gradually over a period of time groups began to work more cooperatively together. The plan

When working as a member of a group remember

Everyone should be made to feel welcome within the group.
Everyone has the right to speak, so offer your point of view.
Everyone has the right to be heard, so listen to other people's ideas.
Everyone should have something worthwhile to do.
Everyone should take part in the decision-making process.
Everyone should share routine jobs.

Figure 7.5   Group Work

did not work immediately but was there as a constant reminder for those who required it.

The research revealed that the majority of children preferred working in groups because of the interaction involved and the confidence acquired:

> *KH:* It's better in groups — you can listen to your ideas and mix them together. You've got your friends' ideas as well.
>
> *JP:* If you don't like your friends' ideas you can either make it the same or go separate.
>
> *KH:* When you're in a small group it's more like a conversation.

Some children liked working in pairs, 'you don't fall out as much', 'you get more chance', 'there's not as many people to make a decision'. No one expressed a preference for working alone. 'I like it in a group but I'd rather work with a partner than alone.' Four was the number declared to be the optimum group size:

> *KH:* You can make two two's if you fall out — obvious!

From the range of responses it has been possible to produce a two-dimensional matrix representing pupil attitudes to class size. This can be found on Figure 7.6.

From the matrix, four categories of workers have emerged depending upon their attitudes to class size. These have been identified as 'workers', 'doers', 'doubters' and 'wasters' for the purposes of analysis and will be discussed briefly below.

Group A — 'Workers'

Children in this category made entirely positive statements irrespective of group size:

> *SS:* It's great 'cos you can do different activities and you can work with who you like.

Pupil attitudes

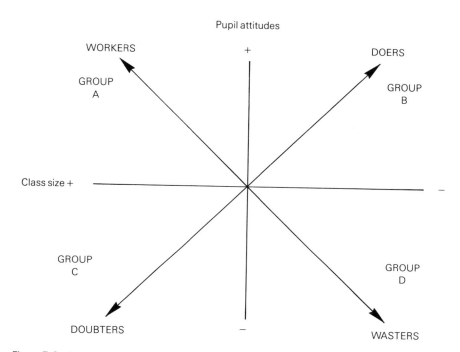

Figure 7.6   Matrix representing pupil attitudes in science to group size

Group B — 'Doers'

Children in this category made positive comments but punctuated these by references to class size:

> KW: I like what we do but it's better in half classes 'cos you can think better. You can work with your friends easier.

Most children in the sample appeared to belong within Group B.

Group C — 'Doubters'

In this category general doubts were expressed but references to group work were positive:

> DW: Sometimes I don't like it, it depends what we're doing. It's OK if you can work with your friends and you don't split us up.

Group D — 'Wasters'

No child in the sample appeared to belong in this category but references were made to other children in the classes who possibly did:

> *SP:* D_____ just messes about. He's not really interested. He just messed about with the cars. He didn't say anything much to join in.

There seem to be four distinct attitudes towards the organization of the science work. This has implications for my teaching within the present system of timetabling. The evidence seems to suggest that in full class situations, working in friendship groups is most likely to enable children to benefit from the curriculum offered.

Conclusion

It was felt that process skills would not develop in isolation or in passing, and therefore, content, though regarded as valuable in its own right, was used as the vehicle for the promotion of process skills. This necessitated the selection of suitably matched, wide ranging and challenging investigations to ensure the continuous provision of opportunities for children to become competent in the use of process skills. A number of pointers to guide practice when adopting this kind of strategy in science were identified from the research. These are summarized below.

1 Children's ideas were always taken seriously and where possible used as starting points for discussions or further investigations. The 'right' idea became regarded as the one that was most helpful to the child as far as could be judged from the evidence. It was recognized that without teacher guidance, existing ideas could result in relevant observations being overlooked or misinterpreted.

2 Children's preferences for working with friends, especially in full class situations, were accommodated after research suggested that children were more likely to benefit from the opportunities offered if they were working in friendship groups.

3 Question and answer sessions were disliked but children were encouraged to raise their own questions. A 'Let's see what we can do to understand it better' approach was developed instead of the previous possibly intimidating requests to 'find out'.

4 Children were also encouraged to make choices, pursue their own enquiries and discuss findings in relation to the evidence in order to provoke new ways of thinking and establish feelings of high self-esteem, increase motivation and create a productive working atmosphere.

5 The classroom organization effectively linked teacher and pupils together in establishing an environment in which process skills could be developed.

6 It was important that appropriate purposes for practical work and the forms that it took were carefully considered in order to avoid inefficient management of time, resources and pupil enthusiam.

7 In effect, my role became that of provider of opportunities and minimizer of constraints such as time, class size and space.

8 Gradually, over time, the children assumed a greater responsibility for managing their own group work in learning situations. Various strategies were introduced to foster a corporate identity, amongst them guidance with the management of group work, discussing planning and evaluating investigations.

Monitoring the development of process skills indicated that the provision of opportunities did not necessarily result in the development of skills, perhaps raising the notion of 'readiness'. Progress was not seen to be consistent, apparent regressions were observed and it is possible that important evidence was not revealed during the research process. It is my intention to continue to improve this approach in the future in light of the National Curriculum. Through the programmes of study, science in the National Curriculum will be open to a multitude of methods that will allow teachers the scope to develop skills and processes which reflect the needs of the individual.

References

ASSESSMENT OF PERFORMANCE UNIT (1983) *Science at Age 11*, Science Report for Teachers: **1**, London. HMSO.

ASSESSMENT OF PERFORMANCE UNIT (1984) *Science Assessment Framework Age 13 and 15*, Science Report for Teachers: **2**, London, HMSO.

BURGESS, M. (1984) *In the Field: An Introduction to Field Research*, London, Allen and Unwin Ltd.

CHAMBERS. D. W. (1983) 'Stereotypical images of the scientist', *Science Education*, **67**, pp. 255–65.

DEPARTMENT OF EDUCATION AND SCIENCE (1982) *Mathematics Counts, Report of the Committee of Inquiry into the Teaching of Mathematics in Schools*. chaired by Dr. W. H. Cockroft, London, HMSO.

DEPARTMENT OF EDUCATION AND SCIENCE (1983) *9–13 Middle Schools: An Illustrative Survey*, HMI Report, London, HMSO.

DEPARTMENT OF EDUCATION AND SCIENCE (1985) *Science 5–16: A Statement of Policy*, London, HMSO.

Virginia Winter

DEPARTMENT OF EDUCATION AND SCIENCE AND THE WELSH OFFICE (1989) *Science in the National Curriculum*, London, HMSO.

DONALDSON. M. (1978) *Children's Minds*, London, Fontana.

DRIVER, R. (1983) *The Pupil as Scientist?*, Milton Keynes, Open University Press.

HARLEN, W. (1987) *Teaching and Learning Primary Science*, London, Harper and Row.

HOPKINS, D. (1985) *A Teacher's Guide to Classroom Research*, Milton Keynes, Open University Press.

ISAACS, N. (1958) *Early Scientific Trends in Children*, London, National Froebel Foundation

McCLELLAND, G. (1970) 'Ausubel's theory of meaningful learning and its implications for primary science, in RICHARDS, C. and HOLFORD, D. (Eds.) *The Teaching of Primary Science: Policy into Practice*, Lewes, Falmer Press.

MARTIN, M.D. (1983) 'Recent trends in the nature of curriculum programmes and materials', in HARLEN. W. (Ed.) *New Trends in Primary School Education*, 1, pp. 55–67.

MILLAR, R. (1988) 'Teaching science processes: The pursuit of the impossible', *Physics Education*, 23, 3, pp. 156–9.

NATIONAL CURRICULUM COUNCIL (1989) *A Framework for the Primary Curriculum*, York, NCC.

NEWSON, J. and NEWSON, E. (1976) *Perspectives on School at Seven Years Old*, London, Unwin.

OSBORNE, R.J. and WITTROCK, M.C. (1983) 'Learning science: A generative process', *Science Education*, 4, pp. 489–508.

PATTON, M.Q. (1980) *Qualitative Evaluation Methods*, Beverley Hills, Sage Publications.

RAPER, G. and STRINGER, J. (1987) *Encouraging Primary Science*, London, Cassell Education.

ROSS, A.M. *et al.*, (1975), *The Curriculum in the Middle Years*, Schools Council Working Paper 55, London, Evans/Methuen.

SCREEN, P. (1986) 'The Warwick Process Science Project', *The School Science Review*, 68, 232, pp. 12–16

SPRADLEY, J.P. (1979) *The Ethnographic Interview*, New York. Holt, Rinehart and Winston.

THIER, H.D. (1973) 'Content and approaches of integrated science programs at the primary and secondary school levels', in RICHMOND, P.E. (Ed.) *New Trends in Integrated Science Teaching*, Vol.II, pp. 53–70.

WOODS, P. (1978) 'Relating to schoolwork: Some pupil perceptions', *Educational Review*, 30, 3, pp. 167–75.

WOODS, P. (1986) *Inside Schools: Ethnography in Educational Research*, London. Routledge and Kegan Paul.

WOOLNOUGH, B. and ALLSOP, T. (1985) *Practical Work in Science*, Cambridge University Education Series, Cambridge University Press.

Chapter eight

Culture and Behaviour:
A Study of Mirpuri Pakistani Infant Pupils

Avrille McCann

A childhood interest in other cultures matured during a twelve year sojourn in Handsworth, Birmingham and was focused on the Mirpuris when I studied English as a Second Language for a certificate at a local college prior to my appointment as home–school liaison teacher in my current school. At this school, 70 per cent of the pupils speak a language other than English at home and the majority of these are Mirpuri Muslims many of whom attend the town centre Sunni Mosque each evening to learn Koranic Arabic and Urdu. House calls form the main part of my brief as a Section 11 funded home–school liaison teacher, visiting new starters and sick children and initiating discussion with families whose children are experiencing difficulties socially or academically. My intention in the research reported here was to investigate the effects of the Mirpuri children's culture on their behaviour in school in order that I could improve my home–school liaison technique and hopefully also improve some of our school practices.

The research was based on observations of children's behaviour in school, home and mosque which were video-taped, noted and discussed with the children, their parents, teachers and other professionals and compared to staff perceptions in a similar school in Bradford, which I visited. Thirty-six families, a Mirpuri doctor and the Mosque Committee were interviewed. Twelve staff and seventy ten-year-old pupils from the adjoining junior school completed questionnaires and bilingual assistants from both schools clarified some findings for me.

Data fell into three discrete categories — those relating to the parents' own upbringing in rural West Pakistan and the effect that has on their own child care practices; the influence of daily classes at the Mosque, and, most pertinently for staff in multicultural schools, the interaction of the Mirpuri pupils with their peer group and teachers in school.

My special responsibility is to interpret the parents' needs to the school and the schools' requests to the parents in order to benefit particularly the children from other cultures. I also act as home-link for the special assessment and monitoring (SAM) register team. This highlights children who need extra care for medical, social or educational reasons. Researching the children's backgrounds in order to be more efficient in both these roles gave me evidence to support Tomlinson's (1983) assertion that:

> There is very little positive literature documenting factors in or out of school which might make for more success among minority children within the existing school system and there is no literature at all documenting particular factors within schools which might make for more effective education for children. (p. 4)

Bearing these comments in mind, I felt justified in presenting as a research question:

> How does the cultural background of the Pakistani Mirpuri child affect behaviour in school and how can staff be alerted to this?

It is this area of misunderstanding of cultural habits which I intended to explore in order to improve my own practice and to act as a source of information for members of staff and other agencies.

Lessons from the Literature

Before collecting data on the behaviour of our Punjabi speaking infants I took Evans' (1978) advice:

> Almost any piece of research should begin with a survey of the existing literature in order to find out and assemble what is known about a particular topic. (p. 15)

A close examination of a translation of the Koran seemed to be an obvious starting point for an understanding of Muslims. This clarified some areas — notably dietary laws, the position of women and a push factor for emigration itself found in Surah IV v. 97 in Pickthall's translation *The Glorious Koran*, where those persecuted for religion are told:

> ... the angels will say, 'Was not Allah's earth spacious that ye could have migrateth therein?' ... except the feeble among men and the women and children who are unable to devise a plan and are not shown a way.
> Who so migrateth for the cause of Allah, Allah wilt pardon them.

Research by Nath (1975), Khan (1979) and Harris (1986) confirmed comments by parents that Mirpuri immigration to this town began after Partition in 1947 when the educated Sikhs and Hindus returned to India leaving the Mirpuri area denuded of leadership. The completion of the Mangla Dam in 1964 and the consequent grants for resettlement gave financial incentive to emigrants who, in Nath's (1975) words:

> turned to Britain with its shortage of labour, the initial stimulus to the chain of migration being provided by pioneers from the villages who had served with the British armed forces in the second world war. (p. 27)

Teenagers are sent to the homeland, returning with cousins as marriage partners, thus expanding the extended families here. Our school had 25 per cent Punjabi speakers in 1975; a decade later the intake was 64 per cent; currently it is 68 per cent. Hence a study of such a large and growing percentage of our school's population would seem to be warranted.

A most fruitful source of written information on the Mirpuri culture has been Khan's (1979) work on migration and social stress, for which information was gleaned by the author during her doctoral research on Mirpuri villagers' lives both in Bradford and in Pakistan. She shows that the change in lifestyle and climate affect behaviour patterns. Many of the points she makes emphasize the need for staff in a multi-ethnic school to be alerted to the cultural aspects of the behaviour of the children in their care. Anwar's (1979) study of the problems of the Mirpuri immigrant in an industrial town also gave further insight into marriage customs and the role of relationships within the extended family.

Troyna and Ball (1986) researching in primary schools found that:

> ...teachers were often unfamiliar with the basic notions of multicultural education. It is not that teachers disapprove of attempts to formulate a policy on these issues for all schools. Much more that they have an over-simplified perception of what is required. (*Education Guardian*, 7.1.86)

An example of this would be the teacher who expressed surprise that the Muslim children knew about Jesus, unaware that Muslims, Christians and Jews all have biblical roots. Not only beliefs and practices but habits and body language patterns appropriate in Pakistan are often misunderstood here. For example, the appeasing smile, which is used under duress, is often misinterpreted as cheekiness — 'And even worse than kicking him is the fact that you're smiling about it' (teacher overheard speaking to a Mirpuri child). Such anomalies need to be demonstrated to staff dealing daily with children from other cultures. Tomlinson (1983) points out:

> Minority children do not simply derive a working class culture from their families and neighbourhood, they are also affected by the specific cultural and racial background of their families and by the way schools perceive and react to their racial and ethnic backgrounds. (p. 62)

Accommodation versus assimilation is an issue also explored by Tomlinson (1984). She feels that Asian parents are interested equally in the problems of achievement and in the school's acceptance of their cultural needs:

> Much of the continuing anxiety about schools on the part of Asian parents has derived from the persistent reluctance of schools genuinely to recognise and accept cultural diversity. Major sources of anxiety for Asian parents are mother-tongue and religious teaching, crucial aspects of cultural identity; dress and food, cultural symbols; single-sex education, PE and swimming for girls . . . crucial areas in relation to the place of women in Asian cultures. (p. 55)

As will be shown later in this chapter, there were many examples of such potential home/school conflicts identified in my research. However, before moving to a consideration of some of the substantive findings, I will say a little about the methodology adopted.

Methodology

The 39-place morning nursery and one of the three Year 2 classes (rising 7-year-olds) were studied for half a term each. The class was chosen because the teacher was a personal friend, appeared interested in the research and of the three teachers was the least nervous about the idea of having a video camera running in her classroom. Given that much of the focus of the research was on the behaviour patterns of Mirpuri children, I wanted to have access to as complete and reliable a record of such behaviour as possible. Thus I also sought permission from parents for their children to be videoed in home, school and the Mosque.

When used in the classroom, the video camera was erected in a corner to give the widest span of the room and directed through the window at playtimes. Occasionally I came in to focus it on a specific work group. The children performed for it when I was there, but appeared to be unaware of the fact that it ran in my absence. On those occasions when I was involved in classroom observation in addition to the camera, I was sometimes called out to sort out an emergency; this was part of my job and therefore took precedence over my research plans. Leaving a video camera running during my absence partly alleviated this problem.

The use of video proved to be a most effective means of eliciting further information from families after viewing their children's behaviour at school and at the Mosque. It gave staff an insight as to how their pupils spent their evenings too. Several visits to the Mosque were consequently planned for staff and pupils. The playground video highlighted several incidents which the head was then able to use as a visual aid for lessons on safe play.

Videoing in the dining room also sowed the seeds of an idea of making a video to show to parents to explain current practices in school. Staff were divided into small groups each of which devised a video script on an aspect of school life: road safety; the cloakroom; changing for PE; school dinners; reading and play. The teachers' centre provided camera and technician, and a bilingual assistant and I provided a voice-over in both Punjabi and English. These videos will be used at parent induction meetings and can be taken out on home visits to illustrate appropriate points to parents. As the 'stars' of these videos are the children and parents themselves, they should have a double impact which we hope will prove beneficial in explaining our school day to those who may have had a very different experience, or indeed no schooling at all.

In addition to the video, when observing in the nursery and classroom I used a battery operated hand tape recorder to note any pertinent reactions and this was also used to record my impressions immediately after interviews. Thirty-six semi-structured interviews were conducted in the children's homes and with children, teachers, doctor and auxiliaries in school.

Translators were avoided as past experience had shown that they were not averse to adding their own point of view to the interpretation, thus invalidating the data. Consequently, the Mirpuri families interviewed were selected because either mother or father spoke adequate English. Thus the data were skewed in favour of well established families and did not cover the views of the few households where no English was spoken.

Rather than provide here a résumé of all the findings, I will focus upon six aspects of the research which resulted directly in changes in school policy. These are leisure pursuits (including play and the use of books) and diet influenced by parents' upbringing; rote learning and rocking behaviour observed in the Mosque; and friendships and celebrations as observed from the school's perspective.

Leisure Pursuits

The generally high daytime temperatures in the Mirpuri area means that our parents, as children, played outdoors. Artificial toys were unnecessary where there was ample sand, mud and small streams and trees to climb. Some fathers mentioned learning to swim in the local canal. Live playmates were freely available among baby calves, goats and chicks, with donkey, bullock and camel carts to ride on and a peer group with which to play, closely supervised by the whole community. Taped comments by children during my classroom and home visits to sick pupils made reference to these animals, the well and rides on carts and tractors. The pre-school playgroup basic course handbook's description of the ideal form of natural play is almost a perfect mirror of the Mirpuri situation:

> Play is nature's way of preparing the young for adult life. Natural play for children includes throwing leaves into streams and stones into the sea, climbing trees, paddling in water, digging holes, playing with sand, clay and soil ... it means learning about animals at first hand, collecting eggs, watching the milking of cows, seeing new born lambs and helping to look after domestic pets. Through practical experience children come to understand size and shape, weight and balance, how to tackle problems, how to cope with their feelings and those of other people. (Nicholls, 1987, p. 2)

In industrial towns here, children are confined in small houses opening on to dangerous roads, with those in our area frequently having no garden at all. The few gardens that do exist open on to busy road routes from the town centre and therefore are not suitable for small children to play in.

Compared with indigenous children, whose parents would open cupboards packed with boxed games to add to the larger toys already apparent round their rooms, Mirpuri children's toys were usually restricted to, for example, a 'bat and ball' with which to play in the backyard (a rag ball and hand-made hockey stick being a traditional village toy). This paucity of toys has repercussions in the classroom. Children who are not used to playing with toys have a tendency to be very possessive, to secrete toys to their person to take home, to handle them very roughly and frequently to fight over favourite ones, all of which adds to the stress of the multicultural classroom. A recent case of petty theft involved a child hiding a packet of toilet tissues to take home to use as tracing paper, just one of many such incidents involving school apparatus. Longer nursery provision might help alleviate this problem.

Mirpuri parents often ask us not to send reading books home with their children as younger siblings tear them. The idea that they should train their toddlers to treat books with respect is difficult to put across. Unlike local born families, Mirpuri parents do not have a tradition of showing their offspring how to draw representations of houses, people, trees and animals. Hence, with a few exceptions, they come to nursery with no pencil skills and several of the 7-year-olds observed would have low scores on the Goodwin 'Draw a Man Test'. This accords with research by Taylor and Hegarty (1985) which 'shows that Asian infants continue to demonstrate lack of familiarity with such objects as books, pencils, scissors and toys and hence may have lower ability in manual dexterity and perceptual skills' (pp. 112–13).

Stories, rhymes and singing games are also notable by their absence. When asked, the only story that was recalled by one mother and by the wife of a Mirpuri doctor was the 'Hare and the Tortoise', which appears in the first Urdu primer used at the Mosque. No one could recall a rhyme or song other than the Mosque prayer chants, although traditional rhymes are sung at pre-wedding parties when the women dance around the bride. A notable exception to this was a father who explained the story behind his son's apparently Irish name, Shamus. It was so lucidly told that I was able to translate it into cartoon form and use it as a basis for a lesson in school, later passing it on to 'Storyline' for inclusion in their English/Urdu Pakistani storybook.

Griffiths, in a Birmingham survey, discovered that only one third of Pakistani mothers read stories, and only 16 per cent told stories, as contrary to the practice on the subcontinent they lacked the older family members to perform this traditional role (cited in Taylor and Hegarty, 1985, p. 105). This lack of evidence of a story-telling tradition was unexpected, as in an illiterate society one would have predicted a stronger emphasis on an oral tradition.

Amin (1984) reports a local coppersmith in Peshawar as attributing the decline of story-telling to the advent of TV:

> Long ago before TV and Radio, people came to Qizza Khawani —
> The Street of Story-tellers — even from Afghanistan to sit here and
> listen to stories. There have been story-tellers here for hundreds of
> years. But nowadays no one has time to listen to stories. All they
> want to do is sit in their houses and watch television. (p. 32)

A bilingual assistant who had returned from a visit to Pakistan explained that:

> the Cinema, which used to be very popular, has almost
> disappeared, but even the poorest homes have videos. Film

making is big business, people like their fantasy worlds when they can't have it in reality. Pakistani TV is only available in the early evening. After 9 pm it's English programmes and there is nothing on in the day.

Here, videos are found even in the poorest home and are often switched on even in the morning. Griffiths in his survey found that:

> 85 per cent of Pakistani babes and infants 'watched' TV for $6\frac{1}{2}$ hours a day. It seems TV is regarded by many as a status symbol and is often a continuous presence in the normal life of the household. (cited in Taylor and Hegarty, 1985, p. 111)

Most of our parents were brought up in villages where there was little opportunity for education and their lack of experience of schooling is often reflected in both their own and their children's behaviour. Among the families interviewed, eight mothers and two fathers had never been to school at all and others had only been for short periods. They would be taught to read in Urdu which is not their mother tongue. One father said he could read a little Urdu but was unable to write anything.

Anwar (1979) has pointed out that 'only those who stayed at school beyond primary level learn English' (p. 20). A newly arrived 17-year-old bride showed me her copybook. She had been practising turning English phrases into Urdu, but the English was quite archaic — 'My brother is a merchant' being the first example. Hill (1976) notes that 'the Pakistani educational system retains the bias towards higher education that was the residue of white-centred British colonial rule . . . the consequences of which being the illiteracy of the majority of the population' (p. 26), given the lack of funding of primary education. Thus, no one interviewed in my study said they could read Punjabi; one father said he had tried to learn it, but it was far more difficult than Urdu. There is no written form of the Mirpuri dialect.

Letters sent out in English and Urdu reach homes where parents are literate in neither language and where children are still struggling with very basic vocabulary. Schools, even in Bradford, do not yet seem to have come to terms with this and persist in informing parents in writing and expecting responses. One mother recently asked for help to fill in a free meals form which turned out to be a nomination form for school governors. I am frequently called on to help with form filling even by families with grown children educated here. DHSS forms and school free meals application forms are far too complex even for those with a minimal degree of literacy.

A recent attempt, however, to offer basic English classes to unemployed Asian fathers was only attended by three fathers, one of whom returned for a second lesson. The two women's classes, however, are well supported with about a dozen students each, though most of them come from outside our catchment area.

Lack of literacy in the home means that the elder children have no model on which to draw, no one to listen constructively while they read, no one to truly appreciate their efforts at writing or drawing. Few homes in the area, with the exception of the polytechnic students, have any books on display and the Mirpuris take no newspapers, magazines or comics. Some parents, however, did show me their children's Mosque Urdu Primer.

As a result of these findings, several initiatives were taken in school. A grant was obtained from the local community council in order to set up a toy and book library. This was initially set up in the Community Centre and parents were encouraged by their children to visit it after school. When the initial enthusiasm for this abated, a new approach was taken. The library was moved into the nursery and teachers asked to send a few children each week to borrow a toy and book to take home. The facility was then extended to nursery parents. A separate scheme was set up in the junior school as a behaviour incentive. Funding was supplied by weekly jumble sales and most toys purchased from car boot sales.

The multi-cultural librarian is now a frequent visitor telling stories in mother-tongue and encouraging parents to bring their children to the town library where there is a selection of books in dual languages. More mothers have been encouraged to join the already established English classes in the Community Centre. This pre-empted the Secretary of State for Education, Mr Kenneth Baker's, exhortation to Section 11 workers to encourage a greater uptake of English classes:

> The ethnic minority communities who come to live in our country add considerably to our society. They wish to be part of it. It is essential to make sure they master the English language. If they do not do that they cannot hope to compete equally. ('Gear funds to minorites', Sue Surkes, *Times Educational Supplement*, 10.3.89)

Diet

The villagers have brought their excellent dietary customs with them, enriching the local choice with samosas and pecora and a multitude of Asian vegetables and herbs available in the neighbourhood's shops. I was interested to find ample evidence of the agricultural background of the Mirpuri. Despite the lack of proper gardens in the area, several families have succeeded in growing traditional foods — such as spinach, coriander and salads — in the small patches between front window and main road. One raised bed, filmed on video, being within a few feet of a major crossroad, was so narrow that it was hidden from the view of the casual passer by, but it grew sufficient herbs to flavour curries through the Summer.

Vegetable and herb cultivation is the traditional occupation of most of our parents of the Milliyard or Jat castes. Perhaps we could utilize it in some way to encourage them to pass on their traditional skills to all our children — a herb stall labelled in English and Urdu prepared for our next festival? Many of our fathers are now unemployed — perhaps some could be encouraged to take up allotment gardening to improve both their own health through exercise and that of their families by improving their intake of fresh vegetables? Since the completion of this research the internal light well in the school has been developed as a mini garden with a rock pool and it is hoped that parents will be involved in supplying, tending and labelling plants.

Unfortunately, the sun rarely shines for long in England and so dependency on the sun for Vitamins C, D and E is ill-placed here and extra sources are required from fresh fruit and raw vegetables as opposed to overcooked curried ones, and from margarine instead of butter or ghee. Despite the appointment of the multicultural dietician and efforts by the School Meals' Service to provide acceptable diets, many families are unaware of the health dangers inherent in a deficient diet.

School meals provide the main dinner of the day for many children and yet the presentation, which is in a way alien to the culture of the majority of the children, means that for many months new starters do not eat much at all. 'My child is coming home hungry. What does she have for lunch?' was often asked. Several Mirpuri parents have queried the provision of meat for their Muslim children. They are not convinced by the term 'Halal' and have to be reassured that it is Pakistani meat from an authorized butcher. The Mirpuri word for such meat is 'Lal', Halal being an Urdu term meaning within the Law, though as all meat would be ritually slaughtered in a Muslim village, perhaps they would not be familiar with a special term for it. Some public relations work in this area was needed.

Mirpuris traditionally eat curry with chappattis, called roti, from tiny bowls and a shared basket, whilst seated on the ground or on bed settees. They do not use chairs or tables. Only three of the families visited possessed a high table and these were homes where the mother had been brought up in England and even here food was offered me on my knee, the tables and chairs appearing to be a status symbol.

Not only are infants expected to eat at a table for the first time in school but they are presented with half a dozen different dishes from which to choose and as many sweets. Another local school tackles the problem by inviting parents to join their children for the first few meals, but as so few of the mothers have been schooled here, this would surely be an even more traumatic experience for them than for their children.

The employment of a roti-making assistant would be the most obvious solution. Roti made from hard flour and water is cheaper, easier to make and more filling than chips, which used to be frequently served. There is a suggestion also, in the 'Commission for Racial Equality Guide to Asian Diets', that anaemia can be caused not only by lack of iron but by deficiency in Vitamin B12 for which an increased use of milk or yoghurt and fresh fruit is recommended and these are now offered as alternatives to sugary cakes or jellies and ice-cream.

Other alternatives now taken up by the cook were to provide more finger food — children were observed eating food wrapped in lettuce leaves in place of roti — and to train dinner nannies to respect children's right to eat food with their right hand as they are taught at home ('right hand for food, left hand for toilet'):

> The Prophet Mohammed (peace be upon him) asked us to eat with the right hand and to wash our hands before and after meals. It is better not to eat so much as to fill the stomach. The Prophet also asked us not to drink water and other soft drinks at one go, rather we should pause in between and it is better to have 3 pauses while having any lawful drink. (Sarwar, 1982, p. 182)

Although by 8 years of age most children can cope well with knives and forks, many infants were observed and videoed putting food in their mouths with a knife or holding the knife and fork in their hand and still managing to push food in with their fingers in an effort to accommodate to both home and school customs. Only one family had cutlery and that was 'never used'; another older brother educated here said 'It's all finger food at home, we don't need forks do we?'

A child care assistant was overheard saying 'It's funny how they all eat American style!' bringing home the fact that there is not an internationally correct way to eat and raising the question as to whether we have the right to insist on children accommodating to our chosen style at the expense of their own. 'Eating out' is not a Muslim custom and they are most likely to take their own style of lunch to the workplace rather than eat in a canteen, and so the argument that we are preparing them for adult life in this country may not hold. It is good to report that a Bengali and two Pakistani dinner nannies are now employed to help the children.

One of the more unfortunate adaptations to the British way of life has been a marked enthusiasm for sweets and coca cola, the latter being served with meals in many homes. Pakistani sweets served at weddings and other celebrations (*matei*) are intensely sticky and sugary but the children have also developed a taste for chocolate bars. Even at the nursery stage, their dental cavities can be observed and rotten stumps are not uncommon. Dental statistics show that 54.8 per cent of our pupils required treatment in January 1986, whereas only 35.5 per cent of children in a neighbouring area with no ethnic minority intake had cavities. However, most of our parents accepted the treatment, which is a positive indicator of our parental response to National Health provision.

A Mirpuri doctor explained the phenomenon of poor dental care by suggesting that first generation parents used local walnut twigs as teeth cleaning implements in the Mirpuri villages. Such twigs are not available here and parents have not yet got used to the idea of buying toothbrushes. Since discovering this, I have obtained a supply of cheap toothbrushes which I sell to nursery parents and carry into the homes. I have also initiated talks on Dental Hygiene and Diet for parent groups with the aid of the multi-cultural dietician and a Punjabi-speaking Environmental Health Officer.

Rote Learning and Rocking

In the Mosque, learning is by rote and the meaning is not taught in the early stages. This is in contrast to teaching techniques in school where children are encouraged to explore meanings and ask questions. The Bradford staff explained their understanding of Koranic learning as Arabic chanting being a sacred language tradition, the benefit derived from the reciting of a holy scripture and not from the meaning itself. A local equivalent in the near past would perhaps be the teaching of ecumenical Latin in Catholic schools, where a child of 7 might well be able to recite most of the Mass in Latin without knowing the meaning of individual phrases.

While reciting the Koran, children were observed rocking to and fro. When questioned about this, the chairman explained 'This is not taught behaviour but some of the children recite the Koran to a rhythm'. I noticed that one of the young male teachers was also rocking — teaching by example.

Rocking is a behaviour observable in school in listening and singing situations like assembly and storytime. It is frequently misinterpreted by staff: 'After a short while he loses interest and can be seen rocking to and fro' (SAM file comment). Because this teacher had not visited the Mosque, she had not made the connection between regular attendance — twelve hours a week at the Mosque — and the rocking habit. Far from being a distracted child, the rocking child is likely to be concentrating hard and showing evidence of devoutness or at least regular attendance at the Mosque. Another factor which might also have a bearing on this is that some mothers recite Urdu poetry at home and rock while doing so, thus providing a further model in the home itself. Although children can be seen rocking on the videos of assemblies and concerts, this behaviour trait has noticeably decreased in the past few years as it is discouraged now at the Mosque by young teachers who are also bilingual assistants in schools.

In the Mosque the Koran is learned by rote and recited in chanting fashion. Children bring this model into the classroom and therefore fail to hit the correct register when pronouncing English sentences. While taping a conversation between a group of children, I was under the impression that one boy was singing a Pakistani song. When I played it back it became obvious that he was chanting details of the piece of work we were doing — ♫ The man was getting on the bus ♫ . When the children have begun to make progress with their Koranic studies, they are allowed to study Urdu and take lessons on Thursdays and Fridays in this:

> Urdu is a phonetic language and once the alphabet is mastered it is possible for a young child to read fluently in a few weeks. (Nath, 1975, p. 89)

This phenomenon gives rise to false expectations on behalf of parents. Their children bring home an Urdu primer and read to them and yet their teachers will say that they are only making slow progress with reading in English. Most parents do not realize, being unable to read either language themselves, that English is so much more complicated to learn. Many parents will cite progress with Koran and Urdu classes as proof that their children are able students and are disappointed to find that they are not yet literate in English. Similarly, a headteacher is quoted by Nath (1975):

> Among the (reception) children we found immigrant parents expected too much of the children. They thought that they should be able to read English school notices and translate to their parents. (p. 130)

Some staff do not realize that by the age of 7 many of our Muslim pupils are coping with four different languages: Punjabi at home, English at school, Arabic for Koran reading and Urdu as their national tongue. At 12, these pupils will be expected to add French to that list. Although much is said in favour of bilingualism, there seems to be a very real danger that many of these children will be only semi-literate in several languages and completely illiterate in their mother tongue, which no-one is attempting to teach them to read or write. The Mother Tongue and Teaching Project Census showed that only 32 per cent of Asian pupils were said by their teachers to be fluent in English (cited in Taylor and Hegarty, 1985, p. 555).

In order to counteract misunderstandings about the Mosque several visits for staff have since been arranged. One teacher found it so interesting that she suggested taking the children to visit all the local places of worship and I was able to negotiate guided tours of the Mosque, Sikh Temple, Church of England, Methodist and Catholic Churches.

Friendships

A friendship sociogram based on a survey of an infant class of rising 7-year-olds showed that sex was the divisive factor, but revealed only two cross-cultural choices — the two extremely popular Punjabi-speaking girls being nominated reciprocally as friends by an English-speaking girl. Interestingly one of these Mirpuri girls has very little English. The only cross-cultural friendship between boys was not known about by the mother. She thought all Muslim boys went to the Mosque after school and did not have time to play. She seemed unaware of the fact that her son sometimes plays at his friend's home. Is it deliberately concealed by the child, aware of parental prejudice, or is the mother uninterested in his whereabouts during out of school hours? The second option seems more likely in that she reported his fear after a fire in a distant adventure playgound that he had visited with a friend.

These two boys live within five minutes' walk from each other close to the school and may well meet to play there in the evenings as the Mirpuri boy is one of the few Punjabi speakers who does not attend the Mosque. Mosque attendance does interfere with cross-cultural friendships as was recognized by this mother of a reception child:

> Who can my little boy play with after school? I am not prejudiced, would be quite happy for him to play with the neighbours' children but they are at the Mosque till 7 pm and even go on Saturday. Where do the other boys live?

There were only two other English-speaking boys in the class, both living at the far end of the catchment area over a major road. The possibility of him playing with peer group girls did not seem to have occurred to them.

Liddell (1985), studying free play in a nursery school also noted that only one cross-sex friendship was seen, though close bonds were made and children coped better than expected in a crowded environment, settling their own disputes often with dominance hierarchies where a female predominated. This has been observed through our school where in free play drama situations, a dominant girl becomes 'mother' and attempts to organize others. Dominant girls tend to be only or eldest children, though in one case she was the fifth child of nine, but the eldest girl in a Punjabi-speaking family.

Friends are greeted with a thumb-to-thumb sign noted in the nursery stage as being assimilated by the indigenous children. A finger-to-finger sign denotes enemy — Koti. The Mirpuri's doctor's wife explained that it could be translated as 'You're not welcome in my house'. An interesting exchange was noted between two 5-year-old boys making the friendship sign by the sand tray: 'You can't come to my house because you're Sikh and I can't come to your house 'cos I'm Muslim but we can be friends here.'

The practice of running sociograms has continued in the primary school and has proved useful in the SAM team discussion and for children requiring statements (a statement signed by a psychologist giving official recognition to a child's special needs). Having a series of sociograms about the same cohort may also provide future research material on the stability of cross-cultural and cross-sex friendships.

Celebrations

Birthdays are not traditionally celebrated by Mirpuris but as knowing one's date of birth is a necessary social skill here, the practice of announcing birthdays in assembly will continue, though this should be done sensitively so that a child who receives no card, present or acknowledgment at home is not embarrassed in public. Birthdays are celebrated in the nursery with a song and a card; in the infant assembly a tapping out the years game is played and a birthday badge is given, sometimes accompanied by questions about birthday festivities. For the Mirpuri child this might well be the first introduction to the idea. Discovering a child's date of birth is not always an easy exercise as it has no significance in Mirpuri culture and thus is only recorded on passports or long-lost birth certificates. No child is now admitted until one or other is produced for school records, as parents' recall of such dates has often been inaccurate. An HMI of Asian origin denounces the practice of public celebration:

> Being hauled out in front of everyone to celebrate a birthday you don't even know about is not on. We don't want it. (Singh, 1987)

However, after an initial shyness, most children not only take part but seem to enjoy wearing their birthday badges. Parents accept 'it's useful knowledge with all the form filling'.

Nevertheless, we must guard against raising unfounded expectations of birthday celebrations in homes where parents are not accustomed to acknowledging such occasions. When visiting a family I asked how old a child was. Mum (Mirpuri partly educated here) said: 'actually, it's his birthday today, he's six'. 'We'll go and buy him a card', replied Dad. Had that child been brought out in front of the assembly that morning and asked about his presents he would have been nonplussed. A child from one of the families being studied wrote a story about a birthday party where the girl was sad because it was her birthday and no one came.

Children with older siblings, however, have assimilated the birthday notion with enthusiasm. A morning off to go to town because it's a birthday, and they've persuaded mum they must have the latest shoes advertised on the television, is not an uncommon story. Families from the larger towns of Jhelum and Lahore do celebrate birthdays with a family party and cake, although this does not extend to card sending or inviting in peer group friends.

Indigenous families tend to the other extreme using the Community Centre and inviting all friends and off-spring to celebrate a birthday with party-fare and gifts. Most indigenous 7-year-old children knew their birthdays; only a few of the Punjabi-speaking children did and very few of their parents can give dates verbatim. However, this does seem to be one aspect of culture which the children will happily take home from school.

Birthdays are heralded weekly but other celebrations also gave cause for concern. The two Eids recognized by 60 per cent of our children were celebrated with a card and a drama, to which parents were invited. Celebrations took an hour at the most and were omitted when Eid fell during a holiday, whereas Christmas and Easter, which always fall in holidays, were celebrated and had a build-up over weeks. Christmas involved a complete change of wall decoration (stories about Santa) and the making of hats, gifts, calendars and decorations.

Children's expectations, as with birthday assemblies, were unrealistically raised during pre-Christmas preparations, although more than half of our pupils do not usually receive gifts at Christmas:

'Did you have a nice Christmas?'

No, the Christmas Father didn't come to our house' (6-year-old girl).

When confronted with this a perplexed teacher responded 'Well, we've got to do it haven't we, it's expected of us'.

The scenario has changed since my research was completed. Both Eid and Christmas are still celebrated with a drama but, for each, parents are invited to bring in a shared feast and they do so with great enthusiasm, so that Asians and English taste each other's party foods. The run up to Christmas has been scaled down and does not now start until December. Classroom wall decorations and friezes have seasonal, rather than religious themes, and festivals of light are used as a cross-curricular topic in the Autumn term.

Conclusion

The cultural background of the child affects behaviour in school to such an extent that some study of it would seem to be a necessity for any staff working in a school with an ethnic minority intake:

> Relationships between homes and schools are not a minor issue,
> they are crucial to the success of a multi-cultural society.
> (Tomlinson, 1984, p. 123)

The single most important change that has been brought about by this research is that the head now sees the importance of home visiting for all staff. She has timetabled herself to cover each class in turn in order that class teachers can accompany the home–school liaison teacher to the homes of those children in their class who are giving most cause for concern. This establishes a personal relationship with the families and allows the teacher an insight into a lifestyle which is markedly different from her own:

> Schools should encourage teachers to see home visiting as an
> integral part of their pastoral responsibilities. (Rampton
> Committee, 1981, DHS Report, p. 80)

New INSET and LEATGS training allowances might be used to finance some staff on Teaching English as a Second Language courses which also detail ethnic minority backgrounds. Alternatively, funding could be used to invite in a lecturer from such a course to pinpoint language anomalies appropriate to our present intake. Teaching materials as well as books could be checked for inappropriate materials or assumptions. A visiting ethnic minority lecturer speaking on 'Bi-cognitive Education' suggested finding common ground on which to base apparatus. An example he gave was cups and saucers. He obviously has not been in a Mirpuri home, because saucers are not used — neither are kettles, teapots nor cutlery. Hence neither reading books nor listening to middle-class experts will fulfil the obligation to find out about our own children's backgrounds and this can only realistically be done by visiting several homes and sharing a meal and joining in some celebrations.

Observing families in depth for the purposes of this research has improved my own understanding of our pupils and made me a more effective link between school and home, heightening my awareness of those issues which need addressing in our community-based parent classes. Improved technical skills, particularly with the videoing, have opened up new avenues of communication for the school.

The headteacher of Cabot Primary School in Bristol is quoted in Twitchin and Demuth (1981) as expressing the opinion that:

> A good school is responsive to its Community. However efficient teaching might be, skill and time must also be given to this. It is part of the Head's job to respond to the needs of the Community as they see it. The Head may lose in dictatorial powers but will gain in educational significance. (p. 30)

In supporting this MA research into the culture of the Mirpuri child, and offering the opportunity at several staff meetings to discuss the findings, the head has enabled the staff to understand better our majority group and to improve communications with them. A cognitive map made as a plan for the writing of the chapter on Mirpur in my MA thesis was enlarged on to a large sheet of card and further elaborated by highlighting in different colours facts, issues and possible areas for future action. This was left on display and was used as a visual aid during discussion at staff meetings.

Some staff made copies for further reference and others requested to read the original thesis. Visitors to the staffroom asked questions about it, and the school psychologist admitted that 'he'd been meaning to do something like it for a while', and asked for a copy. A multicultural teacher suggested a talk to all E2L teachers as she felt it put things in perspective and alleviated prejudices. Such comments have made the effort worthwhile and justified the time spent researching the effects of culture on behaviour.

References

AMIN, M. (1984) *We Live in Pakistan*, Hove, Wayland.
ANWAR, M. (1979) *Myth of Return: Pakistanis in Britain*, London, Heinemann.
EVANS, K. M. (1978) *Small Scale Research*, revised edn., Slough, NFER.

HARRIS, J. (1986) *Subject Choice and the Transition from School to Work. Asian Pupils Survey; Parents' Survey*, Research and Intelligence Unit publication, Cleveland.

HILL, D. (1976) *Teaching in Multiracial Schools*, London, Methuen.

KHAN, V. S. (Ed.) (1979) *Minority Families in Britain: Support and Stress*, London, Methuen.

LIDDELL, C. (1985) 'Free play in a high density setting, (Pretoria)'. Paper given at British Psychological Society Conference, Swansea.

NATH, K. K. (1975) 'Problems of Indian and Pakistani Immigrants in the Educational System of their Host Country'. Unpublished MA, University of Hull.

NICHOLLS, R. (1987) *Play at Home for Under Fives*, Cleveland, Pre-School Playgroup Association.

PICKTHALL, M. M. (1985) *The Meaning of the Glorious Koran*, Delhi, Taj Company.

RAMPTON, A. (1981) *West Indian Children in our Schools*, London, HMSO.

SARWAR, G. (1982) *Islam, Beliefs and Teaching*, London, Muslim Educational Trust.

SINGH, B. R. (1987) 'Bi-Cognitive Education', Talk given at a Cleveland multicultural centre.

SURKES, S. (1989) 'Gear funds to minorities', *Times Educational Supplement*, 10.3.89.

TAYLOR, M. J. and HEGARTY, S. (1985) *The Best of Both Worlds? A Review of Research into the Education of Pupils of South Asian Origin*, Windsor, NFER Nelson.

TOMLINSON, S. (1983) *Ethnic Minorities in British Schools: A Review of the Literature, 1960–82*, London, Heinemann.

TOMLINSON, S. (1984) *Home and School in Multicultural Britain* London, Batsford Academic.

TROYNA, B. and BALL, W. (1986) Views from the chalk face: school responses to an LEA's policy on multicultural education. Paper from Centre for Research on Ethnic Relations, University of Warwick, reviewed in *Education Guardian*, 7.1.86.

TWITCHIN, J. and DEMUTH, C. (1981) *Multicultural Education: Views from the Classroom*, London, BBC Publications.

Chapter nine

Towards a Policy of Equal Opportunities through Research

Jenny Vickers

Developing a meaningful Equal Opportunities Policy in an educational establishment can be a daunting, often frustrating, process for the person with designated responsibility. I propose in this chapter to explain how, through practitioner research, I addressed the issue by involving the people whom the eventual policy would represent. I will outline how I came to be involved in such a venture, highlight the issues to emerge and develop specifically the role of the mother and the influence of the community in creating an effective policy. In conclusion, I will offer a framework which could provide a useful way forward for teachers introducing or evaluating an Equal Opportunities Policy within their own school.

Reflecting on the research I carried out from my present position as headteacher of a school in a very similar area, I am acutely aware of the significant effect the whole process has had and is still having on me and in particular on my role as a policy maker in times of rapid, far-reaching change.

I was appointed as deputy head to Reed School in 1983. The area has an historical tradition of severe social problems and has in recent years become renowned as the victim of high unemployment, domestic difficulties and petty crime. Before going to work at the school, which is in the centre of its local community, I had many preconceived ideas about the function of education in such an area, but it was not until I had been there for some time that I appreciated the extent of the impact which the community identity and mores have on staff, children and parents. The expectations and assumptions of all concerned are greatly affected by the situation and to ignore it would be to undermine the influence it has on the educational process of the participants involved.

I was given, as part of my job specification, a directive to respond to from the Education Committee. They stipulated that every educational establishment in the county must produce and implement an Equal Opportunities Policy. Schools were specifically asked to concentrate on looking at the equal opportunities for girls and boys by assessing the constraints of gender. Discrimination and lack of opportunities for particular groups, such as ethnic minorities, disadvantaged social classes and children from rural areas, were to be considered at a later date.

My initial reaction was to base a policy for Reed School on my own experience and perspective, reinforced by pertinent background reading. I did not need much discussion with colleagues or reconsideration of my motives to recognize that such a document would merely be an academic response. It would also be totally meaningless to the very people it was supposed to represent and whose opportunities it was intended to improve. The alternative was to tread a path very new to me and research the issues with all relevant parties.

I was given tremendous support in making this feasible when I enrolled as a part-time MA student on the first outstation which the University of York ran at the local Middlesbrough Education Development Centre. In addition to providing the necessary information on research design and data gathering techniques, it gave me access to teachers involved in similar work and to the expertise of academic staff.

Planning the Research

I considered what breadth of investigation was necessary before a relevant policy could be formulated. The temptation was for me to decide the issues and then narrow their scope down to the educational arena. After discussion with some other members of staff, it was felt that to restrict the parameters in the early stages of investigation would probably result in a very school-centred policy. What was needed was consideration of all aspects of gender within school and the community. To be totally school orientated would eliminate any chance of gaining an insight into the thinking of the women on the estate and an understanding of the traditional mores which had socialized them into the acceptance of, or resistance to, their apparent role.

A group of staff formed a working party to discuss general aspects of equal opportunities in school. They acted as a monitoring body throughout my study in an effort to ensure that what I was doing was relevant to the participants in particular and to the school in general. I knew that any contribution made by the mothers of the pupils could prove of great value. I was in no doubt about their strength and spheres of influence, not only in the home, but in the community. Connell *et al.* (1982) argue that:

It is not a question of one gender pattern in a school and another in a work place, all independent of each other. They are related: they mesh with each other to make an overall pattern, one of the most general and powerful structures in our society. (p. 72)

One cannot deny that the influences of school are strong on some children, but undoubtedly the predominant influence is the family. Having accepted the value of including mothers in my research, I next gave consideration to fathers. I had met very few of them but felt I knew their 'type' from information given to me by mothers and children on the role of the man or men in the family unit. I was aware that my impressions of a 'time-lock', with men clinging desperately to their identity as breadwinner, disciplinarian, drinker, free-agent and head of household, was based more on my prejudiced view than on real evidence. While recognizing the need to involve them at some stage in the development of an Equal Opportunities Policy or at least in its sphere of influence, I did not feel sufficiently confident to include them during the initial process of data collection.

Staff were obviously going to be crucial to the development of the policy and much of its implementation and eventual influence would depend on their attitude towards it. If they did not see it as important and want to participate in its formulation, then its chances of having even a limited effect would be almost nil. Many staff passed comment on their lack of more than a superficial knowledge of the subject. Some voiced concern about the quality of the contribution which they could make, but all said, in various ways, that they thought it was essential to raise and investigate the issues. The commitment, energy and creative thinking of the majority of staff, in various facets of the school's development, encouraged me to believe they would aim to generate the necessary force needed, not just to formulate and implement the policy, but to extend its area of influence beyond the school's walls.

During the thinking and planning stages of my study, I became very concerned with how the girls in the school viewed their gender. I felt it was necessary to investigate whether or not it was, in fact, something the girls thought about, and if so, what their thoughts and feelings were. I was particularly interested in how they viewed their relationships with males in the immediate family circle and in their general day-to-day life. I also felt that it was important to discover if my assumptions about the influence of the family on sex-stereotyping were on target. I decided that girls in the upper rather than the lower part of the school would probably be the most suitable, as I was looking for participation through discussion rather than observation. I considered that 11-year-old girls, due to transfer to comprehensive school, would have the ability to articulate their thoughts, ideas and experiences relating to sexism. Acknowledging the important contribution girls could make to my research, I then had to give consideration to the inclusion of boys. I decided that if I failed to consider the thoughts, feelings and influences of boys, who, after all, were probably going to have to change their perception of gender roles, if the Equal Opportunities Policy was to be effective, I would lose a very valuable perspective. Accepting that 11-year-old girls were an appropriate age group, I decided, for similar reasons, to select the same age boys. If the policy was to be meaningful, recognition had to be given in the early stages to the very different levels of awareness and greatly varying degrees of interest in the issue. I needed, therefore, to find out just where people stood in their attitude towards sexism and its effect, if any, on their lives.

In formulating guidelines as a structure for the methodological aspects of the research, I was very conscious of the need to gain detailed information on attitudes and values through an appropriate technique of data collection. I considered the most suitable to be an in-depth case-study approach. Cohen and Manion (1980) describe it as follows:

> The case study researcher quickly observes the characteristics of an individual unit — a child, a clique, a class, a school or community. The purpose of such observation is to probe deeply, to analyse intensively the multi-various phenomena that constitute the life-cycle of the unit, with a view to establishing generalizations about the wider population to which that unit belongs. (p. 99)

Ways of gaining data which appeared most appropriate were through the use of questionnaires or interviews. I quickly rejected the idea of any form of questionnaires, acknowledging the reluctance of mothers to fill in a form of any kind and understanding the barriers such a format would create. When considering the possibility of using interviewing, I was conscious of the considerable amount of time it would take both to interview and transcribe. The difficulties of keeping on target could also be a problem and there was a danger of unduly influencing the issues for discussion. The possibility of inhibiting some participants because of my position in school was also a consideration. However, I felt that the advantages made such a method the most pertinent. Oracy is the mode most natural to all participants and through a series of wide-ranging questions the opportunity could be provided to elicit valuable data in a relaxed, non-threatening situation. Through this interpersonal encounter, people disclosed aspects of thoughts, feelings and values which would never have emerged in a more formal situation. The choice of method was justified by the valuable data of a very personal nature which I received. I would certainly never have designed a questionnaire to broach such sensitive areas for fear of infringing privacy.

Purposive sampling appeared the most appropriate to ensure that the sample involved would reflect the views held within the school and community population. The following categories were representative: a single parent, a family receiving support from one or more external agencies, a stable family unit, all ability ranges and emotional/behavioural difficulties. When considering mothers for inclusion, the same specific categories with the addition of those supportive of or anti school were used. In order to eliminate bias from me, the class teachers used the criteria to select a sample of pupils and mothers.

The constraint of time limited the number of participants I could interview. It was only through the goodwill of staff agreeing to give me time out of school that enabled me to interview them all. I was able to interview a 25 per cent sample of the sixty pupils in the 11-year-old age group and sixteen representing 4 per cent of the mothers from the whole age range on the school roll. In addition to these in-depth interviews, a considerable amount of additional information was gained from mothers in casual conversation when they heard about my interest in the gender issue.

The framework, which I set in preparation for the interviews, served as a useful mechanism throughout. A choice of venue was offered to all participants to ensure they felt at their ease in the setting. Questions were simple and clearly defined carrying out interviews as far as possible in blocks to aid continuity. All interviews were held at a time which would offer the minimum constraints allowing for a period of note-taking immediately afterwards. A tone and atmosphere was created to give the interviewee an opportunity to set the pace.

The first group with whom I had discussions were the pupils. The starting point was a brief talk on the meaning of equal opportunities and the possible implications of a school policy for children and adults in the school and community. Literature and posters from the Equal Opportunities Commission stimulated discussion leading to an explanation of how they could help by giving information which could assist in changing issues relating to gender with which they were dissatisfied. All participants entered with confidence into the excercise. It did, however, need considerable input from me to help keep discussions on target whilst being constantly aware of guarding against using my position to direct responses to specific areas. On analysis of the data, the content of those who posed most supplementary questions were often less relevant than those who addressed the issues in quite simple terms.

Interviewing staff proved easier in many ways and more difficult in others. All knew of my interest in equal opportunities, not only in education, but also its wider ramifications in society. This made me handle the interviews more sensitively, trying to keep on a low-key and remain an impartial interviewer, whilst recognizing that they were carrying this knowledge with them and were probably affected by it to some degree. The group of interviews which I anticipated presenting the most problems were those with mothers. This was probably because of my lack of confidence and experience in this area. Many of the wide range of difficulties predicted did not in fact arise. Lack of inhibition by people I knew only superficially in answering questions of a personal nature helped considerably. Their incisive and detailed contributions were of tremendous value to the whole project.

On analysis of the data from all participants the following categories emerged as the most significant for further examination: the importance of the socialization process on sex-stereotyping; gender relationships and sexism; the role of self-image and identity; the effect of gender in the lives of pupils, staff and mothers; the influence of the traditions and expectations of Reed community and all participants (see Vickers, 1986). Although most of the data received provided fascinating insight into the influences which determine attitudes towards sexism, it is impossible, in one chapter, to examine all my findings in depth. Whilst acknowledging the significance of the contributions made by pupils and staff, it was the potency of that which I received from mothers which illustrated for me the vital role which they play in perpetuating gender identity often against their will. Consequently in this chapter I intend to concentrate on the significance of the formulating influences on mothers' lives and how, in turn, they contribute to the socialization process of their children, setting this in the context of home, school and community.

Socialization and Self-Image

In this era of awareness of sexism and its influences, people are reluctant to acknowledge any responsibility for initiating or perpetuating stereotyped gender identity or behaviour in children. In discussion with teachers, they tended to lay the blame firmly with the working-class tradition of male supremacy which they thought dominated homes on the Reed Estate. Mothers felt that they were preparing their children to fit into the role expected of them by the community in which they lived and would grow up. Children, by the age of 11, appeared to have rapidly accepted their gender identity and the constraints which it placed on them. Both staff and mothers made many comments on biological differences. Some thought that this was of far more significance than any socialisation process could be. Deem (1978) suggests that this is not so:

Sexism and sex-stereotyping of roles have been shown by many anthropological studies to vary in their context from one society to another which suggests that cultural factors in behaviour and thought do override biological factors. (p. 26)

All the mothers interviewed, whilst accepting that socialization did have some influence on children's gender identity and sex-stereotyping, felt that the pre-school and primary years were not very important in this process. The majority found it perfectly normal that young girls and boys were treated differently by their parents and several mentioned that they thought it would be more unnatural to treat them the same. Mothers spoke extensively about their childhood and youth and, although not actually saying this had been an unhappy period, most dwelt on what they saw as milestones in these formative years which had had a scarring rather than a positive developmental influence. It appears to have been during these years when most started to be aware of differing expectations of the males and females in the family at school and in the community. Many comments were made indicating that the identity assigned to them was based on gender rather than personality, ability, age or position in the family. Acceptance, yet resentment of this, appeared to prevail. The amount of heavy responsibility taken on at a remarkably early age was seen by the majority of mothers as having a negative rather than good influence on the development of their self-image. Although all spoke in a rational way about the reasons for having to shoulder so much responsibility, the emotional factors surrounding such circumstances had obviously had a devastating affect. The most commonly mentioned were the death of a parent, ill health or nervous stability of a parent, absence from the home of one or both parents for a variety of reasons and major financial difficulties necessitating their involvement in pawning, borrowing or working illegally to help ease the domestic pressures. All who spoke about such circumstances said that they had to take a leading role in keeping the family together because they were the only girl at home or the eldest girl in the family. They did not appear to consider this anything but natural even when older or more able or healthier males were in the family. They said they would have found it difficult to understand if they, as an available female, had not been expected to take on the role of home-maker and all which that entails:

I was 12 when my mother died and I just had to take over. My dad was working and I was the eldest girl. We didn't want to break the family up so I just got on with it. When I look back, I have never known what it is like not to have family worries. I never had a childhood or any youth.

Throughout interviews with mothers, staff and pupils, I was aware of the importance attached by them to self-image and how they thought their own had developed. Almost all those who participated made some significant comment and several made it the basis of the interview. It was not until I analyzed the data that I appreciated the extent of the concern about having a positive or negative self-image and the effect which this was having on day-to-day life. Every facet of functioning, relationships, aspirations, health, status and ability to cope with the complexity of demands to be dealt with, was seen to be influenced. Frequent references were made to the significance of gender and both adults and children saw it as a vital force to the process of developing a self-image.

The institutions of education had a very obvious influence on all participants. Most mothers referred to schools more as systems, establishments or a symbol of authority than an educational process in which they had any real participation. All felt some regret that they had left school without any certificates. Although not blaming the school entirely, they felt that it had provided them with little of relevance. Some acknowledged that poor attendance and a negative or anti attitude by them had been a major factor in their social life. Most, however, felt bitterness and resentment against a system which was loaded against them and their ilk. They were in no doubt that this had had a long-term effect on their self-image and some felt that they had never really recovered from the poor start in life which education had given them. Mothers were very concerned that they should appear strong, caring and understanding to their children but nearly all said that they could not really live up to this image which disappointed them and undermined their confidence. In some cases, it had had quite a devastating effect creating physical and mental health problems. The worst cases of confidence crisis appeared to be in homes where the mother felt isolated with her burden of responsibilities having either no man or one who, instead of offering support, made further demands on her.

The Role of the Mother

The major influence on any woman's approach to motherhood is usually the relationship she has had with her own mother and her perception of her mother's success or lack of it as mother to the family she has developed and grown up in. This was certainly evident in my discussions with all the mothers I interviewed. The most discussed area of contention by daughters about mothers centred around the lack of support for them through schooling and the presumption that they would be satisfied with the same lifestyle as their mothers. Even those who felt that they had had a good relationship with their mother resented their lack of aspirations for them and thought that, in some ways, it had impeded their development as women. The majority spoke lovingly of the valued support given them by their mothers, and described this as a response to a crisis, a haven from disaster. All interviewed accepted that their relationship with their own mother did have a direct effect on relationships with their children. Some voiced regret at the influence, others valued it, but all agreed that it was a factor which could not be ignored.

The most positive emotional and optimistic comment came from mothers discussing their own motherhood. Nobody saw it in glamorized terms; in fact, many spoke of periods of great self-doubt, financial hardship, insecurity and despair but there was evidence of a conviction that despite difficulties this role was their most fulfilling:

> I do wish at times I hadn't started a family so young. I had three kids by the time I was 20 which was stupid. I wouldn't be without them though. It's great now. They are getting up a bit. I really enjoy them now.

Comments made about motherhood were frequently bound up with perceptions of accepted behaviour and responsibilities assigned to the female gender. There was no evidence of resentment that so much was expected under difficult circumstances of the mother of the family. It appeared that it was often a mother herself who willingly took on more and more, either to prove herself, or because she had reason to assume that if she did not, nobody else would and the family would suffer. The need to be a constant figure in the lives of their children was particularly felt by single parents, but even those from a stable family unit expressed the conviction that they, at the centre of the home, should always be available to their children.

Analysis of the data showed many areas of conflict experienced by mothers who often felt that they were trying to be the perfect mother and adequately meet the very differing demands of several children and a man. The need to be constantly making decisions and managing difficult domestic affairs with little or no support took its toll. Dependence on tranquillizers, bouts of depression, nervous disorders and ill health were discussed by many of the mothers. Even those who themselves did not express concern in this area spoke of women close to them who were having serious problems.

When asked about how they considered their quality of life, all said it was not something they really thought about, because they either did not have the time or thought it best not to dwell on such matters in case it provoked depression. Lack of aspirations and ambitions for themselves made those which they had for their children particularly strong:

> I desparately want my children to do well. As long as the kids end up with good jobs, I will be happy. I don't want much for myself but I am determined my kids will get all the chances I didn't have.

Such comments were typical of many, made with great feeling. When asked about the relationship they had with their children, perceptive statements were made about the role of gender in the complexity of feelings and attitudes. Some said that they had always been aware of this, whereas others admitted never considering it until that day.

Parental Expectations

When considering in detail the socialization influences of the home and the community, it should not really be surprising that, by the time children are admitted to nursery school, sexism underlies behaviour, play, attitudes and relationships. However, had comments by staff showed that, even though they had anticipated it, they were still shocked by its extreme manifestations in the 3-year-olds. When observing children at play, nursery staff saw evidence of very strong sex-stereotyping. This is probably why all the staff, but especially those involved with younger children, recognize the import-ance of the early years of socialization. Without some positive intervention to show alternative models of behaviour, by the time the child gets into full-time education, it appeared almost impossible to promote or effect change. Hodgeon (1984) found in her research that during the time children spend in the nursery they are learning a great deal about the attitudes of such an institution towards their gender:

1 Girls are learning that schooling, while interesting, is something that is really for boys.
2 Boys are learning that the adults' attention and careful rationalization are for them.
3 If boys are actually slower in language acquisition, they are catching up fast in the nursery years. Their school performance at 3 and 4 is in general as good as that of girls. Adults are compensating too much. (p. 38)

In interviews with pupils of 11, it was evident that they were already aware of the constraints placed on them by their families' view of them because of their gender. Comments from girls such as 'I always have to do the washing up, our Garry never does', and 'I'm not allowed out at nights but Dad lets Steven go where he wants, when he wants' were typical. Several boys spoke with great sensitivity and perception about the mould they would be expected to fit as a male member of Reed Estate. Although the majority appeared quite happy about their anticipated role, when asked if there was anything they would particularly like to do, if they were not a boy, many of the comments provided an insight into the constraints that they felt were on them:

> I love little kids. If I was a girl, that's what I'd do. Look after them. You can have good fun with them. I know it sounds daft but I have always wanted to be able to knit. I used to watch our gran doing it. If I was a woman I'd knit loads of things.

After some probing to find out why they felt such activities, which would be quite acceptable male pursuits in many homes, were forbidden to them, all made similar comments — 'It's too soft for a boy. Our dad would laugh at me. My mates would think I was a sissy'.

One thing which did emerge was that mothers do not want their daughters to have the same lifestyle as them. They saw the major way of ensuring this did not happen as the prevention of pregnancy at an early age. In an area of high illegitimacy this is a very obvious concern. Unfortunately, whilst not wanting their daughters to take on the domestic responsibilities with which they are burdened, they are expecting sons to find wives who will keep them in the style to which they have become accustomed:

> I wouldn't want our Paul to have a wife who only thought about herself. I hope he gets a good wife. One who will really look after him properly. The right wife is important. I want my sons to have wives who will be home-birds, not the type who want to be out and about all the time.

If such wives are not to be from amongst the daughters of those I interviewed, one can only wonder where they might be found. Such diametrically opposed ideas for one's own daughters and the daughters of others who will become the wives of one's sons did not seem strange when the issue was raised:

> Well it's natural to want the best for your own. I'm not looking for somebody perfect. I just know he's the type who needs a caring wife.

The Influence of the Community

All the mothers interviewed were very community orientated and the majority had lived within or near this particular estate all their lives and envisaged spending their future years in the same house or one nearby. When they spoke of those families who had moved out to newer homes on the outskirts of town, they all quoted people who had returned to Reed because either they did not like the people, they missed close contact with family and friends or they were unable to afford the higher bus fares into town. This is certainly born out by pupils returning to school after a short time of leaving. The most positive comments made about life on Reed Estate were about the matriarchal strengths, the close family network and value of neighbours. Even those who spoke of it in anti or dismissive terms, could not ignore its influences and its expectations of them. All discussed at some length what was expected of them as the woman of the house by the com - munity at large. When discussing what was expected of them by the community, they repeatedly referred to 'it' and 'they' — ' "They" think one's place is in the home, making sure everything is alright. "They" think a woman should have all the worries and responsibility of the family be-cause that's the way it has always been'. All found it difficult to define who they meant exactly by 'it' and 'they'. The nearest they came to clarification was through comments such as — 'well, everybody; all those who live round here; other women'. When asked if they included themselves in the attitudes and expectations of the 'it' and 'they', the response was very mixed, ranging along the full continuum from the extreme of stereotyped roles based on gender to total opposition towards the role and identity allocated to women. Although most of us have some such attitudes determined by socialization, it is the extreme element which appears to create a polarization of gender attributes in men and women in the Reed Estate.

In addition to the image which men have of the women in their lives, resulting in a constraint placed on personal development and functioning of many females, the effects of similar damaging attitudes can be seen in many men. Particularly vulnerable were those who were unable or unwilling to fit the stereotype mould expected of them within the community. There was evidence of considerable strains in marital and family relationships over recent years directly due to unemployment. Many men have lost status, dignity and purpose along with their jobs and have found great difficulty in finding a new role within their changed circumstances:

> I would love it if he could just find some kind of work. Anything as long as he gets from under my feet. I feel he is watching me all the

time. I know he has nothing else to do but I have and he thinks I should just sit with him all day.

The attitude towards husbands and lovers varied very much depending a great deal on particular experiences and circumstances. One theme which did emerge constantly was that a man in the house, regardless of marital arrangements, was a very necessary status symbol. Those without one, even though they protested that they would not have one because of the problems they inevitably brought with them, did comment that they frequently felt out of it as a single parent:

It's not easy without a man in the house. I know I'm better off without a man but sometimes I do feel it. It's just me and our Lisa.

Many women on the Reed Estate ask for or expect very little for themselves. Unfortunately, a too ready understanding of their man's expectations of them, results in personal needs and developments ceasing to exist. This is often not just to the detriment to themselves but also has the long-term effect of perpetuating such patterns of life through their children. The majority of children, like their parents, will continue to live within a limited radius of their childhood homes. This will restrict external influences on the development of their expectations and assumptions about gender identity and relationships. Boys, in particular, seem to be enjoying the fruits of a privileged position because their mothers were conditioned into assuming that this was the natural way of things. All the mothers interviewed discussed in some detail the influence which the community had on their children. Some mothers considered the acceptance of their children by the community as recognition of them having done a good job. There was much evidence of pride from mothers who felt that their children could handle themselves against the rough, often violent, element on the estate:

At least he can fight well. I have made sure he can. If he ever came in crying when he was a toddler saying the big lads are hitting me, I just threw him back out and told him the door was locked until he had hit them back. He'll take anybody on now. They're all frightened of him round here.

The need for sons to project a macho image came through very strongly from all mothers. Some discussed it in a very low-key way but others spoke quite heatedly about the absolute necessity for boys to have this image if they were to be accepted by the community and either become an acknowledged peer leader or somebody safer left alone. The sexuality of boys was discussed much more explicitly than that of the girls. With daughters it was very much

— 'I hope she doesn't get pregnant when she is still at school. I'll make sure I put our Susan on the pill at 14'. Boys, however, tended to be spoken of with pride, humour and to a certain extent excitement:

> He's very well endowed. Have you seen him down below? Our lad says he'll have impregnated half the girls on the estate by the time he's 16. I said to him that there's no chance of him waiting until he's 16, he'll be at it by the time he's 10.

It was evident, from the data, that schools and the home are not only failing girls but they are also failing boys by giving them the impression that regardless of ability or attitudes they are in some way superior to females. This can in some instances have serious repercussions for the all–round development of both sexes. One of the areas of concern seems to be the effect on aspirations. The domestic arena, after a short period in a typical female job, was the extent of ambition for all but one of the girls:

> I want to be a hairdresser for a bit, then get married and have a family.
> I'd like to work in a shop before I get married.
> I wouldn't mind it if I didn't get a job, because I want to get married when I'm young.

Although several of the girls lived in a home where there was no permanent father figure, not one saw themselves in any kind of independent role. Once again the lack of appropriate female role models was evident. Girls were not sufficiently aware of the possibility of gaining financial independence through a well paid job. They spoke of mothers and neighbours who, if they had to work, it was in a low status job, totally lacking in glamour or attraction. Boys, in contrast, appeared to have much broader horizons. Although several of them interviewed had unemployed fathers and all made some comment on the difficulty in obtaining work during a recession, they viewed the future with optimism and a confidence that they would succeed:

> I'm not sure what kind of job I'll get but I want a good one so I can make lots of money.
> When I leave school, I'm going to work in the works and make as much money as I can.
> Before I get married, I want to do a lot of things and make as much money as I can.

Many of the boys are probably under a misconception when anticipating their future quality of life. However, through a confident, aspiring approach to life, they are likely to achieve more than the less ambitious girls.

The majority of participants felt that there was a need for some changes in the development and socialization of boys and girls. All mothers spoke strongly about not wanting their daughters to repeat their mistakes and live a life similar to their own. Girls, whilst accepting that they would lead a life almost identical to their mothers, wanted some changes. They all mentioned in various ways the need for an element of freedom and flexibility in their lives which they did not see their mothers having. Boys spoke proudly of their fathers and the way of life they led regardless of their existence in the home or the length of time since they had seen them. The majority did, however, acknowledge the need for some changes, seeing certain situations between the sexes as not quite right:

> Our dad helps nobody. He never helps our mam or gran at all. He could do a bit to help our mam but he doesn't. I don't think that's fair. I won't be like our dad with my wife. I'll help her to do the work in the house, then we can go out together, instead of me going to the pub on my own.

Staff were probably the most aware of the need for changes and we were all prepared to work hard at offering alternative models. The main obstacle was seen as the strong tradition of clearly defined gender roles within the Reed Estate. Some of the staff discussed this situation in pessimistic tones, suggesting that although willing to work towards a change in attitudes, they held out little real hope of fundamental shifts from those traditionally held. Others spoke of areas of hope and the possibility of affecting some children if they could only observe alternative models to those present in the community.

On close examination of the data, there was evidence which indicated suitable starting points for a better understanding of the community, its corporate identity and the various individuals within it. It appears that the most hope can be derived from the fact that, generally speaking, parents saw the school as having a very relevant function within the community. Staff, although probably needing to reassess their assumptions chiefly based on prejudices about areas such as Reed, were all positive about their commitment to the community and had a sensitivity to the many needs of the children. All the pupils spoke in positive terms about aspects of school life and the relationships within it. Although many saw school and the community as having very separate identities and expectations, several overlaps were discussed. It would be totally impractical and morally suspect for any school to try and change all the traditions and cultural mores of the community which it serves, but there was clear evidence from mothers and pupils that schools should at least help them to examine what they accept as the status quo. The main reason for this from mothers was the feeling that they want their children to be given the same opportunities as those in the so called up–market areas. Nobody was looking for drastic changes, but there was certainly a desire for some shift in attitudes which will hopefully help to create a better quality of life for future generations. It was evident that the hearts and minds of many people in Reed School and its community were open to changes in stereotyped gender identity and relationships and that they were looking for a better understanding of the issues involved and the ways forward which will be of particular benefit to the children in their care.

Redefining an Equal Opportunities Policy

It was on this basis of acceptance by all participants that school had a crucial role to play in the promotion of equal opportunities that a beginning in constructive changes was tentatively started. Having collected, analyzed and interpreted the data it was tempting to produce a definitive Equal Opportunities Policy for Reed School based on my conclusions. This would, however, have been both presumptious and inappropriate. I recognized that if my research was to form a worthwhile foundation for a relevant policy, it needed to be seen in the context of a framework which could develop into a series of inter-related strategies devised as a result of the experiences and perceptions of several individuals and groups.

It was evident to all staff that the policy must acknowledge the significance of the mother's influence and utilization of this resource was seen as a fundamental force for change. I was both surprised and excited by the influence the data which they had contributed had on the various initiatives planned to raise awareness within the school community. The most significant effect of the research for most staff, including myself, was the clear evidence linking our own socialization process to sex–stereotyping and the influence of this on our approach to, and expectations of, pupils in school. As a result of this research, we were able, as a staff, to devise a framework for a policy towards equal opportunities which included parents, pupils and staff in a variety of initiatives affecting curriculum, resources, practice, organization and communication.

Although the working document which resulted from my research was unique to a particular school and community, I feel it can provide an insight and guidance to others in a similar position to go forward with confidence in their task of developing an appropriate Equal Opportunities Policy or evaluating one already in existence. It is impossible for one teacher responsible for Equal Opportunities Policy to be effective without the commitment of every member of staff and the active support of the senior management team. It is essential that a public policy statement reflecting the school's intentions is made not only to the staff but to pupils, parents and the various outside agencies working within the school. The early stages of establishing a policy needs to be handled in a very sensitive manner. Any feelings of threat, or atmosphere of insecurity, will inhibit people from contributing at their level of interest and ability. Although short- and long-term plans will need to be incorporated into a fairly rigid timescale if progress is to be made, I feel it is essential to spend time examining feelings, fears and doubts in the early stages. This process is invaluable to the eventual context and implementation of the policy.

The formation of a representative working party is crucial to ensure that all departments and phases are fully informed and have easy access to influence and modify suggested initiatives. The size, management style and stage of development of the school will determine the most appropriate ways forward but it is necessary to clarify relevant terminology and, through in-service, support people in honestly considering personal awareness of sexism, sex-stereotyping and gender relations. There is much commercial material available to assist in this but only the working party can decide within a school if participants would find this less threatening than a package devised specifically for their own situation. The chances of a successful awareness-raising programme are greatly increased by the inclusion of all who will be involved in or influenced by the policy from the very early stages. Through a consultative process at this stage, it is possible to develop an appropriate in-service programme to meet the varying needs for a wide spectrum of people.

Pilot schemes are a useful way of gathering specific information or trialling an idea for whole-school development, but they must be planned with specific aims and objectives. Staff are under a multitude of pressures in the classroom and are often unwilling to take on anything new which they feel is not necessary. Clear guidance and reasons must be given with the opportunity to have some control and influence over the eventual results and how they will be used. I found the least threatening, very influential starting points were through an evaluation of resources and examination of school organization and administration. Staff were so surprised by the evidence of institutionalized sexism that many were happy and willing to devise pilot schemes relevant to their particular subject area or age group. The monitoring of girls' and boys' attitudes through specific initiatives or use of resources proved straightforward starting points. The most difficult schemes to introduce were those actually involving staff's own use of language or methods of implementing curriculum content. Some staff had grown acutely aware of their differences in approach to boys and girls and were sensitive about it. I found the most effective way of managing this was through staff working with a trusted colleague and observing each other in the classroom. Even the most reluctant participated at a minimum level and its effect as an awareness-raising exercise made further developments much easier. Reassessment of praise and reward systems was a natural progression because staff had realized how much they were using these as a mechanism for control of the most difficult boys, often ignoring the passive, hard-working girls.

Ways of involving mothers will vary according to the extent and quality of the interaction they already have in the life of the school. I found it easier and more practical starting with a group who already met regularly in school. Through their developing interest in the issue, they were able to influence others in informal one-to-one situations, either in the parents' room in school or through home-based contacts. Some schools might find it more appropriate to initiate a group with the specific aim of raising awareness with, and getting relevant information from, other parents. A great deal will depend on the catchment area of the school and the role parents have taken in policy making in the past. The method of consultation is not important but their partnership with the Equal Opportunities Policy is vital to its success.

Evaluation of any policies within schools is not easy and frequently mechanisms which are devised are ineffective. It is essential that a very structured, clearly defined process of evaluation is an implicit part of an Equal Opportunities Policy. Whether equal opportunities will be encompassed as an inherent part of all curriculum policies or will retain its own identity will depend on the school's approach. If evaluation and modification is not seen as an important, integral part, the energy and enthusiasm for early initiatives will soon dissipate and the issue will quickly lose focus and priority in the deluge of demands faced by staff.

Initiating and implementing change is difficult and challenging in any context, but I can recommend the role of practitioner researcher as a method of addressing a complex issue involving a range of people, experiences and ideas. Personally, I felt my project was the most exciting I had ever been involved in. It helped me reassess my own thinking and whole approach to incorporating all who were influenced by school policies in the process of formulating and implementing them. Its most important long-term effect has been the commitment which I have developed to making policies reflect the opinions and needs of those they represent. Whilst recognizing this as a fundamental educational principle throughout my career, it had been purely rhetoric on my behalf. I have participated in many working parties to devise what I thought, at the time, were enlightened policies, but the constraints of time and the pressure to commit to paper tended to translate high ideals into dull documents. Meeting a requirement has invariably been the priority with little status or relevance being given to the process. Often, on completion, policy documents and statements are shelved and rarely, if ever, used as a stimulus or framework to improve the quality of education of the children or the involvement of parents in the educational partnership. This research has reaffirmed the importance of the process of policy-making to me. It does take time but the benefits gained are tremendous for all those involved. Empowering pupils, parents and staff by involving them in determining school policies adds potency which inevitably makes them alive and pertinent to all participants and a developmental force within the school community.

All staff in every school have recently been under much pressure to respond to National Curriculum documents, formulate school development plans and devise guidelines for the introduction of the National Curriculum. The tendency in such a situation is invariably to take short cuts and get the necessary rhetoric in place. This approach, although understandable, can cause people to ignore or devalue their own experiences and pay scant attention to research findings. Once involved in practitioner research, I have found that most people like myself change fundamentally as a teacher and retain a confidence in their ability to act in accordance with their findings rather than in response to the pressures of the situation.

In the next few years, when the radical changes of the Education Act 1988 are being implemented and evaluated, teachers are going to play an essential role in ensuring that an effective education is delivered to the children in partnership with all involved within the school community. The practitioner researcher within a school could play a crucial role in testing out the rhetoric of an imposed curriculum against the practical reality faced by the classroom teacher who is attempting to meet numerous requirements and ensure that a happy, purposeful atmosphere in which children can learn and fully develop all aspects of their nature is sustained. So much time and energy has been invested in the preparation and implementation of the Education Act 1988 that there is a danger that policies made in haste will not be evaluated and modified accordingly. The member of staff who can make the time to stand back from the situation and assess what is actually happening, rather than what is perceived, could play a crucial role in supporting colleagues and ensuring that children are actually receiving the best that the school can deliver.

References

COHEN, L. and MANION, L. (1980) *Research Methods in Education*, London, Croom Helm.

CONNELL, R. W. *et al* (1982) *Making the Difference*, London, George Allen and Unwin.

DEEM, R. (1978) *Women and Schooling*, London, Routledge and Kegan Paul.

HODGEON, J. (1984) 'A Woman's World?', EOC/CLEA.

VICKERS, J. E. (1986) *Towards a Policy of Educational Equality*, Unpublished MA thesis, University of York.

Chapter ten

Procedural Rules in the Management of Pupils in the Primary School

Alastair Horbury

The methodological and substantive themes that are embodied and developed in this chapter are the product of research carried out in four primary schools in the North of England. The chapter is divided into two sections. The first section — a methodological note — turns on the difficult business of analyzing data. Consideration is given over to how data were analyzed and to some of the attendant problems of this process. The discussion is directly related to some of the ideas which are developed in the substantive section. This second section identifies a set of classroom-based rules which both infant and junior teachers use to bring about and sustain social order and control in the classroom. Such a set of rules can be seen as part of a process of child socialization into becoming an 'effective' member of a class. One purpose of such rules is to facilitate group management. The research was conducted in four schools: 'Riverside'; 'Home'; 'Market'; and 'Parkside'. In total over forty teachers were involved in this research. As many of the ideas embraced within this chapter came from 'Riverside' school, where I spent three months as a full-time researcher, a brief mention will be made of it.

'Riverside' school had ten full-time members of staff including the headteacher. One was a nursery assistant who took a small pre-reception morning group, who also worked with three infant classes in the afternoon on a rota basis. A part-time teacher assisted with children who were considered to have learning difficulties. The staff were 'mature', several of whom had been at 'Riverside' since the commencement of their careers. All but two full-time members of staff had been at the school for not less than ten years. 'Riverside' is a large school with a rather austere appearance, typical of many such Victorian establishments found in city areas in the North of England.

A Methodological Note

In the first instance, my research developed out of an interest in considering some of the processes which occur between teachers and pupils in the primary school. In a more specific respect, the impetus for doing my research, of which this chapter is a small part, was two-fold. Firstly, at the time of being a primary school teacher, I was eager to study, with a degree of critical distance, the nature of the daily round of processes and procedures which occurred between teachers and pupils. My research was spurred, therefore, in part, by a desire to understand more about social processes and events engaged in by teachers and pupils and for such an understanding to be developed through *their* perspectives of such processes and events.

The second reason for undertaking research was born of a feeling that many of my colleagues felt some resistance to research and educational theory because there was a perceived gap between research and practice in that the research which they had come across did not inform their practice. Although I was sympathetic to this feeling, the little I knew of the case-study tradition fuelled my interest in undertaking research and developing an understanding of classroom life in the primary school from those parties who were the key participants in the day to day activities of that setting. In looking at the taken-for-granted, daily round of activities in which teachers and children engage and by using a research strategy which was sensitive to probing their perspectives, it was hoped that such a study would be personally insightful and hopefully useful to others.

To illustrate exactly how categories emerged in this research is in some respects difficult. This is not to say that the data were not looked at systematically nor that the procedures by which categories were formed were not consistent, but rather, to say that simply to indicate that the categories were 'grounded' in the empirical material (Glaser and Strauss, 1967) is not sufficient. Categories do not simply 'emerge' from data, nor do they stand out strikingly without analysis. The ideas developed from this study were in part the consequence of the research design and the selection of the data collected. Ideas were formulated in the early stages and often reformulated as more data were amassed and so analysis and interpretation took place throughout the period of research and not as a separate procedure at the end of the data collection. In this respect it is consistent with Hammersley and Atkinson's (1983) idea when they state:

> . . . the analysis of data is not a distinct stage of the research. It begins in the pre-fieldwork phase, in the formulation and clarification of research problems, and continues in the process of

> writing up . . . Theory building and data collection are dialectically
> linked. (p. 174)

This illustrates the pervasive nature of analysis and hints, in one sense, at the
difficulty of indicating precisely how, where and when analysis took place.
But what makes the task more complex is the role that 'creativity' plays in
the formulation of ideas. As C. Wright Mills (1959) suggests:

> It is the imagination, of course, that sets off the social scientist
> from the mere technician. Adequate technicians can be trained in
> a few years. The sociological imagination can also be cultivated;
> certainly it seldom occurs without a great deal of often routine
> work. Yet there is an unexpected quality about it, perhaps because
> its essence is the combination of ideas that no one expected were
> combinable.
> . . . There is a playfulness of mindback (sic) of such combining as
> well as a truly fierce drive to make sense of the world
> . . . (pp. 232–3)

There were undoubtedly times during the study that a 'leap of
imagination' (Ford, 1975) would occur when abstractions from the new data
would be made. Advice has been given on how to achieve this state of mind
(see Denzin, 1978; Becker, Geer, Hughes and Strauss, 1961; Sjoberg and
Nett, 1968). Feyerabend (1970) advocates an extreme form of 'playfulness'
through his principles of 'proliferation' and 'counterinduction' (p. 26),
which are aspects of his anarchistic methodology where 'anything goes'.
Moving from the extreme, the issue of successful and fruitful category
construction would seem to be a balance between creative flexibility and
methodological discipline, for as Woods (1985) suggests:

> Most agree that the ideal-typical circumstances in which ideas
> emerge is a mixture of, on the one hand, dedication to the task,
> scrupulous attention to detail and method, and knowledge, and,
> on the other, the ability to 'let go' of the hold of this rigorous
> application, to rise above it as it were and to 'play' with it,
> experimenting with new combinations and patterns. (p. 70)

It is precisely this oscillation between methodological rigour and
imaginative flexibility which makes the task of explaining how the emergent
categories were arrived at difficult. However, one aspect of this emergence
can be explained through an example from my work where the 'sociological
imagination' in the first instance was a little too fertile and how a balance was
achieved through the counter action of methodological discipline.

As I will mention in the second part of this chapter, the categories which emerged from this research were developed at a level of generality higher in conceptual abstraction than the empirical data themselves. The categories of procedural and moral rules emerged early in the research, but it was soon realized that the 'leap of imagination' had been overstretched. The two categories were at such a level of generality that they were all-encompassing and, as such, most of the data collected 'fitted' into one of the two categories. As the study progressed and more data were collected, subdivisions in the form of minor categories were developed within the overarching categories. These proved more useful as analytical tools in providing means of progressively focusing on what emerged as important issues. With the procedural rules category, for example, the focus of attention was initially wide and only when subdivisions emerged, such as the organization of time, space and the transfer of knowledge was the research focus given more point.

The development of the procedural rules was arrived at by moving through a number of stages. The following extract from my fieldnotes illustrates an embryonic awareness of the category:

First-Year Infant Class: start of the day.

There's a lot of movement in the classroom. One child moves around the room on a big red tractor. Another child with arms outstretched makes the noise of an aeroplane and runs between the desks. The class teacher doesn't like this second activity and says 'I don't think that's a nice way to play'. As an outsider (previously a junior teacher) much of this activity is bewildering to me, there is a strange combination of apparent chaos and order. Activities seem to be rule-governed but it is not at all clear to me what they are.

Further observations of infant and junior classes led me to see such rule-bounded activities as classroom procedural rules. The category was so broad, however, that almost all the activities I observed seemed to 'fit' into the category: the imagination was flying but it embraced little analytical thrust.

I then began to look at similarities and differences between rule-constitution with infant and junior classes. Later fieldnotes state:

In some sense it strikes me there's a world of difference in how the enterprise of teaching is constituted between infant and junior teachers. The rules are constituted differently and everything's organized differently.

The organization of time, space and transfer of knowledge struck me as immediate differences and these then became more analytically prosperous subdivisions of the procedural rules category.

It was the initial leap from the raw data which provided the abstract idea which then turned back on the data and refashioned them, and in so doing, the analytic concepts were developed which gave more shape to the abstract category of procedural rules. It was then, through a dialectical relationship between the data collected and the subsequent abstract category, mediated by both methodological rigour and creative flexibility, that substantive theory was developed.

Methodological discipline took the form of constantly looking for continuities and discontinuities in the data collected in the different classes that were observed. For this, two initial categories were found which were procedural and moral rule categories. These were close to what Blumer (1954, p. 7) calls 'sensitizing concepts'. Thereafter, each segment of data was compared to the categories generated and its relation to those categories and other data in the categories was noted. This was a form of 'constant comparison', a method advocated by Glaser and Strauss (1967). In this way the breadth and depth of the categories were charted and the relations between categories were identified. As a result of the process of sifting through the data, the properties of the categories became more striking and the relationships between the categories developed clarity, in ways which are illustrated later in this chapter.

Procedural Rules of Classroom Management

In this section apparent elements of a rule-bound process of child socialization will be identified. This process appears to turn on a series of teacher-pupil interactions which are rule-orientated. These rules seem to be introduced and inculcated by the teachers from the moment of a child's arrival into the school and concurrently the process of pupil assimilation of such rule-governed interaction commences. At this stage it is important to state that emphasis is placed on identifying apparent mechanisms by which socialization into the institution of the school occurs, but *no* claims about its effectiveness are made. Specifically, this section identifies a number of procedural rules of classroom practice. The classroom practice of teachers is considered in terms of the organization of the 'transfer of knowledge', time and space. It is argued that the constitution of such rules vary with educational practices and that trends in the constitution of procedural rules appear to exist as between infant and junior teachers.

Before the discussion can proceed a working definition of the overarching concept of socialization is required. As the ideas and emergent categories are the result of empirical research, it would seem inappropriate simply to impose an existing conceptual framework which may be irrelevant to the findings and interpretations based on the work carried out in four schools. So, just as the emergent categories of procedural and moral rules have been inductively generated, so too has the following definition: socialization is a *rule*-based process of cultural induction, where certain interactional requisites are assimilated. By 'cultural' I mean those values, attitudes and beliefs no matter how loosely configured, that are held by a group.

In keeping with the research findings this definition emphasizes the rule-based nature of the enterprise rather than the superficial manifestations of it. Speier (1970) defines socialization as 'the acquisition of interactional competences' (p. 182). This definition could be seen as deficient in that it describes only the surface features of such processes, whereas the former, it is argued, locates such features in a deeper-seated rule-governed matrix.

Most of the evidence which is used to identify the process of socialization is taken from the research undertaken at 'Riverside' School — the first of the four research schools. It must be said, however, that what is presented here was also influenced by further investigations in the other schools in which research was undertaken.

From my research the rules governing the form and direction of teacher-pupil behaviour appeared to be of two types: procedural and moral rules. These two groups are mutually distinct in that the emphasis of each is different: procedural rules have a classroom specific orientation but the moral rules are more pervasive in their sphere of influence. Both, however, contribute towards modifying the behaviour of children and so the difference between the two is considered to be one of emphasis rather than one of kind. The two groups of rules are therefore seen as being mutually dependent rather than mutually exclusive. In this chapter only features of the procedural rules category will be identified.

The procedural rules are classroom specific and as such are manifested through the perspectives of teachers. By perspective I mean those general informed attitudes which characterize a particular orientation, in this case to the business of teaching. Importantly, with regard to infant and junior teacher perspectives, there seemed to be a difference in emphasis between them. Basically, both infant and junior teachers had a concern for children learning how to get on with one another and with acquiring curriculum knowledge. *Trends* in the data indicated that infant teachers emphasized the development of social skills, while junior teachers appeared to give more weight to the curriculum aspects of classroom life. Aspects of such practices appear to be illustrated through a variety of organizational classroom forms: the management of time, space and the transfer of knowledge. Implicit within such 'organizational properties', there is a rationalization for what counts as appropriate behaviour. With the differing arrangements of the 'organizational properties' it is found that differing rationales for appropriate behaviour also appear to be evident. I suggest that the rules forming the basis of classroom interaction are not a static and unchanging collection. Although it is argued that continuities exist within the procedural rules category, the rules themselves appear to be constituted differently according to the educational practices of each teacher and the age of the children taught.

It is further contended that the procedural rules, regardless of their constitution, appear to be a mechanism of effective cohort management. From my research it is suggested that teachers' time is a scarce resource and so the procedural rules inculcated by teachers can be interpreted as a coping strategy adopted by them to accommodate their notion of lack of time plus other factors such as the organization of materials and discipline control. Coping strategy is used here in a way which is consistent with Hargreaves (1979) and Pollard (1980, 1982 and 1985).

With further analysis the procedural rules category was subdivided into a number of smaller categories. These categories will be dealt with individually, though they are to be viewed holistically, that is, as being interrelated rather than independent from each other.

Transfer of Knowledge

In comparing different classes within and between 'Riverside' and the other schools, it was found that there were a number of continuities and discontinuities between the learning situations that teachers facilitated. The greatest differences were found between the infant and junior classes. Differences were found in the organization of what I term 'social learning opportunities'. 'Activities' is a teacher generated category which is used to label collectively the sorts of events in which the infant children are engaged (predominently in the afternoon sessions). These are contrasted with similar events (though constituted differently) in junior classes. A feature common to both infant and junior lessons is that they are constructed by the teacher to allow, at least in part, the children to interact with one another. These events were designed according to infant teachers to 'let them socialize', 'give them a chance to get on with each other', 'work together and learn to share' and, particularly according to junior teachers, 'to work as a team'. It would seem, therefore, that a thread of continuity between both infant and junior teachers in providing such experiences was allied to the notion of promoting cooperation between children. An interesting feature of this, however, is the different constitution of such events.

An important aspect of an infant 'activity' is that it tended to be selected by the children, whereas in junior classes the context and form of an event tended to be more structured and controlled by the teachers. There were many activities from which an infant child could choose: construction models, jigsaws, sand, water, bricks, to name a few. The child was allowed to select an activity which tended to be closely associated with also choosing a friend. The kind of activity selected, however, was within a range of teacher defined possibilities. The control imposed by the infant teachers seemed to be minimal, though it was manifest, first, in the choice of play materials and, second, in the number of children allowed to engage in a given activity at any one time.

The nearest junior equivalent seemed to be art/craft lessons. Teacher control over content was often strongly manifested even when apparent permission had been given to draw something of their own choice. The following extract from a junior art lesson illustrates this point where, in the teacher's preamble, the only explicit pre-condition about the children's work was that their drawings had to be related to a profession:

Teacher: Off you go then, (draw) anything you like.
 (Some minutes later)
 Child: Can I draw a rock star at a concert?
 Teacher: Don't be silly, that's just being daft.

Though freedom had apparently been given, limitations of what was appropriate content were clearly defined for the teacher, and made clear to the children when the boundaries of the teacher's tacit definition was exceeded.

Further discontinuities between the 'social learning opportunities' of infant and junior children can be highlighted. The infant children initiated and directed their own activities whereas this responsibility was taken by the teacher in junior classes. Though infant play was child directed, it took place within certain limits which the teacher defined. An example of this was a group of boys play-acting in the hall, using large building blocks to construct a 'boat', thereafter running and sliding around the hall pretending to be chased by a shark. In conversation with their teacher after the event, she condoned their actions and considered their experience as 'valuable' because they were being 'creative' and 'developing language'. A short time later, two boys from the same group were running around the classroom and were sanctioned by the teacher saying 'I don't think that's a very nice way to play'.

The point being made is that although the term 'play' employed by the teacher and children implies a degree of freedom, it is situation specific and so what counts as appropriate play varies from one situation to another. As with other infant teachers, Mrs S considered that learning through play was an important part of schooling, and indeed the amount of time given to such activities per day would seem to support this. Such an attitude is consistent with one of the principles which has traditionally been valued in early years initial teacher training and is advocated by 'great infant educators' such as Froebel, Montessori and Steiner. The following extracts are accounts of an infant teacher and child's interpretation respectively of an 'activities' session:

AH: What's happening here?

Mrs S: This is where they get a chance to play — it's only a short lesson so I don't get the big things out.

AH: Why do you have this kind of lesson?

Mrs S: Well, they can make things, construct — good for thinking and manipulative skills — and the language, that's important too. The social side too — they learn to play together, they're very different when they come in you know.

Conversation with a 6-year-old boy, playing with small bricks:

AH: What's happening here Darren?

D: What do you mean?

AH: Well, this isn't a maths lesson is it?

D: (laughter) No, it's play.

AH: What kinds of things can you do in play?

D: All kinds (pause — he starts to play) you can build or paint.

AH: You can do all kinds of things in the class can you?

D: Yes.

AH: Is there anything you can do in the playground but not in here?

D: Yeah, run and things and play fights.

The conversation with Darren illustrates his already 'sophisticated' understanding of the situation-specific nature of behaviour. Darren is seen by the teacher as 'quite mature for his age'. It is argued here that such a statement is aligned to his ability to appreciate what counts as proper behaviour in different situations. He has begun to distinguish play as a word meaning different sorts of action peculiar to specific contexts. His relative sophistication can be contrasted with the new entrants — a reception/nursery teacher gives her impressions:

AH: Can you tell me what your impressions are of children when you get them at first?

Mrs W: They come in at about four and a half years and most of them have been to playgroup or some kind of nursery, so the social problem isn't what it used to be years ago when children didn't necessarily want to come to school and cried, and we don't get many children crying . . . but the playgroup tends to make them a bit wild . . . so we have to cool it a bit because they're very boisterous and use all the space for a bit of running.

This extract indicates a lack of knowledge on the part of new entrants about the school rules. It seems that when they arrive the word 'play' for them is relatively context free and only gradually do they begin to take on board some of the rules appropriate to school behaviour. Here Darren (unlike new entrants) is not only developing a sense of cooperating with others through play activities, but he is also learning that rules governing play are context specific. What is being acquired, through what could be called a heuristic approach, is an understanding of what counts as appropriate behaviour, and the rules governing that behaviour change from situation to situation. He is learning that the term 'play' means to act differently when it is associated with a playground, hall, corridor or classroom context. Furthermore, the rules which constitute each teacher-defined play activity are implicit and remain so until one or more are contravened.

The teacher does not start each day by making explicit the rules that are appropriate for the activities to be carried out during that day, but only makes explicit a rule when it is breached. This is why the term heuristic is used to describe the phenomenon of rule assimilation. It is through trial and error that the rules appropriate to a given situation appear to be learned.

A child is made aware of breaking a rule by 'sanctioning'; this is carried out by the teacher when such a rule is breached and it is considered necessary that action should be taken. The severity of the sanction is determined by the teacher's view of the severity of the offence. The nature of the sanction and the way it is ratified varies. Sometimes the teacher sanctions a child, referring directly to the breach of rule and on other occasions, as in the earlier example (boy running about the classroom 'I don't think that's a very nice way to play!'), indirect references to the rule are made. I believe that the discontinuity in ratification is related more to the teacher's expectation of a child knowing the rule rather than the severity of the rule that is broken. By this I mean that when the teacher assumes a child has knowledge of the rule that has been contravened, only indirect reference need be made for it to be re-affirmed. Conversely, if the teacher's expectation is such that a child has broken a rule, but has acted innocently, then explicit reference to the rule is made — for example, 'Don't run around like that!'. This kind of statement is often associated with an adjoining rationalization of the rule such as '. . . it's dangerous, you might hurt yourself or knock something over'.

Classroom Organization of Time and Space

It has been suggested earlier that the perspectives of teachers seemed to be manifested through a number of 'organizational properties'. From my research, nowhere is this more apparent than in the way time and space are managed within the classroom. Related to these properties is a rationalization for what counts as appropriate knowledge.

In 'Riverside', significant differences were found in the way space was used between infant and junior classes; the infant children were group based with usually six to a group, whereas the junior children were in rows. It should be made clear at this point that all infant classes operated a group system whereas three of the junior classes (J3, J4, J5) operated a row system. First year juniors were in groups and the second year junior class was mixed (both groups and rows).

It became apparent as the categories developed that there were a number of continuities and discontinuities between the classes studied, both in the organization of time and space. I made no conscious effort to seek out differences between infant and junior classes *per se* but with the development of the above categories it became clear that such differences appeared to be evident. I feel that the arrangement of furniture and the structure of the timetable were so inextricably interwoven with the teachers' ideas of what counted as appropriate knowledge, that the 'knowledge' property will be dealt with alongside the above categories.

In the infant class, the division of time was reasonably uncomplicated as the following comments from an infant teacher indicate:

AH: Can you tell me how you normally divide up time during a day?

Mrs S: There are usually three things — three main parts to the day. We always try to do some maths, English and creative work activities. These make up the major parts of the day but also these are interwoven with television programmes and radio.

AH: Why do you have these three things every day?

Mrs S: Well one has to have continuity — if we didn't have maths and English every day they would quickly forget what they had been doing previously. And the activities are important for the language, physical and social skills. It may look as if they're just playing but they are developing various skills.

It seems that the teacher sees as her main priority the development of a number of general skills (numeracy, literacy and 'social skills') and as such organizes time around their development. The 'social skills', as they are described, are not developed only during the 'activities' period, but appear to occur throughout the day, so therefore, during a maths lesson, because of the group arrangement, the children are continually engaged in conversation, negotiating between one another for pencils, crayons and talking about their work.

As a result of a number of skills being developed simultaneously, freedom of movement was much more evident than in junior classes. During a maths lesson, infant children would frequently leave their seats sometimes looking for mathematical apparatus, at other times, for a conversation with a friend. It is suggested that this action was permitted on two counts. Firstly, with the teacher's notion of a multiplicity of skills being learned simultaneously, such multiplicity of action is consonant with the development of such skills and, secondly, the teacher has an expectation that the concentration of a child at this age is short and so it is of little surprise to the teacher to observe several children walking about the classroom at any one time during a maths lesson. The perspectives of the teachers, aspects of which appear to be manifested through such organizational properties as mentioned above, offer a rationalization for what counts as appropriate behaviour.

As mentioned earlier a number of discontinuities were noted between the infant and junior classes. In the junior class where an intensive study was undertaken, the organization of time, space and a rationale for the constitution of knowledge and behaviour, were very different. An extract from the 'official' document or school 'brochure' given to parents of new entrants is given below:

> ... basic reading, writing and maths skills are essential for future development ... We also provide a basis for the development of concepts in the social sciences and humanities (History, Geography and Environmental Studies) and in Primary Science ...

The curriculum areas outlined above were more easily identified in junior than in infant classes as their timetables were divided into a number of discrete activities carried out each day. A major discontinuity between infant and junior teachers' practices is that infant work tends to be 'skill' based and junior work is 'knowledge' based. In conversation with a fourth year junior teacher the 'knowledge' based element is emphasized:

> *AH*: Infant teachers seem to spend a lot of time developing what they call social skills. Do you do any of this?
>
> *Mr D*: They do it for a different reason. When you say a social bit, I don't really do a social bit, I have learning bits.
>
> *AH*: Yes right.
>
> *Mr D*: I don't have bits, the main objective being that we are learning to get on with each other and things like that, I don't really have that sort of thing.
>
> *AH*: So what kinds of things do you have in place of that?
>
> *Mr D*: I try to give them topics and opportunities to learn about other things . . . I don't have a social thing, it's an opportunity to learn.

This extract illustrates a significant difference — that the junior teachers are predominantly concerned with the transfer of knowledge as contrasted with the development of social skills in the infant classes. I am not suggesting that junior teachers perceive social skills as being incidental or contingent to their teaching operations, but it does seem that it is assumed that junior children — through their passage through infant classes — have already acquired such skills, which allows junior teachers to do other things. As a result, these perspectives are reflected in the way the timetable and classroom space are organized. Further, this affects the kinds of behaviour/movement that is expected.

'Going for a walk are we?' This was a typical remark made by many junior teachers who have been observed, where such movement around the classroom was seen as unnecessary. A consequence of the assimilation of the 'no walking about' rule is that many junior children spend much of their time sitting at their desks, being sanctioned if the rule is breached.

I argue that a feature of different teacher perspectives being current in a school is that certain action which is fostered and encouraged by some teachers (talking, socializing involving movement) is antithetically opposed by other teachers at later periods in the child's primary school career. This is a point made by King (1988) where he touches on ideological tensions between the two different historical traditions from which infant and junior education have emerged, with their consonant differences in emphasis regarding practice. Consequently, the children have to learn as they move from class to class that not only is their behaviour rule governed and that the rules are situation specific, but also age specific. What counts as appropriate behaviour then is not only a question of the assimilation of context specific rules but also an internalization of age specific teacher expectancies.

Recurrent throughout the whole of the research has been a theme of differential teacher expectations towards children on what appeared to be a notion of 'normative' development. The teachers defined their situations in relation to their interaction with children on the basis of an 'ages and stages' sequence of development. Children were expected to act and be able to perform certain 'intellectual' tasks according to their age. Furthermore, such a notion of normative development appeared to act in part as a rationale for what constituted appropriate knowledge at different ages. The following extracts illustrate this — the first is a conversation with a junior teacher, the second, with an infant teacher:

AH: I was chatting with an infant teacher who said that part of the reason her children sit in groups is so that they can talk.

Mr D: Yes, that's right, but I think they have command of the language by now, and as far as the social chit chat is concerned 'Did you see E. T.?' — well this is no place for that in my mind. But I can understand in the infants still learning their skills, building up their vocabulary, but by this time (10/11 years) they are able to communicate.

AH: Do you think other teachers think like this?

Mr D: Yes, as they go through the school, the way we treat them is different. There is this, 'You should be at this stage by now because we must get you ready for when you move', and it is a move a big move for them.

Such statements and classroom observation notes indicate that the 'normative' rationale acts as a justification for the skill-based infant work and the more knowledge-orientated components of junior classwork. In keeping with the junior teacher's comments it did appear that most teachers operated within such a conceptual scheme. An infant teacher compares a junior maths lesson with that of her own:

AH: In junior classes the children don't move around much.

Mrs S: No, but most of their work is recorded on paper and they are working from books or the blackboard — they don't need to move they've got everything to hand. Anyway, they can sit for long periods because they have got more concentration. My children can't sit for long — they can't concentrate — anyway they're continually on the move fetching and using apparatus.

Such comments appear to be common amongst these teachers and as mentioned earlier, offer a 'yardstick' on which to base their teaching decisions.

The procedural rules as an effective form of cohort management will now be considered. Normally it is assumed that it is the teacher who establishes control and manages the classroom situation and only when there is a failure to do so do children grasp the opportunity to negotiate the definition of the situation (Pollard, 1979; Stebbins, 1981; Woods, 1978). Davies (1983) suggests that pupils collaborate with their teachers in the establishment of order in their classrooms. I contend that the strategies adopted and expectancies held therein do not require negotiation, at least in the sense that there are a number of fundamental procedures which teachers *demand* of their pupils. The following extract illustrates that infant teachers have a number of expectations of children's behaviour which *require* them to act in certain ways:

> *Mrs P*: I think school is an entity on its own, with its own code of conduct within a classroom, and those children (new entrants) have not been in the regimented classroom conditions — now I don't mean that they are very strictly applied here, but it is different from being at home or at play school.
>
> *AH*: In what way is it different?
>
> *Mrs P*: Well they have to learn to listen, which a lot of them are not used to doing.
>
> *AH*: What does this involve?
>
> *Mrs P*: Well cooperating with each other . . . listening carefully to what is actually being said to them and learning how to carry out these instructions correctly . . .

The teacher recognizes that to become a member of the school, the children have to acquire and assimilate certain rules which, when followed, promote behaviour which is consonant with the expectations of the teachers. Further, there is an awareness that certain classroom-specific rules have to be followed. Some of these rules are listed below:

1 Listening rule — when the teacher speaks.
2 Cooperation rule — this is inter-child. It is assumed that the child will cooperate with the teacher and in the vast majority of cases observed this did *appear* to happen.
3 Carry out instructions rule.
4 'Hands up' rule.

Because of the age of the children (an implicit assumption of infant teachers being their relatively emotional insecurity) and because of their school experiences being their first induction into an institution which is potentially alienating, the infant children on the whole are not in a position to bargain or negotiate for the definition of the situation. The infant teachers would appear to be in an 'all powerful' position to define the situation through laying down the rules of classroom procedure and making them explicit when necessary. As the children move from year to year, they internalize these rules so that when they are breached in a fourth year junior class, for example, teachers need only make implicit reference to them for a child to realize that the teacher is aware of a breach of rule.

As an illustration, I will now consider the ways in which the 'hands up' rule (which was universally acknowledged and applied by teachers) assisted in the accomplishment of the teacher's task of cohort management. It had three functions: (1) Orderliness; (2) Feedback; and (3) Efficient mechanism of questioning. When a question is asked, only one child may answer at a time and to do so their hands must be raised. This effectively manages and keeps order in a group. If a question is asked by the teacher and only three from a group of thirty know the answer, the remaining twenty-seven are controlled because only by hand raising and being selected to respond are the children legitimately allowed to speak. By hand raising in response to a teacher's question, the teacher is immediately able to establish from the number of raised hands the degree of immediately available participation in response to the question. Hand raising is seen by teachers as an *efficient* mechanism of questioning with a large group. This, it seems, is an indication of a coping strategy adopted by teachers (where they see their time as a scarce resource) to 'get the job done' in the most effective and efficient means at their disposal.

These findings are consistent with the work of Payne and Hustler (1980), though they make no reference to the 'hands up' rule as being a coping strategy where teacher's time is seen as a scarce resource. They state:

> . . . the teacher makes a reference to the pupils raising their hands. He asks the whole class a question and he is, we argue, using the raising of the hands as a desire both to enable him to select the next speaker from the class and to give him some feedback on the pupils' involvement in the activity. Additionally of course, it is a device which facilitates the preservation of orderliness of the occasion, through providing for the preservation of the 'one person talks at a time' rule. (p. 59)

The following is a tape extract from the beginning of an infant lesson. The children are told to 'sit on the carpet', where they are then given the opportunity to show toys to the rest of the class and tell their 'news':

(1) *Mrs S*:   Right come along quickly and sit down.
            (Children chat as they sit down, facing the teacher)

(2)   First of all, are we ready? Vicki are you ready?

(3)   I don't think you'll see very well over there, Darren.

(4)   Right, can I have everyone looking this way.
         (virtual silence)
         You danced out of the hall beautifully this morning.
         Who came to the disco last night?

    Voices: Me, me.

    Mrs S: What a lot of you! See if anybody can tell me about it.

(5)   (Teacher scans group, three hands are raised) Rebecca!

    Rebecca: It was dark and they had flashing lights.
             (Noise from other children talking)

(6) *Mrs S*:   Shhh — if you want to say something put up your hand.

1   This illustrates the teacher collecting the children together to allow for easy management of the class. Mrs S is aware that for discussion purposes, group management is easier when the children are not dispersed — 'it's much easier to bring them all together and talk on the carpet than to have them scattered about the room'.

2   I suggest that this is a commencement signal or cue, where the teacher is bringing the listening rule into operation.

3   Darren is standing a few metres away from the group, the rest of whom are sitting on the carpet. Such distance makes him physically dislocated from the group and as such efficient group management cannot be accomplished until he has been called back to the remainder of the class.

4   After the interruption the teacher requires attention again and needs to reinforce the listening rule, for as she said, 'with Darren not being where he should have been they became restless while he sat down, so I had to get them ready again'.

5   The teacher scans the group getting feedback from the question which is allowing efficient passage to the next question. What I am suggesting here is that Rebecca was asked and she responded. Had the 'hands up' rule not been operating, a number of children might have been asked thus wasting time, until one with a positive response was found. Further, had the rule not been operating and a number of children knew the answer, orderliness might have been lost with those people 'shouting out' simultaneously, again wasting time re-establishing order.

6   The rule is reinforced and the orderliness function is applied

'. . . providing for the preservation of one person talks at a time rule'
(Payne and Hustler, 1980, p. 59).

The analysis of the above extract illustrates how and when the rules are
brought into operation, highlighting their importance as rules of procedure
and how they function as a successful mechanism in achieving group
management.

I argue that from the following statements, the 'hands up' rule is
assimilated by children as a result of the teacher making such a rule explicit.
As the children move from year to year the rules become internalized and the
teachers then need only reinforce them occasionally through implicit
reference to sustain effective cohort management:

4th Year junior teacher

> *AH*: How do they know not to shout out but put up their
> hands instead?
>
> *MD*: I don't know really. I suppose M . . . (J3) tells them
> before they come up to me. They all know what to do
> anyway. It just seems to happen, I've never really
> thought about that.

Infant teacher

> They're just at the learning stage at the moment, they're
> very egocentric. Sometimes they've got to shout out if
> they know the answer.

Infant children

> *AH*: Why do you put your hands up when Mrs S asks a
> question?
>
> *Various* Because she tells us to — I don't know — because she
> *Respondents*: says she wouldn't be able to hear us if we all shouted at
> once.

4th Year junior children

> You learn it (to put up your hand) as you go from class to
> class. The infant teachers aren't very hard on you at first
> but then it gets harder and harder for you, they shout a
> bit more . . . most of the teachers know the rules.
>
> *AH*: How do you know?

> Well you can just hear them 'cos as soon as you start running with one teacher they tell you to walk, and other teachers tell you to walk, and other teachers tell you to walk as well — they say 'pick up that litter!'

AH: Do infant teachers know the rules?

> Yeah most of them know the rules.

AH: Why didn't they get angry when you didn't put up your hand?

> We were small and it might have upset us — infants don't underestand them, they've only been in school for a few years.

Earlier in this chapter I proposed that different teacher perspectives and notions of 'normative' child development produced two apparent patterns to teaching and learning; infant skill-based learning and junior knowledge-based learning. From the above comments it can be seen that the infant teacher gives an explanation of the 'hands up' rule but the junior teacher, because of his knowledge-based domain, is less certain as to how this is accomplished. Infant teachers appear to be actively promoting the development of the rules whereas the junior teachers take for granted that the assimilation of such rules has been accomplished. Infant teachers make explicit reference to the rules when they are breached, while junior teachers make only implicit reference. Given that the effective management of a group requires the internalization of the procedural rules and, further, that internalization means that explicit reference to those rules need rarely be made by the teacher, it is therefore not surprising that junior teachers manage their classes but at the same time are unsure exactly how it is they do it. It is the successful socialization of the children in their infant years which allows the junior teachers to accomplish the rule-governed nature of their classroom enterprises in a taken-for-granted manner.

This is illustrated by the following summary of a junior teacher and children in a conversation — the teacher and the group of children were interviewed separately. The teacher frequently started lessons by saying, 'Right! I've got a job for you'. Following this comment his class would appear to be ready to commence work:

Teacher's interpretation

Teacher: Oh it doesn't mean anything really, I just use it like any other word. I say it at home, 'I've got some jobs to do'.

AH: So you don't use it to give the children an extra sense of purpose in what they're about to do or to get them to listen?

Teacher: No, if I wanted to do that I might use the word 'task', that's more appropriate isn't it?

Children's interpretation

The children interpreted the 'Right! I've got a job for you' as a cue for a specific course of action to be taken. From the interview four significant behaviour responses emerged:

1 Sit in your place.
2 Stop talking to your neighbour.
3 Take out from desks, pens and rulers.
4 Adopt a 'work attitude'.

It would seem that the children see the 'doing a job' as an implicit reference to the 'listening' rule employed by the infant teachers. But, because of its implicit nature and furthermore because the children 'read' the cue/rule correctly, it becomes part of and one of many rules in the repertoire of taken for granted strategies adopted by junior teachers in attempting effective cohort management.

Conclusion

In conclusion, it would appear that a process of socialization can be identified which turns on a series of teacher-pupil interactions which are rule-based. The first set of rules that has been identified (procedural) are classroom specific. They are manifested through the perspectives of each teacher — aspects of such practice are illustrated through a number of organizational classroom forms: the management of time; the management of space; and the transfer of knowledge. Aligned to these specific organizational properties appear to be specific teacher rationales for what counts as appropriate knowledge and behaviour, such a rationalization being based on a 'normative' notion of child development. As such, though continuities exist within the procedural rules category, the rules appear to be constituted differently, according to the practices of the teacher and the age of the children that are taught. The most significant differences in rule constitution appear to be between junior and infant classes. An important caveat here is that what has so far been discussed are apparent regularities that occur typically and, as such, allow distinctions to be made between the actions of infant and junior teachers. I do not want to suggest that such regularities are 'universal' in the sense that they operate for all teachers, all of the time. Nor do I wish to suggest that all the rules are applied by all teachers, to all children, at all times. The procedural rules can be seen, however, as a mechanism and function of effective cohort management. They may be also seen as a coping strategy where teachers' time is interpreted as a scarce resource. The classroom specific rules therefore allow potentially for the most effective management, given the constraint of teachers' time, of a large group of children.

The teachers in the schools in which the research was undertaken had a strong sense of children of different ages, moving through different stages of development. Such a notion seemed to have a significant impact on organization and pedagogy. Teachers seemed to have a fairly definite understanding of what could be expected of children at different ages and this affected their responses to children, particularly with regard to classroom procedures. Teachers of infant children seemed to initiate their pupils in a variety of classroom procedures as gently as possible, but a tension existed between facilitating this initiation gently and smoothly while trying to complete this process as quickly as possible for the purposes of having an ordered and orderly class. Teachers recognized that such experiences were often bewildering, in the initial stages, for their pupils and, as such, were sympathetic, but they also perceived the speedy acquisition of the rules of classroom procedure as essential if 'effective' teaching was to proceed. It is not surprising, therefore, that teachers of infant children tended to make frequent and explicit reference to the procedural rules of classroom interaction and that junior teachers assumed that when children had reached the junior 'stage' such basic understandings of how to act while in a group had been assimilated and therefore they need only make implicit reference to such rules.

References

BECKER, H. S., GEER, B., HUGHES, E. C. and STRAUSS, A. L. (1961) *Boys in White*, Chicago, University of Chicago Press.

BLUMER, H. (1954) 'What is going wrong with social theory?', *American Sociological Review*, 18, pp. 3–10.

DAVIES, B. (1983) 'The role pupils play in the social construction of classroom order', *British Journal of Sociology of Education*, 4, pp. 55–69.

DENZIN, N. K. (1978) 'The logic of naturalistic inquiry', in DENZIN, M. K. (Ed.) *Sociological Methods: A Source Book*, New York, McGraw-Hill.

FEYERABEND, P. K. (1970) 'Against method: Outline of an anarchistic theory', *Minnesota Studies in the Philosophy of Science*, 4, pp. 17–30.

FORD, J. (1975) *Paradigms and Fairy Tales*, London, Routledge and Kegan Paul.

GLASER, B. G. and STRAUSS, A. L. (1967) *The Discovery of Grounded Theory*, London, Weidenfeld and Nicolson.

HAMMERSLEY, M. and ATKINSON, P. (1983) *Ethnography: Principles in Practice*, London, Tavistock Publications.

HARGREAVES, A. (1979) 'Strategies, decisions and control: Interaction in a middle school classroom', in EGGLESTON, J. (Ed.) *Teacher Decision-making in the Classroom*, London, Routledge and Kegan Paul.

KING, R. (1988) 'Informality, ideology and infants' schooling', in BLYTH, A. (Ed.) *Informal Primary Education Today*, Lewes, Falmer Press.

MILLS, C. W. (1959) *The Sociological Imagination*, Oxford, Oxford University Press.

PAYNE, G. and HUSTLER, D. (1980) 'Teaching the class: The practical management of a cohort', *British Journal of Sociology of Education*, 1, pp. 49–66.

POLLARD, A. (1979) 'Negotiating deviance and "getting done" in primary school classrooms', in BARTON, L. and MEIGHAN, R. (Eds.) *Schools, Pupils and Deviance*, Nafferton, Nafferton Books.

POLLARD, A. (1980) 'Teacher interests and changing situations of survival threat in primary school classrooms', in WOODS, P. (Ed.) *Teacher Strategies*, London, Croom Helm.

POLLARD, A. (1982) 'A model of coping strategies', *British Journal of Sociology of Education*, 3, pp. 19–37.

POLLARD, A. (1985) *The Social World of the Primary School*, London, Holt, Rinehart and Winston.

SJOBERG, G. and NETT, R. (1968) *A Methodology for Social Research*, London, Harper and Row.

SPEIER, M. (1970) 'The everyday world of the child', in DOUGLAS, J. (Ed.) *Understanding Everyday Life*, London, Routledge and Kegan Paul.

STEBBINS, R. A. (1981) 'Classroom ethnography and definition of the situation', in BARTON, L. and WALKER, S. (Eds) *Schools, Teachers and Teaching*, London, Falmer Press.

WOODS, P. (1978) 'Negotiating the demands of schoolwork', *Journal of Curriculum Studies*, 10, pp. 309–27.

WOODS, P. (1985) 'Ethnography and theory construction in educational research', in BURGESS, R. (Ed.) *Field Methods in the Study of Education*, Lewes, Falmer Press.

Chapter eleven

The Processes and Purposes of Practitioner Research

Rosemary Webb

The first part of this chapter is on research processes and the second part reviews the range of purposes that practitioner research may serve. Consideration is given to what is involved in translating a particular interest or concern into a feasible research project. Data gathering and analysis are briefly discussed and the issues raised through the research experiences portrayed by the contributors are brought together. Although within this chapter these issues cannot be treated in depth, their importance will be reiterated and the reader who wishes for more information can obtain it through the references to relevant literature supplied in this and the preceding chapters.

As the book illustrates, professional development is a major outcome of practitioner research. The personal benefits and disadvantages of embarking on practitioner research are therefore examined. The main reason for carrying out practitioner research, as is demonstrated by the studies in this book, is to bring about changes in classroom practice and school policies. However, it is also argued that such research has the potential to fulfill a wider role by contributing to pedagogic theory and to policy at LEA and national level. While looking at the various roles of practitioner research the chapter identifies the research agenda created by the National Curriculum.

Designing the Research

Shumsky (1956) suggests that teachers' anxieties about how they are perceived by others can cause them to select 'safe' topics to investigate which allow them to demonstrate competence rather than topics related to unspoken, unacknowledged problems. However, topics which may have been considered 'safe' at the outset are likely to rapidly cease to be so once opened up to scrutiny. For this reason data on 'safe' topics have the potential to be more threatening and stressful for the practitioner researcher than topics anticipated from the outset as inevitably giving rise to personally disturbing information. Gregson reflects on how the unanticipated initial effects of innovation on pupils' attitudes and behaviour so undermined her confidence in her teaching skills that she almost abandoned the project on topic work (p. 37). Experience on the Outstation Programme suggests that while teachers may avoid researching areas in which they believe they are alone in encountering major difficulties, they certainly select topics which are acknowledged throughout the school as problematic. They view the research as a vehicle for gaining a deeper understanding of the problems and to explore possible solutions.

The process of devising a feasible project is ultimately shaped by each individual's status and role within the school. This is because it is these factors which determine access to data, how, when and where such data may be collected and the ability to implement and monitor changes at classroom or whole school level. Consequently, the topics selected by headteachers and deputy headteachers (see, for example, Vickers' research to produce an Equal Opportunities Policy) tend to reflect their managerial function and concern with policy issues, their privileged access to data down the hierachy and the possibility of some non-contact time for data collection both within and outside the school. Class teachers usually prefer to research their own classrooms. While this is predominantly because understanding the effects of their own practice on pupils' learning is the major concern for them, it also avoids encountering problems of lack of non-contact time and negotiating access to appropriate data, which could present an unnecessary threat to the successful completion of the research. Furthermore, it means that if they so wish they are in a position to implement changes — either as part of an action-research cycle or suggested as desirable by the research findings.

Douglass (1987) in his research on participants' perceptions of the Cleveland II Outstation Programme found that despite differences in roles and hierarchical status, individuals usually viewed their own positions as 'the best' for facilitating the research:

> I think the teacher I was involved with would perhaps feel less likely to let me observe her if I hadn't been a deputy. I think it certainly helped in terms of other schools because the headteacher — I'm friendly with him — he's been very very helpful towards me and perhaps he mightn't have been that helpful if I had been Scale 1 or 2 or something like that.
>
> I'm not a member of the hierarchy and most of my colleagues don't see me as threatening. I think that's been positive. (p. 3)

If practitioners can operationalize their position in the school to the advantage of the research then it is likely to progress more smoothly.

Once an initial research concern is identified the next stage in getting started is to formulate some research questions. Oberg and McCutcheon (1989) comment that:

> The stickiest part of teaching teachers to do action research — or any kind of research, for that matter — is helping them develop the knack of asking the right questions. The question is important not only to limit the focus of the inquiry and make it manageable, but more significantly because it often determines what is taken for granted and what is made problematic. (p. 124)

The need to assist Outstation course members to ask research questions led Lewis and Munn (1987) to produce a booklet offering guidance. They suggest that there are five main sources which can be used to generate research questions:

1 The purpose to be served by the research.
2 The particular features of the school, department, or classroom in which the research is to be undertaken.
3 The views of colleagues, especially colleagues who do not share your own views.
4 Your own position in the school may provide you with information which alerts you to the focus of the research into a specific topic.
5 Published material, reporting the experience of other schools and teachers, and more general material relating to the area of your research. (p. 12)

As Lewis and Munn observe 'it is unlikely that the first set of research questions you produce will be the set you finally use' (p. 12).

Also, during the initial stages of the research it often becomes apparent that additional research questions need to be added to the list or that the original research questions are missing the point because the nub of the problem being investigated is emerging as something quite different from that expected. For example, Wright, whose research arose from a growing awareness of some children's difficulties in coping with the language of mathematics lessons, describes how the research questions on the detailed list that she drew up to guide data collection assumed greater or lesser importance as the fieldwork progressed (p. 127–128).

Simultaneously with drawing up research questions, as discussed by Vickers (p. 203–6), consideration needs to be given to the techniques of data collection to be used, the criteria determining the selection of the sample who are to be researched and the timescale within which the evidence must be gathered, analyzed and written up. All the contributors describe the sample from which they gathered data for their research. Guides to conducting research, such as Patton (1980, pp. 98–107), discuss the alternative kinds of sampling available to qualitative researchers and the rationale underpinning them. Hammersley and Atkinson (1983), who emphasize the need to make the criteria employed in selecting a sample as explicit and systematic as possible, provide a useful discussion of the three major dimensions along which sampling within cases occurs: time, people and context (pp. 45–53).

According to Walker (1985), researcher's abilities and preferences are the major determinant in the selection of data-gathering techniques:

> Just as an instrumentalist will not change from playing the clarinet to playing the trumpet because a particular piece demands it, but will instead usually turn to another piece of music, so researchers generally give a lot of time and thought to the formulation of possible and potential research problems, looking for those that appear to fit their interests and preferred methods. (p. 47)

Ideally, decisions about the research design — including the choice of data-gathering techniques — should be based on the perceived best way of generating relevant data in response to the research questions. However, in practice, in practitioner research and in research generally, such decisions have to be shaped by pragmatic considerations such as who is actually available to be researched, how data can most readily be gathered and what is feasible in terms of other school commitments.

Data Collection and Analysis

Practitioner research builds on those skills of data gathering that practitioner researchers have already developed as part of their work and which inform their routine judgments and decision-making. However, the data thus gathered are usually impressionistic, subjective and often assimilated subconsciously or collected sporadically. If the research undertaken by practitioners is to be valid and to penetrate below the surface features of teaching and learning it is essential that the collection and analysis of data should be systematic and rigorous. Pollard and Tann (1987) suggest four key characteristics of data gathered to inform reflective teaching which are also central to practitioner research. Data should be:

descriptive (rather than judgmental)
dispassionate (and not based on suspicions and prejudice)
discerning (so that they are forward-looking)
diagnostic (so that they lead us into better action)
(p. 27)

Information gathering and analysis are currently being advocated as the basis for a range of activities in relation to school-focused research, curriculum evaluation and development, school-based in-service, monitoring pupil progress, achieving effective school management and conducting teacher appraisal for professional development. Over the last decade this has led to a steadily expanding literature providing advice on alternative techniques available for data collection (see, for example, Bell, 1987; Bell, Bush, Fox, Goodey and Goulding, 1984; Hopkins, 1985; Patton, 1980; Pollard and Tann, 1987; Walker, 1985; Woods, 1986). Consequently in this chapter it suffices to briefly review the main techniques of interviewing, observation and document analysis which were used by the practitioner researchers in this book.

Most practitioner research involves the use of some form of open-ended interviewing which allows interviewees the freedom to elaborate on the questions asked and to introduce their own issues as well as respond to those identified by the interviewer. The kind of interview which was most frequently used by the contributors is often referred to as semi-structured. Patton (1980), who identifies and describes three types of open-ended interview, labels it 'the general interview guide approach' (pp. 200–2). It involves drawing up in advance of the interview a checklist of issues to be covered. The phrasing of the questions addressing these issues and the order in which they are asked will vary from one interviewee to another, and particular follow-up probing questions are used with some interviewees but not with others. This interviewing approach is more likely to be adopted where the researcher has a limited number of general issues to explore rather than a wide range of precise questions.

In all forms of interviewing the language used, the ways in which the questions are phrased and the reaction of the interviewer to the responses given will affect the nature of the information obtained. For example, Winter discusses how listening to the transcripts of her pupil interviews revealed inadequacies in her interviewing technique which prevented her from obtaining the kind of information that she wanted (p. 161–2). The quality of interview data is also determined by contextual factors such as the relationship between the interviewer and the interviewees, procedures of anonymity and confidentiality, the venue and the method of recording adopted (see, for example, Measor, 1985).

Participant observation as a method of data gathering in classrooms (see, for example, Ball, 1985; Hook, 1981; Pollard, 1984; Woods, 1986) was central to all research reported in the book with the exception of Vickers — at least in the part of her research reported here. It is an essentially exploratory and open-ended method of data gathering, although as the fieldwork progresses and the research questions become more specific it is likely to become narrower in its focus (see, Russell p. 78). Horbury, Reed and I, as outsiders to our research schools, observed in other practitioners' classrooms. This required access to and release of data to be cautiously and sensitively negotiated. For Reed, gaining and maintaining access was a major methodological concern throughout the research period and she describes how this was accomplished and how she coped with the element of tension that she felt was ever present.

Practitioners collecting data in their own schools usually experience few difficulties — other than practical ones such as finding opportunities to conduct interviews — in gaining access to the staff perceptions and school events that they wish to research. However, decisions about the use of data and their possible effects on research participants and staff relationships invariably pose dilemmas. Consequently, McTaggart and Kemmis (1982, pp. 43–4) stress the importance of such practitioner researchers adhering to ethical principles which not only respect the confidentiality of data and anonymity of research participants but also set down procedures for the conduct of the research that should be accepted in advance by all involved. The fact that these practitioner researchers need to preserve the goodwill and trust of colleagues in order to maintain their professional role both during and after the research can be viewed as a constraint likely to distort the findings. However, as Winter (1989) suggests, it can be advantageous for the research by imposing 'a rigorous intellectual discipline, ensuring that the conclusions of the work are broadly based, balanced, and comprehensively grounded in the perceptions of a variety of others' (p. 23).

For the contributors engaged in researching their own practice there were some fundamental differences in the nature of the observation process and the challenges it presented. For example, Winter (p. 159) describes the frustrations of having time allocated to classroom observation used up in dealing with enquiries and interruptions by teachers and pupils from other classes. She also found it difficult to concentrate on the group doing science when pupils from other groups needed help — a problem she solved by enlisting the assistance of a colleague as 'an extra pair of hands'. Russell, who also encountered this problem, both took advantage of the headteacher's offer to take the rest of the class and made use of an 'invisible cloak' to indicate to the children when she did not wish to be disturbed. Gregson's research demonstrates the potential advantages of team teaching for practitioner research as she and the class teacher were able to collaborate to use a variety of strategies to gain access to the pupils' experiences — particularly working alongside them on the set tasks.

Audio-recording often accompanies observations as was the case in the fieldwork that I conducted for my research into topic work. Such taping provides valuable insights into peer group interaction and captures the vocabulary and language that the children actually use to describe their experience. It also reveals the amount, nature and distribution of teacher talk which, as Wright found, can be a very salutory experience. I found taping was effective in those parts of lessons where the teacher was in a didactic role or carrying out a question and answer session with the class. Owing to background noise and the general hum of conversation it is difficult to make audible recordings of groups of children working together in informal teaching situations. Wright also encountered this difficulty and speculates on how this limitation on the kind of data that she could collect may have shaped her findings (pp. 129 and 133). Russell overcame it by working with the groups being researched for part of the time while the headteacher took out the rest of the class. However, she acknowledges that this created a very different work atmosphere for the children than was the norm, thus probably having a distorting effect on the data (p. 78).

McCann describes how video-recording enabled her to gain data on the behaviour patterns of the Mirpuri children at home, in school and in the Mosque. She was also able to use extracts from the video tape to elicit further information from families about their children's experience in school and at the Mosque and to inform and stimulate staff discussion. Video-recording can assist in alleviating the classroom organizational problems mentioned earlier that are posed for teacher researchers who wish to examine their own practice or to record in detail the interactions of a particular group while they are working with the rest of the class. Video-recording also offers the possibilities of capturing those non-verbal expressions and behaviour that are often very revealing. Initially the use of audio and video recorders is likely to have a distorting effect on the data by influencing the behaviour of both teachers and children. However, as Russell (p. 79) discovered, the novelty soon wears off and behaviour returns to normal as all the parties involved become accustomed to being recorded. The main disadvantage of such recording is that going through it and making notes or transcribing key sections is immensely time consuming.

Research diaries, which were referred to by some of the contributors (see, for example, Winter, p. 158–9), provide important contextual inform-ation about the lessons and activities observed and log key events such as important staff meetings, industrial action and government legislation, as well as charting difficulties encountered in the research process, initial ideas, hypotheses and speculations. They can also serve as a record of ongoing reflections and learning in relation to the subject of the research and as an *aide memoiré* for analyzing the data more fully (for a discussion of the nature and purposes of research diaries, see Burgess, 1984).

The principal forms of documentation used as data sources by the practitioner researchers in this book are teaching materials — either made by the practitioners or published resources — and the work produced by pupils (see, for example, Gregson, Reed, Wright and Winter). School documentation can often prove a very useful source of data, particularly in the early stages of the research. For example, school brochures provide clues through the content, tone and language used of relationships with parents; school development plans indicate school commitments and intentions; policy documents provide insights on the aims and values of those who wrote them; schemes of work reveal assumptions about the nature of knowledge and the way children learn. Reflections on the rhetoric of documents and the reality of what actually happens in school, on the intended curriculum as portrayed in policy documents and schemes of work and the reality observed in classrooms can generate intitial research questions and form the focus of interviews and staff meetings. Further discussions of the particular contributions that documents can make to research and the factors to consider when evaluating their reliability and validity as data sources are provided by Hammersley and Atkinson (1983), Hitchcock and Hughes (1989) and Plummer (1983).

Through the process of triangulation (Elliott and Adelman, 1976) the contributors compared and contrasted the various interpretations of the same event or particular issue which were gained from different participants and alternative data sources. For example, I checked inferences from the observation data gathered in the museum on the 'How We Used To Live' lesson with the perspectives of the pupils, class teacher, museum teacher and Director of the Museum Education Service and noted where accounts agreed and disagreed. Where interpretations disagreed I checked them against the transcript of the lesson and where issues emerged that required clarifying or expanding I went back to those interviewed with further questions (for example, in relation to the issue of the museum teacher's use of questioning, pp. 106–7). I also circulated initial drafts of material which would ultimately form the case studies. These drafts became the subject of some year group meetings which provided me with additional perceptions of events. However, Hammersley and Atkinson (1983) warn us that:

> . . . triangulation is not a simple test. Even if the results tally, this provides no guarantee that the inferences involved are correct. It may be that all the inferences are invalid, that as a result of systematic or even random error they may lead to the same, incorrect conclusion. What is involved in triangulation is not the combination of different kinds of data *per se*, but rather an attempt to relate different sorts of data in such a way as to counteract various possible threats to the validity of our analysis. (p. 199)

When several practitioners are working together on a research project there is the possibility of triangulating between the observations and interpretations of different researchers. For example, Wright drew on the observations made by a team colleague on the mathematical ability of the pupils that she researched.

The process of analysis is a difficult and demanding one which needs maximum time and effort to ensure that the final research account is not merely a description of events, however lucid and well-ordered this might be. The literature on the methods of conducting qualitative educational research provides little advice on how to do analysis and researcher accounts of the process are also relatively rare. An interesting exception to this is Winter (1989), who suggests six principles for the conduct of action research, of which the first two (reflexive and dialectical critique) address data analysis, and then illustrates how these principles underpin his own research and writing. He suggests that the lack of attention given to analysis is due to misleading notions that 'reflection is tacitly assumed to be a straightforward familiar process, or one where the comprehensiveness of the data automatically guarantees the validity of the interpretation, or one which action research can simply borrow from elsewhere, i.e., from 'common sense' or from conventional research methods' (p. 25). I suspect that it is also because of its very complexity, interrelatedness with other aspects of the research and — in practice if not in theory — its essentially non-linear, untidy nature. Therefore, researchers have difficulty in recalling and verbalizing exactly how and when ideas emerged if they have not systematically charted the process recording the sticking points, blind alleys and backtracking as well as the leaps forward. As practitioner researchers, now that we have made our data-gathering techniques more systematic and rigorous, our next priority must be to critically reflect on, make explicit and share the ways in which we approach data analysis. From this knowledge and experience we can then offer alternative appropriate approaches that have been developed within practitioner research itself.

A handout produced for the Outstation Programme offers the following advice on how to get started on analysis:

1 Categorize your data in relation to your research questions. Some data may be clearly relevant to one question. Other data may be relevant to more than one. The first stage provides a basis for deriving an overall picture of the data.

2 Look in more detail at each category. Are there any issues, themes, trends which form sub-categories/sub-patterns within it? Are some of these more widespread than others?

3 Look for similarities and differences in terms of who is saying or doing what — for example, differences between the attitudes of subject coordinators and the headteacher, the preferences of girls and boys.

4 Look for omissions in the data. Were there issues that you expected to come up but did not? How might you explain this? Could it be related to the way you conducted the research?

5 Make explicit the rules by which you have categorized/coded your data. If possible ask a team colleague to code an interview transcript or fieldnotes according to the rules that you are operating. Re-examine the rules if there is a substantial variation in analysis.

6 Have a 'rag-bag' category into which data which does not directly relate to your research questions can be placed for it may be needed as your research proceeds.

7 Suggest interpretations of the data and from these interpretations develop hypotheses or grounded theories.

8 Search for exceptions or negative cases which will help refine or disprove emerging hypotheses.

9 Compare findings with those of related research and seek to explain the similarities and differences between the theories forwarded and your grounded theories.

10 Consider how your findings/theories at the local, micro-level of the school relate to national, macro-level trends and events.

While data analysis assumes greatest importance at the end of the fieldwork stage, as stressed by Horbury (pp. 223–4), it is an ongoing process throughout the research. He describes how his categories were formed as a result of the framework created by the original research design, the actual process of data gathering which shaped the data collected and the creative experimentation with ideas which generated possible alternative meanings for the data. Once he had identified categories he refined them and clarified the relationships between them through the use of the constant comparative method of analysis advocated by the American sociologists Glaser and Strauss (1967). Their book on *The Discovery of Grounded Theory* (1967), which criticizes research traditions where hypotheses are formulated before the research begins and argues for new theories to be 'discovered' in the data during the research process, has proved popular with proponents of practitioner research (see, for example, Hopkins, 1987).

The ongoing analysis of data as they are gathered and reflected upon is essential to guide progressive focusing — the continual funnelling process which limits and clarifies the scope, subject and structure of a research project. For example, in her study of her science teaching Winter moves from general observations to examining behaviours which inform her about pupil interest, acquisition of process skills and the effect of the organizational and social context on children's progress (pp. 159–160). As mentioned earlier, initial research questions are often transformed as the fieldwork progresses and this is usually a consequence of continual progressive focusing on what emerge as the central issues. The ongoing analysis of data throughout the fieldwork stage also assists in the process of grounded theorizing.

The physical process of recording the analysis as it develops is a matter of personal preference. In carrying out analysis Horbury finds it useful to build up his coding system on large sheets of paper. The first sheet depicts the various emerging themes and their interrelationship and subsequent sheets chart the range and variety of evidence within the sub-categories/patterns. Perhaps, as a response to sharing an office at CARE with a friend and fellow PhD student, whose fieldwork was completed before mine and who enthusiastically papered every available surface with data analysis sheets, I developed a preference for using marker pens to colour code different categories of data on transcripts and fieldnotes and to pencil analytic memos (Elliott, 1981) in the margins. Alternatively, access to a word processor and/or simple computer data-base programme can make recording the analysis speedier and more flexible.

Writing up research invariably takes longer than was anticipated and in the latter stages often becomes regarded as a somewhat laborious chore. All of the contributors here admit to identifying with the criticisms levelled by Bogdan and Biklen which I am sure do not only apply to novice writers:

> Novice writers are big procrastinators. They find countless reasons not to get started. Even when they finally get themselves seated at their desks, they always seem to find diversions: make the coffee, sharpen the pencil, go to the bathroom, thumb through more literature, sometimes even get up and return to the field.

> Remember that you are never ready to write; writing is something you must make a conscious decision to do and then discipline yourself to follow through. (Quoted in Bell, 1987, p. 172)

One of the reasons writing up can be such a struggle is because often it is not solely a question of reporting carefully worked out ideas but rather is a central process in the clarification and development of those ideas. When these formulate slowly through successive rejected drafts it is easy to get depressed through seeming lack of progress. It is probably helpful to draw up a writing plan incorporating the kinds of features suggested by Bell (1987, p. 125), such as stopping at a point where it will be easy to resume writing rather than just before a difficult section.

A Climate for Practitioner Research

Although research may be undertaken individually (for example, Horbury and Reed) or as part of a team engaged in related projects (for example, Winter and Wright) practitioner research always involves others — pupils, teachers, parents, governors. It is always a collaborative undertaking in that to varying degrees data collection depends on the cooperation of the parties to the research problem. While Gregson also derived moral support and information from members of her team she worked collaboratively on her project with a class teacher. From this experience she came to appreciate the need for partners in action research to give and take constructive criticism and the degree of understanding, trust and goodwill required to see a project through to a successful conclusion (pp. 37–9). Access to data, the ways in which they will be collected, the uses to which they are put and ethical issues such as confidentiality and ownership of data have to be negotiated with those involved. Also, as discussed in Chapter 1 (pp. 18–9), if the implications of school-based research are to be understood and their importance acknowledged and appropriately acted upon by members of staff other than those involved in the data collection, then they have to be kept informed of, or actively engaged in, the research project.

Cassidy (1986) claims that 'co-ordinated action research can be a powerful tool for generating school-wide curriculum change, the professional development of staff, and quite radical changes to the ethos of the school' (p. 134). Shumsky (1956) views collaboration as essential both for the well-being of the researcher and the resulting quality of the thought and action. He identifies five major ways in which collaboration contributes to the success of practitioner research:

— Working together on a common problem is a source of security, status and recognition.
— The stimulation that comes from group contact helps to overcome inertia and self-defeatist attitudes.
— The fear of failure is lessened and an attempt to embark on an intelligent action is more possible.
— Group work is conducive to the release of potential creativity and in promoting social vision, inspiration and critical thinking.
— A promising way of initiating and securing change is by involving the potential consumers of the research results in the planning, analysis and interpretation of the research data. (pp. 183–4)

The message to those engaged in practitioner research, which aims to initiate and sustain change going beyond the individual classroom, is that if it is to have maximum impact an appropriate environment has to be created. Such an environment requires collaborative relationships to span heirarchies and enable ideas, information and decision-making to be shared throughout the institution. Besides being supportive it also needs to be capable of sustaining reflection that is both self-critical and critical of the school and the wider educational context and enables teachers 'to break out of the "survival" cycle' (Gregson, p. 53). This runs counter to the prevailing school culture which displays a powerful cult of individualism (Hargreaves, 1980, p. 142) and leads to the physical isolation of teachers and to norms of not sharing, observing or discussing one another's work (Lortie, 1975, p. 164). To take steps to change this culture is a difficult and complex process which is dependent on the support of the head. Consequently, individual practitioner researchers sometimes feel disillusioned and alienated from their colleagues:

Unless you are working with colleagues who are genuinely interested in education and who do not see extra study as simply a means of gaining a qualification for promotion you will become isolated from, and disappointed with, them. Since my MA I have turned down an appointment as Assistant Head of Upper school and have asked for redeployment. (Outstation evaluation questionnaire response, 1989)

Those who are researching as part of a group may resort to developing their own subculture to support their research, thus reducing the possibility of other staff being influenced by their work. This is illustrated by the Action Research on Change in Schools (ARCS) Project (Oja and Pine, 1989), which involved university researchers from the National Institute of Education,

USA, working with teachers from two public middle/junior high schools. The project aimed to determine the effect on teachers' personal and professional development of participation in collaborative action research and in what ways the experience might influence teachers' ability to initiate future change in practice. A major finding was that 'the action research teams created their own operational contexts which contrasted markedly with the operational context of their schools' (p. 111).

Increasingly there is a thrust towards creating operational contexts in schools which emphasize staff collaboration and participation in decision-making and have the potential to create the kinds of conditions in which practitioner research can flourish. For example, in order to establish school curriculum development plans, schools are being asked to reflect corporately on where they are now, where they need to get to and how this might be accomplished. Also, a whole school approach to planning for the National Curriculum is advocated which promotes:

> a shared understanding of, and commitment to, curricular goals; real participation of all staff in curriculum policy-making; clear and explicit delegation of curriculum leadership. (NCC, 1989, p. 12)

The implementation of the National Curriculum has undoubtedly increased and enhanced the quality of debate both on new issues and on those long recognized as problematic. It also appears to have greatly increased the amount of collaborative curriculum planning and review that is taking place in primary schools. This can be viewed in a negative light as teachers uniting to assist each other through the stresses and strains of a current educational crisis. Alternatively, it may be viewed as a positive response to the challenge posed by the National Curriculum which is breaking down the 'individualist culture' of schools. The National Curriculum together with Local Management of Schools and the pace at which these initiatives are being introduced makes it not only desirable but necessary that primary headteachers delegate curriculum leadership, representation on in-service courses and LEA training days and the arrangement of school-based INSET to their staff. Initially, headteachers may find this difficult if it requires a major shift in the way they interpret their role, their self-image and the expectations that staff have of them. However, ultimately this could provide teachers with more power over decision-making and therefore more ways in which to use their research to influence school policy and practice. A school environment conducive to sharing the aims, values and processes of practitioner research might enable such research to become generally understood and accessible to all, rather than the preserve of an elite or subversive subculture as has tended to happen in the past.

Personal and Professional Development

The contributors all feel that the research in which they engaged contributed in varying ways to their personal and professional development. However, as they are all proponents of practitioner research, in order to evaluate this claim in a wider context it seems appropriate to briefly consider some of the findings of a questionnaire survey that a colleague and I conducted in the Spring Term 1989. The questionnaire was sent to all the past Outstation students and the students on the two current Outstations in order to gain their perceptions of the personal and professional effects of course participation. We received 127 returns which represented an 80 per cent response rate.

The survey identified more advantages to research involvement than disadvantages and stressed the value of the personal gains. However, certain negative effects were recurrent in the data relating to the time-consuming, all-demanding and therefore stressful nature of carrying out research. A few teachers felt that commitment to their research projects had resulted in aspects of their teaching receiving inadequate attention which was a cause for guilt and anxiety. Many commented on the way the research had encroached on their social life reducing opportunites for leisure pursuits and time spent with their partners and children. For most this was viewed as a temporary sacrifice but for about a fifth of the sample at various stages in the research it was a serious problem:

> I felt exhausted and physically ill by the end. Every holiday I worked on my research so I felt that I hardly ever had a break. Family life suffered.

A few found that the extra burden of work placed an additional unacceptable stress on family life which left either permanent scars or contributed to a complete breakdown in relationships. Clearly commitment to practitioner research which can have such personal repercussions is not something to be embarked on without careful consideration, particularly in the current climate which is making new demands of teachers.

Having examined the potential personal difficulties that can arise from any substantial piece of practitioner research I shall now turn to the major personal benefits which were identified in the questionnaire responses and echoed in the follow-up interviews to the survey and earlier Outstation evaluations. An increase in confidence was identified as the major contribution of participation in the research process. Confidence was thought to have been improved in a range of differing contexts: contributing to educational debate whether in the staffroom or other forums; making a critical appraisal of the implications of school policies; developing a personal philosophy on teaching and learning; trying out new ideas in the classroom; relating to pupils and carrying out self-evaluation. Linked to this was a commonly expressed 'feeling of self-satisfaction' thought to be particularly important 'as the job doesn't always do this nowadays'. 'In a profession where it seems there are few tangible rewards' their research provided the teachers with a valued opportunity to experience success. Other frequently mentioned areas of personal gain, for which the teachers who were interviewed supplied examples, were heightened awareness of alternative perspectives on issues, a willingness to question existing assumptions and predilections, a more analytical approach to problems and open-mindedness to new ideas.

The possession of these competencies and the confidence to put them into practice can assist individuals to carry out their responsibilities to their personal satisfaction, benefit the schools and help to create the kind of open-minded collaborative, critically reflective school environment that was advocated in the previous section. Thus Vickers' research enabled her to meet her job specification and draw up an Equal Opportunities Policy and Winter's action research into process-based science helped her to fulfill her responsibilities as the school's science coordinator. An evaluation into consultancy-based INSET that I carried out (Webb, 1989) revealed that headteachers in primary schools felt that there was a considerable need for staff to acquire the appropriate skills to initiate and carry out curriculum review and development activities and communicate the findings to staff. Vickers believes that teachers practised in the art of collecting, analyzing and acting upon evidence will be in a strong position to evaluate the effects of the implementation of the National Curriculum on teaching and learning and to enquire into and tackle the classroom problems and policy issues that may be identified. Also, as Wright suggests in relation to her own experience, the skills developed through the close study of children learning will assist in the process of monitoring pupil progress through the National Curriculum.

Changing Classroom Practice

Many practitioners, like the majority of participants in the Outstation Programme, undertake case study and action research in order to gain insights into problematic aspects of classroom life and to inform their judgments on the way forward. As Rowland (1986) claims:

> ...the in-depth study of selected samples of activity from our classrooms can lead us to challenge, modify and at times radically alter those assumptions from which we work when we interact with children in the classroom. It can help us build an understanding of the learning process and of the concerns of children which are expressed and developed through that process (p. 29)

The contributors' research accounts demonstrate to varying degrees and in different ways how the critical reflection on practice through the collection and analysis of data challenged their preconceptions, provided new insights, influenced their thinking and suggested practical courses of action.

However, practitioner research has relevance and value beyond the particular situation that gives rise to it. In various ways accounts such as those in this book have the potential to exert a wider influence on classroom practice. Readers may generalize from the situations portrayed by the contributors to their own experience and in doing so critically reflect on their own practice. For example, reading about Russell's discovery that the children believed that the only reason for writing activities was to please her, might serve to alert readers to the need to devise 'real' opportunities for children to write for diverse audiences and to ensure that they understand the purposes behind set tasks. As well as provoking questions the research accounts also provide ideas to assist in the development of classroom practice — for example the activities enjoyed by the children in the study of information gathering in Chapter 5 and its concluding suggestions (pp. 119–23).

An important role of practitioner research is to generate pedagogic theory which is of direct relevance to teachers because it offers them alternative ways of understanding and acting in their own situations. Gregson takes the reader through her experiences and in doing so leads them to challenge some of the assumptions that they may have shared with her. She documents that a major insight for her was the recognition that she often responded to pupil behaviour which was symptomatic of learning difficulties rather than trying to find out the underlying cause of the behaviour. For example, her impressions that the children lacked both the motivation to work on topic tasks and the necessary skills to use the school library and reference books were replaced by an understanding of the limitations of the resources on offer and the subsequent appropriateness of the pupils' coping strategies. She describes how her observations called her to look for reasons behind the claims made by Lunzer and Gardner (1979) that while pupils could verbalize strategies for information retrieval they could not put them into practice. Through analysis of the data gathered on pupils' difficulties with the text that she presented them she came to theorise about the ways in which learning contexts rather than children's abilities give rise to 'more or less able' readers. Her emerging theories of teaching and learning contribute to pedagogic understanding and can inform the thinking of other teachers experiencing similar difficulties or wishing to review practice in relation to developing pupils' reference skills. Similarly in Winter's portrayal of the science activities that she devised and monitored the reader is given access to her developing pedagogic theory about the factors which promote and hinder learning through a process-based approach. Readers can regard her pedagogic theories as hypotheses to be tested out, challenged and refined in their own classrooms. In so doing the learning that has occurred for one teacher in one situation can contribute to the professional development of others in a range of related situations.

In trying to achieve change in schools and classrooms it is essential that 'professional development must focus on a need' (Fullan, 1982, p. 264) and that the resultant innovation should embody criteria which render it 'practical' (Doyle and Ponder, 1977–8). This has been borne out in the assistance and support for research projects given to members of the Outstation Programme by their school colleagues. Where projects addressed generally held concerns and/or reflected national and LEA initiatives — such as pupil profiling and record keeping, the use of IT and primary science — staff interest and involvement was easier to generate and to maintain. Interest in projects focusing upon the concerns of individual teacher researchers tended to be quickly supplanted by more pressing and global issues.

The implementation of the National Curriculum has created an array of 'practical' needs to form an important agenda for practitioner research. Writing in *Junior Education* (July, 1989), Campbell says:

> I prefer to think about the National Curriculum in terms . . . of an experiment whose outcome is uncertain and whose hypotheses are to be put to the test in schools. What we have is a set of hunches in search of evidence — evidence that can only be provided by schools, governors and LEA inspectors adopting an open-minded attitude to it, as it is introduced. (p. 10)

He suggests four fundamental issues about which evidence needs to be collected: the levels at which the attainment targets have been pitched; the ordering of the levels of attainment within the core subjects; feasible ways of collecting reliable evidence that attainment targets have been reached and teaching the National Curriculum through integrated topics or themes.

Legitimation for practitioner researchers to regard the National Curriculum as something to be tried out, critically examined and developed can be found in both the DES documentation and that of the National Curriculum Council (NCC). In the back of the statutory orders (see, for example DES and the Welsh Office, 1989, pp. 7–8) it states that 'in formulating the statements of attainment which define the levels, the working assumption, which will need to be tested in practice, has been that the pupils should typically be capable of achieving around levels 2, 4, 5/6 or 6/7 respectively at or near the reporting ages of 7, 11, 14 and 16'. An acknowledgment that 'The introduction of the National Curriculum raises questions which do not have easy answers, nor will they be solved overnight' is made in *A Framework for the Primary Curriculum* (NCC, 1989, p. 2). It points out the need for the NCC to develop close links with schools and LEAs because 'There will be many joint lessons to be learned from the work to be done over the next few years' (p. 22).

As the statutory orders for each National Curriculum subject are formulated they will pose specific challenges for practitioner researchers. There are likely to be other projects like the one carried out by Winter which address the teaching of science through investigative work. Data handling in mathematics and speaking and listening in English may be areas where teachers feel the need for research to inform curriculum development. Also, as identified above by Campbell (1989), teaching the National Curriculum through topic work is likely to provide an important focus for teacher enquiry. As discussed in Chapter 5, although initially the subject-based National Curriculum was viewed as a threat to topic work, its requirements and accompanying assessment procedures can be viewed as a means of achieving the structure, continuity, progression and systematic monitoring and record keeping that has been lacking. Practitioner research could develop a range of alternative models of topic work for teaching the National Curriculum which both build on the best of existing topics and explore planning new topics starting from the programmes of study. The models might include subject-specific topics and topics which only span a few elements of two or three of the foundation subjects as well as topics that incorporate a wide range of subjects which is probably the most common approach. These models could be evaluated in practice in terms of their advantages and disadvantages for meeting and monitoring National Curriculum requirements and for providing opportunities which allow pupils to experience depth in learning as well as breadth. Also, a number of skills will re-occur in all subjects as they are formulated, such as study/information skills, discussion learning, question posing, problem-solving, the use of IT and pupil self-evaluation. Practitioner research might explore the ways in which these can be combined and developed within topic work.

Bennett, Desforges, Cockburn and Wilkinson (1984) claim that teachers typically adopt a 'crisis mangement style':

> This requires that they be all things to all pupils at all times. The consequences of this style include constant interruptions, divided teacher attention, lack of adequate class supervision, lack of opportunity for adequate diagnosis and explanation and, in many instances, teacher frustration. In short, a learning environment which is far from optimal for teacher or taught. (p. 219)

The National Curriculum which requires an 'optimal learning environment' has created a demanding agenda for research on classroom organization and teaching and learning styles. There is a need for practitioner research to develop and improve a range of different kinds of groupwork within various forms of curriculum organization. *A Framework for the Primary Curriculum* (NCC, 1989) recognizes that teachers already arrange their classes in a variety of groups such as friendship groups, mixed age groups, age groups, mixed ability groups and groups of pupils of similar ability (pp. 10–11). It stresses the value of different strategies for grouping pupils in terms of assisting in the effective use of resources and deployment of teacher time and in improving the quality of learning experiences for pupils. The need to provide varied opportunities for pupils to work in groups in order to develop the skills of working cooperatively, leadership, clarifying and developing ideas through sharing, problem-solving and speaking and listening is an important part of the Programmes of Study for the core subjects and featured in the Statements of Attainment. However, research has revealed that, even in primary schools, pupils often sit in groups but work individually although they are tackling the same task (see, for example, Galton and Simon, 1980; Tann, 1988).

The National Curriculum also focuses attention on the need to diagnose pupils' abilities in order to set them tasks which make appropriate practical and intellectual demands. The research carried out by Bennett *et al.* (1984) demonstrates that this is a difficult process:

> In both number and language work at infant level teachers were able to provide a match on approximately 40% of tasks. About a third were too difficult for the child and a little over a quarter were too easy . . . It was also very clear that the quality of matching varied in relation to the children's intellectual standing in the

classroom. High attainers were underestimated on over 40% of tasks assigned to them ... But an equally clear pattern of overestimation was found for low attainers. Of their assigned tasks 44% were overestimated in both language and number work. (pp. 214–15)

Therefore, another area for practitioner research to explore and develop is that of differentiation. Research questions could usefully be asked about the ways in which learning opportunities might be better matched to individuals' needs and experiences through employing various types of tasks and a range of teaching strategies and resources.

At the moment, the area of greatest speculation, contention and anxiety is that of assessment. Anxieties over the possible negative outcomes of the new national assessment procedures continue to abound in this period of uncertainty, as educationalists speculate on the form that these procedures might take. The development of Teacher Assessment and the effects on teaching and learning of the Standard Assessment Tasks (SATs) are likely to be the focus of much practitioner research. As has been demonstrated (Treacher, 1989) practitioner researchers can make invaluable contributions to school assessment policies through action research projects which examine the ways in which staff evaluate pupils' learning and the criteria that they use.

Influencing Policy

Many practitioner researchers prefer to engage in the kinds of classroom-focused research described in the previous section because it addresses their practical concerns and is likely to be of immediate benefit to their teaching. However, others may set out to influence policy-makers at school or LEA level. McCann explains how her research influenced home–school relations and led to policies which took account of the culture of the Mirpuri pupils, such as the setting up of a toy and book library, visits by the multicultural librarian telling stories in mother tongue, the provision of alternative food for lunch and less time and attention being given to Christmas festivities. In describing the process of drawing up an Equal Opportunities Policy Vickers shows how the research process can make a valuable contribution to the production of informed workable policies. The implementation of the National Curriculum will mean that policies for equal opportunities and multicultural education will need reviewing and updating. Other important policy issues likely to require research and development are the factors constraining and promoting collaborative planning within and between schools, the ability of school-based in-service training to meet individual staff and school needs, the role and effectiveness of subject coordinators, record keeping and the training and influence of school governors.

Through seeking to understand school problems in order to pose solutions, practitioner research inevitably raises questions with implications beyond the school, which are about the nature and origins of the problems, the values and beliefs underpinning proposed solutions and the consequences to which these give rise. Encouraging teachers to critique the contexts of their practices Pollard and Tann (1987) state that:

> They should speak out if they view particular aims and policies as being impracticable, educationally unsound or morally questionable. In such circumstances, the professional skills, knowledge and judgements of teachers should be brought to bear on policy-makers directly. (p. 6)

Adelman and Young (1985) are very pessimistic about the possibility of practitioner research having any effect on policy-making beyond the level of the school. They regard all research as based:

> On the assumption that careful, systematic enquiry into a publicly acknowledged, valid problem will be seriously considered by policy makers and others with influence in educational matters. That assumption has little to support it. Educational research by and large is ignored or taken up within political expediences. It rarely informs or extends public debate. (p. 52)

Pollard (1984), while acknowledging that the nature and focus of ethnographic work means that it is most likely to inform policy-makers only within schools, believes that its impact could be more widespread. As much practitioner research has its roots in anthropological and sociological ethnography and shares the same techniques of data gathering it is useful to consider the way forward that he suggests. He proposes that the respectability of ethnography should be increased by a more rigorous approach to methodology, where appropriate quantitative and qualitative methods should be combined and case studies on related themes should be cumulated in order to enable theory generated from a specific case to be verified and developed across multiple cases. The implementation of the National Curriculum has created a situation where many practitioners are likely to be embarked on similar, or closely related, projects and a dialogue about these has already started. This could serve to encourage a more coordinated and cumulative approach. Networks of practitioner researchers, such as the well-established Classroom Action Research Network (CARN) and the newly-formed regional groups of the Association for the Study of Primary Education (ASPE) could have an important role in encouraging this to happen.

Finch (1986), in her analysis of the ways in which politicians and administrators actually use research findings, argues that it is unrealistic to expect policy-makers to make direct use of research in the way envisaged by Adelman and Young (1985). She attributes this to the difference in values and interests between researchers and policy-makers and the fact that the net result of various findings is a complex and diverse picture of the situation, which does not provide straightforward policy guidance. Rather, she suggests that ethnographic research has the potential to have a significant indirect influence on policy through providing new conceptualizations, which 'redefine the terms of the debate, refashion its boundaries and illuminate features which have previously been hidden' (Finch, 1988, p. 196). She suggests three main ways in which these new conceptualizations might be achieved:

> Showing how much change actually occurs in practice; identifying the unintended consequences of policy initiatives; exposing the contradictions in policy which are apparent when it is implemented. (1988, p. 190)

These are highly relevant to practitioner research on aspects of the National Curriculum, as I will now briefly indicate.

The National Curriculum employs a range of new terms (see glossary in DES, 1989, Annex B), with which most teachers are now very familiar, to describe the educational process. Critics of the National Curriculum predict the impoverished nature of education in the future on the basis of the production line language used by many of its proponents to characterize its 'delivery'. How far does this new language represent substantive changes in practice and how far is it merely a change of labels? During the spring and summer terms of 1989, schools and LEAs worked hard to translate programmes of study into schemes of work. Now practitioner researchers need to consider how far the reality of classroom practice matches the rhetoric of the new documentation. The advantages and the disadvantages of the new content and ways of working for all those involved need to be identified.

As we move towards the 1990s, all schools will undergo a considerable amount of change in various ways, to different degrees and at different speeds as a result of the 1988 Education Reform Act. Although we can predict change with certainty, we can only speculate on its effects and on how far it will fulfill the intentions of policy-makers at all levels in the system.

Practitioner evaluations of particular school policies and the resulting changes in practice will reveal both the intended and the unintended outcomes of the various facets of the National Curriculum.

Finally, practitioner research not only demonstrates the strengths and weaknesses of policies in practice, but reveals tensions between aims and outcomes and contradictions within the policies themselves. One area where potential tension exists and which is therefore a likely subject for practitioner research is the effect on pupils with special educational needs of the National Curriculum and Local Management of Schools. On the one hand, the principle of participation is stressed (see Circular 5, NCC, 1989) as it is intended that the quality of educational provision in ordinary schools should be enhanced for these pupils by giving them access to a broader and more balanced curriculum in a context which stresses both the need to match tasks to individual competencies and to monitor individual progress. On the other hand, there are fears that the publication of schools' performances on Standard Assessment Tasks could lead to the principle of participation being abandoned as schools respond to market forces by trying to attract able pupils in order to achieve better results and by allocating less time and fewer resources for pupils with learning difficulties.

As Fullan (1982) points out 'neglect of the phenomenology of change — that is, how people actually experience change as distinct from how it might have been intended — is at the heart of the spectacular lack of success of most reforms' (p. 4). The National Curriculum is an extremely complex innovation which is occurring simultaneously with other fundamental changes such as Local Management of Schools and the current training initiatives to overcome teacher shortages. Practitioner research, which is currently being undertaken, can provide insights into the ways in which one innovation influences the implementation of another and the combined effects of multiple innovations on schools. It can portray the 'realities' of classroom life and the perspectives on the changes of teachers and pupils. Also, it can identify the factors at school, LEA and national level which facilitate and constrain the plans for change laid down by local and national policy-makers. Thus, it has the potential to make a powerful contribution to our understanding of the current situation and the further development of theory on the process of educational change.

Conclusion

As has been argued and demonstrated throughout this book practitioner research can promote the development of the critical and creative powers of individual teachers. The confidence, knowledge and skills thus acquired empower them to both implement current initiatives in an exploratory and constructive way and to offer an open-minded critically reflective response based on evidence. Although practitioner research can be carried out by individuals, it is always dependent to varying degrees on the cooperation of others and is most influential when it has whole school support or involvement. The current emphasis in British primary schools on collaborative planning, together with the increasing acknowledgment of the value of collecting evidence to inform decison-making, should assist in creating a school climate which strengthens the influence of practitioner research and encourages its findings to be acted upon.

The provision of research-based higher degree courses whether focusing on professional learning, curriculum development, school management or evaluation and assessment continues to expand. Initial worries that applications for the York Outstation Programme might diminish because of teachers' increased workloads have proved unfounded since practitioner research has been viewed as assisting applicants to fulfil their professional roles. As has been illustrated in relation to the demands made on primary schools by the National Curriculum, the current research agenda is a full and challenging one. To adequately address the breadth and diversity of issues which that agenda encompasses will require imaginative research designs and the full range of methodologies available and appropriate to practitioner research.

We are in a period of great change, which can be seen as a crisis creating anxiety and tension. However, a time of change is also a time of excitement, creating opportunities and new possibilities, and this seems particularly the case for practitioner researchers. Thus the current situation offers an unparalleled opportunity for them to assume a more central role in curriculum evaluation and development and to contribute to policy-making at school, LEA and national levels. This book demonstrates what can be achieved through practitioner research, contributes to the debate on its origins, methods and purposes and will hopefully encourage readers who have not participated in such research before to wish to do so.

References

ADELMAN, C. and YOUNG, M. F. D. (1985) 'The assumptions of educational research: The last twenty years', in SHIPMAN, M. (Ed.) *Educational Research: Principles, Policies and Practices*, Lewes, Falmer Press.
BALL, S. J. (1985) 'Participant observation with pupils', in BURGESS, R. G. (Ed.) *Strategies of Educational Research: Qualitative Methods*, Lewes, Falmer Press.

BELL, J. (1987) *Doing Your Research Project*, Milton Keynes, Open University Press.

BELL, J., BUSH T., FOX A., GOODEY, J. and GOULDING, S. (Eds.) (1984) *Conducting Small-Scale Investigations in Educational Management*, London, Harper and Row in association with the Open University.

BENNETT, N., DESFORGES, C., COCKBURN, A. and WILKINSON, B. (1984) *The Quality of Pupil Learning Experiences*, New Jersey, Lawrence Erlbaum Associates.

BURGESS, R. (1984) 'Keeping a Research Diary', in BELL, J., BUSH, T., FOX, A., GOODEY, J. and GOULDING, S. (Eds.) *Conducting Small-Scale Investigations in Educational Management*, London, Harper and Row in association with the Open University.

CAMPBELL, J. (1989) 'In search of evidence', *Junior Education*, July, pp. 10–11.

CASSIDY, T. (1986) 'Initiating and encouraging action research in comprehensive schools', in HUSTLER, D., CASSIDY, T., and CUFF, T. (Eds.) *Action Research in Classrooms and Schools*, London, Allen and Unwin.

DEPARTMENT OF EDUCATION AND SCIENCE (1989) *From Policy to Practice*, London, DES.

DEPARTMENT OF EDUCATION AND SCIENCE AND THE WELSH OFFICE (1989) *Science in the National Curriculum*, London, HMSO.

DOYLE, W. and PONDER, G. (1977–78) 'The practicality ethic in teacher decision making', *Interchange*, **8**, 3, pp. 1–12.

DOUGLASS, J. (1987) 'Professional Benefits from the MA'. Unpublished paper on the second Cleveland Outstation.

ELLIOTT, J. (1981) 'Teacher–Pupil Interaction and the Quality of Learning Project', Working Paper, No. 1, London Schools Council (mimeo).

ELLIOT, J. and ADELMAN, C. (1976) *Innovation at Classroom Level: A Case Study of the Ford Teaching Project*, Unit 28, Open University Course E203: Curriculum Design and Development, Milton Keynes, Open University Press.

FINCH, J. (1986) *Research and Policy: The Uses of Qualitative Methods in Social and Educational Research*, Lewes, Falmer Press.

FINCH, J. (1988) 'Ethnography and public policy' in POLLARD, A. *et al.* (Eds.) *Education, Training and the New Vocationalism*, Milton Keynes, Open University Press.

FULLAN, M. (1982) *The Meaning of Educational Change*, Ontario, OISE Press.

GALTON, M. and SIMON, B. (1980) (Eds.) *Progress and Performance in the Primary Classroom*, London, Routledge and Kegan Paul.

GLASER, B. and STRAUSS, A. L. (1967) *The Discovery of Grounded Theory*, Chicago, Aldine.

HAMMERSLEY, M. and ATKINSON, P. (1983) *Ethnography, Principles in Practice*, London, Tavistock.

HARGREAVES, D. (1980) 'The occupational culture of teachers', in WOODS, P. (Ed.) *Teacher Strategies*, Beckenham, Croom Helm.

HITCHCOCK, G. and HUGHES, D. (1989) *Research and the Teacher*, London, Routledge.

HOOK, C. (1981) *Studying Classrooms*, Victoria, Deakin University.

HOPKINS, D. (1985) *A Teacher's Guide to Classroom Research*, Milton Keynes, Open University Press.

HOPKINS, D. (1987) 'Enhancing validity in action research', in RUDDUCK, J., HOPKINS, D., SANGER, J. and LINCOLN, P. *Collaborative Enquiry and Information Skills*, London, British Library.

LEWIS, I. and MUNN, P. (1987) *So You Want To Do Research*, Edinburgh, The Scottish Council for Research in Education.

LORTIE, D. (1975) *Schoolteacher: A Sociological Study*, Chicago, Ill., University of Chicago Press.

LUNZER, E. and GARDNER, K. (Eds.) (1979) *The Effective Use of Reading*, London, Heinemann.

MCTAGGART, R. and KEMMIS, S. (1982) *The Action Research Planner*, Geelong, Deakin University.

MEASOR, L. (1985) 'Interviewing: a strategy in qualitative research', in BURGESS, R. G. *Strategies of Educational Research: Qualitative Methods*, Lewes, Falmer Press.

NATIONAL CURRICULUM COUNCIL (1989) *A Framework for the Primary Curriculum*, Curriculum Guidance No. 1, York, NCC.

OBERG, A. and MCCUTCHEON, G. (1989) 'Teachers' experience doing action research', *Peabody Journal of Education*, **64**, 2, pp. 116–27.

OJA, S.N. and PINE, G.J. (1989) 'Collaborative action research: teachers' stages of development and school contexts', *Peabody Journal of Education*, **64**, 2, pp. 96–113.

PATTON, M. Q. (1980) *Qualitative Evaluation Methods*, London, Sage Publications.

PLUMMER, K. (1983) *Documents of Life*, London, George Allen and Unwin.

POLLARD, A. (1984) 'Ethnography and social policy for classroom practice', in BARTON, L. and WALKER, S. (Eds.) *Social Crisis and Educational Research*, London, Croom Helm.

POLLARD, A. and TANN, S. (1987) *Reflective Teaching in the Primary School*, London, Cassell.

ROWLAND, S. (1986) 'Classroom enquiry: An approach to understanding children', in HUSTLER, D., CASSIDY, T. and CUFF, T. (Eds.) *Action Research in Classrooms and Schools*, London, Allen and Unwin.

SHUMSKY, A. (1956) 'Co-operation in action research: A rationale', *Journal of Educational Sociology*, **30**, pp. 180–5.

TANN, S. C. (Ed.) (1988) *Developing Topic Work in the Primary School*, Lewes, Falmer Press.

TREACHER, V. (Ed.) (1989) *Assessment and Evaluation in the Arts*, Berkshire LEA SCDC Arts in Schools Project, Reading, Berkshire Local Education Authority.

WALKER, R. (1985) *Doing Research: A Handbook for Teachers*, London, Methuen.

WEBB, R. (1989) 'Changing practice through consultancy-based INSET', *School Organisation*, **9**, 1, pp. 39–52.

WINTER, R. (1989) *Learning from Experience: Principles and Practice in Action-Research*, Lewes, Falmer Press.

WOODS, P. (1986) *Inside Schools, Ethnography in Educational Research*, London, Routledge and Kegan Paul.

Notes on Contributors

Doreen Gregson began her career as a primary school teacher. Later she specialized in the teaching of reading and moved into the peripatetic remedial reading service. She is now an advisory teacher for language in Kirklees.

Alastair Horbury is the lecturer responsible for running the Outstation Programme at the Department of Education, University of York. Prior to joining the Department in 1986 he worked as a primary school teacher.

Avrille McCann is a home–school liaison teacher for an infant and a junior school. Her varied teaching career includes experience of teaching in all sectors of education from preschool playgroups to adult classes.

Beatrice Reed spent ten years teaching in primary schools in both England and Canada and latterly she worked as a support teacher for travelling children. In 1989 she took up her current position as lecturer in primary education at Newcastle upon Tyne Polytechnic.

Linda Russell became a deputy headteacher of an infant and nursery school in 1989 after five years varied experience of teaching infants in Kirklees.

Jenny Vickers is now a headteacher of a primary school in a social priority area in Cleveland. She has spent much of her career working in a similar school in the same area, although prior to this she spent six years teaching in Germany and Hong Kong.

Rosemary Webb taught for ten years in infant, primary and middle schools. She joined the Education Department at the University of York in 1985 and subsequently took over the running of the Outstation Programme. Since the research for this book she has been appointed to the National Curriculum Council as a Professional Officer for Primary Education.

Virginia Winter began her teaching career in secondary schools in the late 1960s and since then she has taught in junior and special schools. Currently, she is working as a science coordinator and a year leader in a Bradford Middle School.

Susan Wright began teaching in a comprehensive school where she was responsible for RE. While her children were small she helped to run a preschool playgroup. She now teaches part-time at a primary school in Calderdale where she specializes in the teaching of mathematics.

Author Index

Abbs, P., 115, 123
Adelman, C., 57, 75, 100, 123
Adelman, C., Jenkins, D. and Kemmis, S., 5, 10, 128, 152
Adelman, C. and Young, M. F. D., 22, 31, 265, 266, 268
Althusser, L., 22, 31
Amin, M., 189, 200
Anning, A., 3, 10, 36, 53
Anwar, M., 185, 190, 200
Assessment of Performance Unit, 154, 157, 181
Association for Science Education, Association for Teachers of Mathematics and National Association for the Teaching of English, 98, 123
Atkinson, P., 133, 152
Avann, P., 97, 104, 116, 123

Ball, S. J., 129, 152, 249, 268
Barnes, D., 136, 146, 152
Bartholomew, J., 21, 31
Bassey, M., 3, 4, 10
Becker, H. S., 71, 75, 100, 123
Becker, H. S., Geer, B., Hughes, E. C. and Strauss, A. L., 224, 242
Bell, G. H., 6, 10
Bell, J., 8, 10, 248, 255, 268
Bell, J., Bush, T., Fox, A., Goodey, J. and Goulding, S., 248, 268
Bennett, N., Desforges, C., Cockburn, A. and Wilkinson, B., 262, 263–264, 269
Bernstein, B., 72, 75
Blank, M., Rose, S. A. and Berlin, L. J., 49, 53
Bloom, W., 96, 123
Blumer, H., 226, 242
Bogdan, R. and Taylor, S. J., 45, 53
Boone, N., 13, 31

Bowles, S. and Gintis, H., 22, 31
Brake, T., 114, 123
Brinton, P. and Shaw, C., 96, 123
Browne, A., 49, 53
Buckingham, B. R., 13, 14, 15, 31
Burgess, R. G., 22, 31, 56, 75, 101, 102, 123, 158, 161, 181, 251, 269

Campbell, J., 261, 262, 269
Carr, W., 27, 28, 31
Carr, W. and Kemmis, S., 18, 20, 31
Carroll, Lewis, 126, 152
Cassidy, T., 255, 269
Chambers, D. W., 163, 181
Cicourel, A. V., 27, 28, 31
Cohen, L. and Manion, L., 205, 221
Collier, J., 17, 31
Connell, R. W., *et al.*, 203, 204, 221
Cope, E. and Gray, J., 23, 31
Corey, S. M., 18, 19, 20, 24, 30, 31
Corrigan, P., 58, 75
Cox, B., 62, 75
Cullingford, C., 87, 95
Cummings, C. and Hustler, D., 36, 54
Czerniewska, P., *et al.*, 93, 95

Dadds, M., 96, 123
Davies, B., 236, 242
Deem, R., 207, 221
Delamont, S., 99, 100, 123
Denscombe, M., 37, 54
Denzin, N. K., 224, 242
Department of Education and Science, 86, 95, 97, 107, 123, 124, 126, 137, 139, 152, 154, 155, 175, 266, 269
Department of Education and Science and the Welsh Office, 98, 122, 124, 131, 152, 155, 175, 177, 182, 262, 269
Dewey, J., 16, 31

Donaldson, M., 150, 152, 182
Douglass, J., 245, 269
Doyle, W. and Ponder, G., 261, 269
Driver, R., 157, 182

Early Years Curriculum Group, 98, 124
Ebbutt, D. and Elliott, J., 15, 32
Edwards, A. and Westgate, D., 132, 152
Elliott, J., 24, 25, 28, 32, 254, 269
Elliott, J. and Adelman, C., 24, 32, 251, 269
Equal Opportunities Commission, 8, 10
Evans, D. M., 121, 124
Evans, K. M., 184, 200

Feyerabend, P. K., 224, 242
Finch, J., 13, 32, 265, 266, 269
Ford, J., 224, 242
Fullan, M., 3, 10, 261, 267, 269

Galton, M. and Simon, B., 263, 269
Galton, M., Simon, B. and Croll, P., 70, 75, 97, 124
Galton, M. and Wilcox, J., 62, 63, 75
Glaser, B. G. and Strauss, A. L., 223, 226, 243, 254, 269
Gorbutt, D., 21, 22, 32
Gordon, C., 42, 54
Gregson, D., 35, 54
Griffin, M., 97, 124
Groundwater-Smith, S., 26, 27, 28, 32, 39, 54
Grundy, S., 8, 10, 27, 32
Gunning, S., Gunning, D. and Wilson, J., 96, 124

Habermas, J., 27, 32
Hammersley, M. and Atkinson, P., 223, 243, 247, 251, 252, 269
Hammersley, M. and Woods, P., 22, 32
Hargreaves, A., 61, 76, 228, 243
Hargreaves, D., 256, 269
Harlen, W., 154, 182
Harris, J., 185, 201
Heather, P., 97, 124
Hill, D., 190, 201
Hill, M., 52, 54
Hitchcock, G. and Hughes, D., 251, 269
Hoare, R. J., 96, 124
Hodgeon, J., 211, 221
Hook, C., 249, 269
Hopkins, D., 158, 182, 248, 254, 269
Hounsell, D. and Martin, E., 20, 32

Holly, P., 19, 32
Hustler, D., Cassidy, T. and Cuff, T., 7, 10, 25, 32

Irving, A. and Snape, W., 20, 32
Isaacs, N., 175, 182

Jackson, P., 100, 124
Jones, J., 121, 124

Kerry, T., Eggleston, J. F. and Bradley, H. W., 97, 124
Kerslake, D., 151, 152
Khan, V. S., 185, 201
King, C., 120, 124
King, R., 100, 124, 234, 243

Labbett, B., 100, 124
Lawn, M. A., 26, 32
Lawn, M. A. and Ozga, J. T., 26, 32
Leith, S., 97, 124
Lewin, K., 16, 17, 32
Lewis, I., 2, 10
Lewis, I. and Munn, P., 246, 269
Liddell, C., 196, 201
Lomax, P., 8, 10
Long, S., 97, 124
Lortie, D., 256, 269
Lunzer, E., Gardner, K., 41, 54, 114, 124, 260, 270
Lunzer, E., Gardner, K., Davies, F. and Greene, T., 49, 54

McClelland, G., 175, 182
KcKernan, J., 15, 17, 32
McLeod, R., 88, 95
McNiff, J., 8, 10, 25, 32
McTaggart, R. and Kemmis, S., 26, 29, 32, 249, 270
Martin, M. D., 154, 182
May, N., 13, 15, 33
May, T. and Williams, S., 122, 124
Measor, L., 248, 270
Meek, M., 71, 76
Michael, B., 89, 95
Millar, R., 153, 182
Mills, C. Wright, 224, 243
Moore, W., 136, 141, 147, 152
Munn, P., 2, 11
Murray, W., 63, 76

Nash, R., 100, 124
Nath, K. K., 185, 195, 201

National Curriculum Council, 122, 124, 155, 182, 257, 262, 263, 267, 270
Newson, J. and Newson, E., 177, 182
Nias, J., 6, 11, 64, 76
Nias, J. and Groundwater-Smith, S., 8, 11
Nicholls, R., 188, 201
Nixon, J. C., 7, 11
Norris, N., 20, 33

Oberg, A. and McCutcheon, G., 5, 7, 11, 15, 33, 246, 270
Obrist, A. J., 88, 95
Oja, S. N. and Pine, G. J., 256, 257, 270
Oliver, R. P. C., 17, 33
Osborne, R. J. and Wittrock, M. C., 157, 182

Paice, S., 40, 54
Passow, A. *et al.*, 18, 33
Patton, M. Q., 100, 124, 161, 182, 247, 248, 270
Payne, G. and Hustler, D., 237, 239, 243
Pickthall, M. M., 184, 201
Plummer, K., 251, 270
Pollard, A., 19, 33, 59, 61, 65, 76, 228, 236, 243, 249, 265, 270
Pollard, A. and Tann, S., 247, 248, 265, 270
Prisk, T., 7, 11

Rampton, A., 199, 201
Rance, P., 96, 124
Raper, G. and Stringer, J., 153, 182
Reed, B. and Horbury, A., 66, 76
Ross, A. M. *et al.*, 153, 182
Rowland, S., 259, 260, 270
Rudduck, J., 37, 54
Rudduck, J., Hopkins, D., Sangar, J. and Lincoln, P., 8, 11, 21, 33

Sangar, J., 20, 33
Sarwar, G., 193, 201
Schools Council, 153, 182
Screen, P., 154, 182
Sharp, R. and Green, A. G., 22, 33, 73, 74, 76, 100, 124
Shuard, H., 143, 144, 152
Shumsky, A., 244, 255, 256, 270
Simons, H., 96, 124
Singh, B. R., 198, 201

Sjoberg, G. and Nett, R., 224, 243
Skilbeck, M., 5, 6, 11
Smith, F., 77, 86, 87, 93, 95
Smith, L. M., 5, 11
Southgate, V., Arnold, H. and Johnson, S., 50, 54
Speier, M., 227, 243
Spradley, J. P., 159, 182
Stebbins, R. A., 236, 243
Stenhouse, L., 1, 6, 11, 14, 24, 33, 53, 54, 96, 125
Surkes, S., 191, 201
Svensson, L., 114, 125

Tabberer, R., 52, 54
Tann, C. S., 97, 125, 263, 270
Taylor, M. J. and Hegarty, S., 189, 190, 196, 201
Thier, H. D., 154, 182
Tomlinson, S., 184, 186, 201
Torbe, M., 136, 152
Torbe, M. and Medway, P., 39, 54
Torbe, M. and Shuard, H., 140, 152
Tough, J., 78, 80, 95
Treacher, V., 6, 7, 11, 264, 270
Troyna, B. and Ball, W., 185, 201
Twitchin, J. and Demuth, C., 200, 201

Vickers, J. E., 207, 221
Vulliamy, G., 21, 33

Walden, R. and Walkerdene, W., 149, 152
Walker, R. 129, 152, 247, 248, 270
Webb, K., 2, 11
Webb, R., 2, 3, 11, 96, 125, 259, 270
Weiner, G., 8, 11
Wells, G., 63, 76
Whitehead, J., 25, 33, 36, 37, 54
Whitty, G., 21, 22, 33
Whyte, J., 149, 152
Winter, R., 7, 11, 249, 252, 270
Woods, P., 22, 33, 156, 161, 182, 224, 236, 243, 248, 249, 270
Woolnough, B. and Allsop, T., 156, 182
Wray, D., 40, 54
Wright, S. J., 130, 152

Young, M. F. D., 21, 33

Subject Index

access
  to data 56–8
action research
  co-operative, 18–19, 37–39, 255–57
  definitions of, 5, 36–37, 158
  emancipatory, 26–29, 30
  origins of, 16–21
  use of action hypotheses in, 18, 24
anthropological strangeness, 99–100, 129
audio-tape recording, 101–102, 128–29,
  160–161, 187, 250

Bath, University of, 25, 30

Cambridge Institute of Education (CIE),
  24–5, 30
case study, 5–6, 7, 78, 96, 205
Centre for Applied Research in Education
  (CARE), 2, 23–25, 30, 96
change resulting from research
  in classroom practice, 52, 93–4, 132,
    140, 151–2, 168–70, 172, 176, 180,
    259–265
  in LEA policy, 264–7
  in national policy, 264–7
  in school policy, 187, 191, 192, 191–4,
    196, 199–200, 217, 264–7
Classroom Action Research Network
  (CARN), 24, 265
classroom organisation, 62–3, 70, 74–5,
  82, 262–4
collaboration
  in Outstation research teams, 3, 126–7,
    151–152, 159, 161, 252
  with school staff, 37–9, 53, 155,
    199–200, 203–4

data
  analysis of, 100, 223–6, 252–4
  key characteristics of, 247–8
Deakin University, 26–29, 30
disciplinary research, 3
document analysis, 233, 251

educational research, teachers' views of, 3,
  12, 13, 16, 36, 223
equal opportunities policy, 217–20

Ford Teaching Project, 24, 28
Frankfurt School of Critical Theorists, 27–9

gender issues
  in practitioner research, 7
  in mathematics learning, 8–9, 13, 149
group work, 177–80

history teaching
  use of anecdote in, 108–10, 121–2
  use of museum visits in, 105–7, 111–14
  use of role play in, 110, 122

Humanities Curriculum Project (HCP),
  23–24

Innovation
  pupils' reactions to, 37
  RD and D model for curriculum, 20
  teachers' reactions to, 64–5
interviewing, 101–2, 161–2, 187, 206, 248

macro-micro debate, 27–28
mathematics teaching
  and maths vocabulary, 136–40

and pupil misunderstandings, 140–5
and pupil questions, 133–5
and pupil understanding, 145–151
and teacher questions, 130–133
use of worksheets in, 135–6, 143–145
multi-cultural education
and celebrations, 197–9
and friendships, 196–7
and the Koran, 184–5
and Mirpuri diet, 191–4
and Mirpuri leisure pursuits, 188–91
and the Mosque, 194–6

National Curriculum
and classroom organisation, 262–4
and communication, 177
and information skills, 97–9, 122–3
and reading, 75
implementation of, 75, 97–9, 220
mathematics, 131, 146, 148
and practitioner research, 152, 257, 259, 261–8
Science, 155, 181
New Sociology of Education, 21–2
note-making
by pupils, 110–16, 121

Outstation Programme, 2–3, 7–8, 126, 203, 245, 256, 258–9, 268
participant observation, 5, 21, 56–8, 78–80, 94, 101, 129, 158–161, 249–251
pedagogic research, 3–5, 100
pilot study, 35, 101, 156–158
positivist research, 13, 23
progressive focusing, 128, 159–160
psycho-statistical paradigm, 13–16

questioning
and the 'hands up' rule, 236–40
by pupils, 102–4, 106–7, 133–5, 167–70
by the teacher, 130–33, 168
in worksheets, 135–6

reading
approaches to teaching, 61–65
and comprehension, 45–52
and factors influencing the teaching of, 60
influence of home background on, 72–4
and 'jumps' in learning, 67–71
and multi-lingualism, 195–6
and pupils' attitudes to, 48–50, 55

and reading schemes, 65–6
and teachers' perceptions of, 58–61, 118–9
and the use of reference books, 39–45, 116–9, 120
research
and the academic community, 4, 6, 7, 13, 14
and award-bearing courses, 2, 4, 6, 268
climate in schools, 28–9, 53, 203–4, 255–7, 267–8
constraints on, 128–9, 159, 206, 258
design, 203–7, 244–7
and emancipation, 24, 26–29, 30
and fieldwork diaries, 35, 101, 129, 139–40, 141, 146, 158–9, 175, 225–226, 250–51
personal effects of, 168, 200, 202, 219–220, 258–60
and pupil diaries, 119–20, 164–5, 172
questions, 35, 100, 127–8, 156–8, 184, 251
and self-questioning, 36, 41–3, 51–2, 53, 93–4, 101, 119, 132, 141, 219
and writing up, 7, 15, 39, 254–5

sampling, 156, 203–5, 206, 247
school library, 39–45, 68–70
schoolwork research, 26, 30
science teaching
collaborative work in, 177–180
and definitions of science process skills, 154
and learning through discussion, 170–4
and pupils' observational skills, 164–7
and pupils' perceptions of science, 162–4
and pupils' questions, 167–70
and pupils' understanding of theory through practical work, 157, 175–6
Scottish Education Data Archive (SEDA), 22–3
sex-stereotyping
community influence on, 213–7
and parental expectations, 211–2
and the role of mothers, 209–11
and socialisation, 207–9
and pupils' perceptions of scientists, 162–4
socialisation
into classroom behaviours, 226–242
into sex-stereotypical roles, 207–9
sociological research in education, 21–3

Teacher-Pupil Interaction and the Quality
  of Learning Project (TIQL), 24–5
theory generation, 3–5, 15, 16, 18, 19–20,
  25, 34, 253–4, 260–261
television
  use in teaching, 107–8, 111
  influence of, 72, 189–90
topic work
  accuracy in 104–5
  criticisms of, 95
  and first-hand experience, 105–7, 119
  and museum visits, 105–7, 111–14
  and the National Curriculum, 97–99,
    122–3
  and pupils' reference skills, 39–45,
    116–9

and pupils' use of text, 45–52
triangulation, 100, 158, 251–2

video recording, 186–7, 250

writing by pupils
  appearance of, 89–93
  collaborative, 87–88
  content of, 85–87
  reasons for, 82–5
  and spelling, 90–92
  talk as an aid to, 80–82
  and vocabulary work, 116–18

York, University of, 2–3, 30–31, 203